Helping
Transfer
Students

Leonard A. Jason
Andrew M. Weine
Joseph H. Johnson
Luann Warren-Sohlberg
Laura Ann Filippelli
Elizabeth Y. Turner
Cecile Lardon

Helping Transfer Students

STRATEGIES FOR EDUCATIONAL AND SOCIAL READJUSTMENT

Jossey-Bass Publishers · San Francisco

For sales outside the United States, contact Maxwell Macmillan International Publishing Group, 866 Third Avenue, New York, New York 10022.

Manufactured in the United States of America.

 The paper used in this book is acid-free and meets the State of California requirements for recycled paper (50 percent recycled waste, including 10 percent postconsumer waste), which are the strictest guidelines for recycled paper currently in use in the United States.

Library of Congress Cataloging-in-Publication Data

Helping transfer students : strategies for educational and social
    readjustment / Leonard A. Jason . . . [et al.].
        p.   cm. — (A joint publication in the Jossey-Bass social and
    behavioral science series and the Jossey-Bass education series)
    Includes bibliographical references and index.
    ISBN 1-55542-452-X
    1. Transfer students — United States.   2. Transfer students — United
States — Services for.   3. Student adjustment — United States.
4. School children — United States — Social conditions.   I. Jason,
Leonard A.   II. Series: Jossey-Bass social and behavioral science
series.   III. Series: Jossey-Bass education series.
LB3064.2.H45   1992
371.2′914′0973 — dc20   92-11510
                                                                                              CIP

FIRST EDITION
HB Printing   10 9 8 7 6 5 4 3 2 1   *Code 9255*

A joint publication in

The Jossey-Bass
Social and Behavioral Science Series

and

The Jossey-Bass
Education Series

Consulting Editors
Psychoeducational Interventions:
Guidebooks for School Practitioners

Charles A. Maher
Rutgers University

Joseph E. Zins
University of Cincinnati

Contents

Preface

This book originated in the experience of the lead author, Leonard A. Jason. As a fifth grader in the New Jersey public school system, he made an unscheduled transfer to a school with higher academic standards than his previous school. Because of this difference, he fell behind as a student and had a difficult time adjusting. With the help of a tutor hired by his mother, he was able to catch up, succeed academically, and avoid becoming a troublesome student. Later, as a professor, Jason found that the educational and psychological literature on transfer students suggested that these children suffered adjustment problems, but almost no one was developing programs to help them.

Most people probably know someone who at some point transferred from one school to another, or they have experienced it themselves. In the course of our research, many people (colleagues, friends, and family) affirmed our concern with school transfer by relating their own difficult experiences. One man recalled that because of his father's job changes when he was growing up, his family frequently had to move to new states. Each time he enrolled in a new school, male classmates picked fights with him and he had to defend himself until a "pecking order" was established. He complained that all too often he had been beaten up.

In our clinical experience, too, we repeatedly see the effects of school transfer. One mother brought her son to a community mental health center for treatment of school behavior problems, including kicking, swearing at teachers, and frequent fighting with peers. At the beginning of treatment, the mother revealed that over the past two years the child had been in three different public schools and was in danger of being moved again if the behavior problems were not resolved. The clinician's role became two-fold; to treat the individual psychological problems of the child and assist in the adjustment to the new school. Addressing the child's psychological problems would ultimately reduce the exertion of negative behaviors in the school, reduce the risk of being transferred again, and allow the child to maintain a stable environment in which he could improve academically and socially.

Another mother sought therapy services for her seventh-grade son. The young adolescent had been performing well in his old school, but when he transferred during the middle of the year to a new school, he quickly fell behind in his classwork and began associating with delinquent youth. Consequently, he began skipping school and shoplifting. This case illustrates the risks of school transitions that take place during critical developmental periods (for example, early adolescence).

In contrast to these difficult school transitions, a woman whose father had been in the military reminisced that she made friends quickly following school moves and always achieved above-average grades. She attributed her success to having a supportive family, which eased the stress of school transitions.

Transfer children may come to the attention of a variety of professionals. In schools, they may emerge after a recent transfer as having behavioral problems and academic lags. Teachers, social workers, and school psychologists confronted with transfer-student problems may benefit from guidance on transition issues. Principals and school administrators may seek to implement programs for students, parents, or teachers. Parents may be concerned about their children's transfer; tutors and other school volunteers may be confronted with newly moved students struggling to succeed. Graduate and undergraduate students in education, social work, and psychology, along with researchers in these areas, may want to deepen their understanding of school problems and their prevention. This book is written for all of these potential audiences.

Overview of the Contents

We have aimed for a difficult and challenging balance of theory and application, guidelines, quantitative and qualitative descriptions, numbers, and case studies. In Part One, we integrate theory and research based on school transition, educational, developmental, and community psychology literatures. Chapter One introduces and explains the phenomenon of school transfer, reviews studies concerning the interaction between life stress and individual adjustment, and describes briefly our School Transition Project (STP)—its goals, methods, participants, and programs. (More detailed program description can be found in Chapters Six, Seven, and Eight.) In Chapter Two, we elaborate on how children cope with stressful life events and chronic adverse circumstances. Our discussion also focuses on students' adjustment to school settings, including their social and academic adaptation. We examine important relationships between transfer students' academic achievement, social competence, and self-concept. Next, Chapter Three explores teacher, peer, and parent support of student adjustment to a new school. We review the small number of programs that have been designed to aid transfer students. In Chapter Four, we examine why children transfer from one school to another, reviewing the literature in this area and analyzing the reasons for school transfer among participants in our program.

Part Two explores the facets of the School Transition Project. In Chapter Five, we lay a theoretical foundation for understanding and preventing school transfer problems. Such a foundation utilizes behavioral, ecological, and transactional theories, among others. Next, in Chapter Six, we describe the STP in greater detail, discussing its goals, personnel, instruction, and communication methods. Two main programs are presented: the School Tutoring Program and the School and Home Tutoring Program, both containing an orientation component and a buddy system. Inevitably, any large-scale preventive intervention encounters implementation hurdles. In Chapter Seven, we discuss such barriers, including selecting tutors, working with challenging children, and negotiating our way through the difficult terrain of differing expectations among principals, teachers, and families. Chapter Eight explains how schools can involve parents in assisting their transfer children by using a team approach, training parents to be tutors, and conducting periodic home visits. The possible influence of school climate is discussed in Chapter Nine; such influences may reflect how warm, supportive, and involved the school is and how the school facility is designed and embellished. Chapter Ten relates results from analyses we have conducted; we consider how children benefited from the programs, delineate subgroups of children, and discuss consumer satisfaction.

Finally, in Part Three, we attempt to envision the future for children who will transfer between schools. Our vision is based on what we know about school transfer from other studies and what we have learned in our interventions. We suggest ways in which all schools can permanently adopt programs that welcome transfer students. The prospects and potential for such widespread attention are considered.

Although some readers may want more material tailored to their own concerns, we hope that our integration of many aspects of school transfer will expand their interests into new areas they may not have considered. Such integration represents an important step in school transition research and in social science research in general, which sometimes suffers from a narrowness of interest, overspecialization, and lack of accessibility.

School transfer is a milestone in child development, affecting some six million children each year. We hope this book helps to raise public awareness of the transfer phenomenon, and that it offers concerned parents, educators, and researchers ways to address the problems that may come with changing schools. As of this writing, there is increasing talk on the national level of allowing parents to choose public schools for their children. Whatever its merits or disadvantages, such choice will certainly result in more transfer. Thus, in a society of increasingly changing and mobile families and careers, one can be sure that school transfer will continue to occur and to warrant our attention and best efforts.

For an updated list of the School Transition Project's articles, write to Leonard A. Jason, Department of Psychology, DePaul University, 2219 North Kenmore Avenue, Chicago, IL 60614.

Acknowledgments

This book and the project we describe would not have been possible without the generous assistance and diligent work of the many people mentioned below. Although this list is organized by the job titles people held, their work was broad and multifaceted, often transcending the confines of their formal roles.

First, over the four years we implemented our project, we benefited from the work of many tutors. We heartily thank the following: Jeanne Arrigo, Levera Banks, Tracey Beater, Kelly Behnke, Elena Bertolucci, Scott Birkhead, Phil Brown, Maria Calvillo, Catherine Chestler, Mary Cradock, Chron Cross, George Demakis, Elizabeth Feret, Gaithri Fernando, Charles Ferrer, Vera Flint, Terill Harrington, Walter Kimmons, Bruce Kitsuse, Theresa Leen, Ray Legler, Veronica Luna, June Mizumoto, Natalie Montefinese, Cheryl Novak, Carrie Nutter, Pamela Orosan, Sally Osborne, Magda Paczut, Derick Patton, Sonia Perez, Linda Serpico, Rachel Singson, Carol Starr, Sharon Thomas, Mary Tyrell, Edgar Urzua, Effy Vega, Kathy Walton, Rachael Weakland, Julie Wright, and Bertha Young. We must make special acknowledgment to Karen Danner, who, in addition to serving as a tutor, acted as research coordinator, picking through data with a fine-tooth comb and helping to organize a bustling enterprise.

We thank the following supervisors, whose encouragement and leadership were greatly valued: Peter Bennett, Corina Garcia, Beth Wilson-Grove, Lisa Neuson, Charles Shinaver, and Suzanne Smith. Also, thanks to data coders, who worked hard to put our many measures on computer: Laura Adler, Tamara Carls, Tina Garipes, Chris Gertner, Berton Hestroffer, Natalie Niles, Christopher Till, and Jill Wiedenfeld. The School Transition Project orientation booklet, shown in part as Resource B, was designed by Suzanne Smith and Laura Filippelli. Illustrations appearing in the original version were drawn by Douglas Aupperpie. We would also like to thank Steven Johnson and Ellen Sachs-Alter for their helpful suggestions and direction during the design phase of the booklet.

In addition, we warmly thank Karen Kurasaki, whose assistance, as data analyst, was critical in meticulously cleaning, organizing, and analyzing data; supervising others; and writing up results. As project director, David Betts helped shape the first two years of the project, and his involvement is greatly appreciated. Michael Anes has been invaluable in his help collecting references, proofreading, and editing.

Thanks also to Brother Don Houde and the Archdiocese of Chicago; to Doreen Koritz; to educational consultants Louise Ferone and Katherine Karsh; to computer consultants Brenda Greiner and Scott Oliver; to research consultants Jane Halpert, Don Hedecker, Steve Jost, and Werner Woethke; and to Mari Brown and Nancy Burgoyne for their assistance as well.

We gratefully acknowledge the helpful comments and advice of our professional colleagues Anne Bogat, Sheldon Cotler, Steve Fawcett, David Glenwick, Jack Glidewell, Steven Hobfoll, Jim Kelly, Chris Keys, John Moritsugu, Olga Reyes, Vicky Sloan, Dick Winett, and Edwin Zolik. At DePaul University, thanks also to Laura Axelson, Barbara Baird, and Marjorie Piechowski.

Last, this project would not have been possible without the generous financial support of the National Institute of Mental Health (Grant No. 40851), the William T. Grant Foundation, and the DePaul University Faculty Research and Development Program. We would also like to thank the members of W. T. Grant Foundation's Consortium on the School-Based Promotion of Social Competence for their constructive comments on many of the ideas expressed in this book.

A final thanks must go to all the principals, teachers, and school secretaries who graciously welcomed us into their schools and to all the students and families with whom we worked.

Chicago   Leonard A. Jason
                                             Andrew M. Weine
                                             Joseph H. Johnson
                                             Luann Warren-Sohlberg
                                             Laura Ann Filippelli
                                             Elizabeth Y. Turner
                                             Cecile Lardon

The Authors

Leonard A. Jason is professor of psychology at DePaul University. He earned his B.A. degree (1971) in psychology from Brandeis University and his Ph.D. degree (1975) in clinical and community psychology from the University of Rochester. Jason is a past president of Division 27 of the American Psychological Association. He has published over 200 articles and chapters on varied topics, including preventive school-based interventions, substance abuse prevention, media interventions, program evaluation, smoking cessation, and behavioral assessment. He is the coauthor of *Preventing Substance Abuse Among Children and Adolescents* (with J. E. Rhodes, 1988). He is also coeditor of several books: *Prevention: Toward a Multidisciplinary Approach* (with R. Hess, R. D. Felner, and J. Moritsuga, 1987), *Preventive Psychology: Theory, Research, and Practice* (with R. D. Felner, J. Moritsugu, and S. S. Farber, 1983), *Behavioral Community Psychology: Progress and Prospects* (with D. S. Glenwick, 1980), *Researching Community Psychology: Issues of Theory and Methods* (with P. Tolan, C. Keys, and F. Chertak, 1990) and *Prevention in the Community: Behavioral Approaches to Intervention* (with D. S. Glenwick, 1992). Jason has received three honorable-mention television-media awards from the American Psychological Association and has served on review committees of the National Institute on Drug Abuse and the National Institute of Mental Health.

Andrew M. Weine is entering a postdoctoral fellowship program at the Center for Children, Youth, and Families at the

Department of Psychiatry, University of Vermont. He earned his B.A. degree (1985) from the University of Michigan in English and his M.A. degree (1990) from DePaul University in clinical psychology. He is receiving his Ph.D. degree (1992) from DePaul University in clinical and community psychology. He worked at the Institute for Social Research in Ann Arbor, Michigan, from 1987 to 1988. Weine has published several studies in psychological journals. His main interests are in community and child psychology.

Joseph (Jay) H. Johnson is currently a psychologist resident in Portland, Oregon. He received his B.S. degree (1983) from the College of William and Mary in psychology and education, and his M.A. (1988) and Ph.D. (1991) degrees from DePaul University in clinical psychology and clinical child psychology, respectively. He has published a book chapter on the role of social competence in education and other articles on issues about school transfer. He specializes in child, adolescent, and family mental health issues.

Luann Warren-Sohlberg is a doctoral candidate in clinical and community psychology at DePaul University. She earned her B.A. degree (1985) from Stanford University in psychology, her M.Ed. degree (1988) from the University of Washington in educational psychology, and her M.A. degree (1990) from DePaul University in clinical psychology. During her graduate work, she specialized in addressing and treating domestic violence for the police department of Bellevue, Washington. Her interests are in school-based prevention programs.

Laura Ann Filippelli received her B.A. (1987) and M.A. (1991) degrees from DePaul University in psychology and in human services and counseling, respectively. As project director of the School Transition Project for two years, she is a coauthor of several articles on transfer children. She is interested in how life events affect the social and academic adjustment of transfer students.

Elizabeth Y. Turner is a doctoral candidate in clinical and child psychology at DePaul University. She received her B.A. degree (1987) from the University of Michigan in psychology and her M.A. degree (1990) from DePaul University in clinical psychology. She has conducted research in the areas of smoking cessation, social skills, and the effects of divorce on adolescents' peer and parental relations.

Cecile Lardon is a graduate student in clinical and community psychology at the University of Illinois at Chicago. She received her B.A. degree (1987) from DePaul University in psychology. She was data manager of the School Transition Project for two years. Her interests include prevention, program development and evaluation, and collaborative research methods.

To the children with whom we have worked and to those who, in the future, will undergo school transfer with greater ease, guided by the care that schools and families can provide

Helping Transfer Students

Part One

Understanding the Effects of School Transfer

1

Changing Schools: A Major Life Event

School transfers have been considered one of the most stressful and frequently occurring major life events children undergo (Coddington, 1972). In the United States, an estimated six million students between the ages of five and thirteen transfer to new schools each year (Cornille, Bayer, & Smyth, 1983; Schaller, 1975). One investigation determined that only 20 percent of the sixth-grade population had been in the same school since first grade (Bensen, Haycraft, Steyaert, & Weigel, 1979). This large number of transfer students must adapt to new peers, meet new academic and behavioral standards, adjust to new curricula, and be accepted by teachers as appropriate classroom members (Holland, Kaplan, & Davis, 1974; Long, 1975). Concerned about these adjustments, educators, researchers, and parents have sought to determine the effects of school transitions on students' achievement and social adjustment.

The research literature is mixed regarding the consequences of school transitions. Several investigators have suggested that few untoward effects should be anticipated provided the transfer student is relatively well adjusted, adaptable, and intelligent, and is supported by a stable family (Turner & McClatchey, 1978; Whalen & Fried, 1973). However, a predominant assumption has been that for some children changing schools may precipitate impairment of academic achievement (Lacey & Blane, 1979) as well as emotional and social problems (Holland et al., 1974; Stubblefield, 1955; Turner & McClatchey, 1978). Even such an unlikely source as the *Wall Street Journal* published a front page story headlined "Endless Transfers Hurt Some Students' Work," which documented the plight of inner-city school children falling behind and starting over each time their parents move (Graham, 1990).

As a result of school transitions, students' educational experience may become repetitive and boring; also, moves may cause them to miss large sections of important academic work (Lacey & Blane, 1979). No matter how good his or her previous performance has been, a transfer student may be required to catch up in some subjects (Long, 1975). Thus, most students new to a school, regardless of their past academic achievement and social development, are thought to experience some difficulty adjusting to a new school system (Brockman & Reeves, 1967; Holland et al., 1974; Panagos, Holmes, Thurman, Yard, & Spaner, 1981).

School transitions are categorized into two types: *scheduled* and *unscheduled*. A scheduled transition occurs when entire groups of students enter school or graduate from elementary or junior high school. Unscheduled school transitions involve students in isolation changing schools. A student transferring to a new school after a summer break is considered an unscheduled transition. A school transfer occurring during the middle of the school year is considered unscheduled as well. During an unscheduled school transition, not only is the student transferring alone but there is also less chance that the newcomer will receive a planned orientation and adjustment period more typical of scheduled transitions (for example, freshman orientation). For these reasons, one might assume that the academic and social adjustment of an unscheduled school transition is generally more difficult than a scheduled one. The time during the year when transitions occur may be critical, too. One study has shown that students who undergo an unscheduled school transition during the summer are less affected academically than those students who transfer during the school year (Brockman & Reeves, 1967).

School systems are becoming more aware that transferring can be traumatic for students. Many have developed orientation programs to facilitate the transition process (Cornille et al., 1983; Donohue & Gullotta, 1981; Jason & Bogat, 1983).

There is still inadequate support for these students, however, especially for the high-risk transfers. To date, there are few comprehensive preventive interventions aimed at these special-needs transfer students (Felner, Ginter, & Primavera, 1982; Jason et al., 1992; Jason et al., 1989; Jason et al., 1990; Panagos et al., 1981). In this book we attempt to provide a broad exploration of the entire phenomenon of school transfer: how children adapt to school transitions, what personal and external resources they possess, and how we may prevent maladjustment and enhance competency. We begin our inquiry by reviewing, in this chapter, studies concerning the interaction between life stress and individual adjustment.

Stress Associated with School Transitions

A guiding etiological hypothesis for many psychology researchers predicts that psychosocial stress is important in the causation of psychopathology (Dohrenwend, 1978). Stress can be defined as a "state in which individuals judge their response capabilities as unable to meet the threat to the loss of desirable experiential states" (Hobfoll, 1988, p. 19). The presence of stress, both acute and chronic, presumably increases the risk of at least short-term psychological disturbance among children, and in general, chronic or prolonged adversities seem to be the most detrimental (Rutter, 1981). Early research on stress focused primarily on the impact of major life events such as a serious illness or divorce (Holmes & Rahe, 1967). Similarly, school transitions have been considered stressful events that potentially lead to poor school adjustment (Coddington, 1972; Filippelli & Jason, in press; Holland et al., 1974; Jason et al., 1989; Jason et al., 1990; Panagos et al., 1981; Turner & McClatchey, 1978). The following discussion examines stress-related issues concerning school transitions.

Investigators have debated whether the positive or negative values attached to particular stressors or life events influence the course of individuals' adjustment. Holmes and Rahe (1967) proposed that a life event is stressful solely as a function of the change it requires in a person's life. Gersten, Langner, Eisenberg, and Simcha-Fagan (1977) countered that individual differences in perceptions of the desirability of an event and in coping styles determine the stressfulness of an event.

In order to assess the influence of stressful life events on individuals' functioning, Gersten and colleagues (1977) examined children and adolescents before and after the onset of a stressful event. Their most striking finding was that, with increasingly rigorous data analytic controls, the association of life events with psychological disorder weakened. They discovered that the undesirability of an event — not change per se — proved to be more predictive of the development of psychopathology in their sample. Other findings indicate that undesirable life events are most strongly associated with behavior problems (Wertlieb, Weigel, & Feldstein, 1987). In relation to school transitions, these findings imply that undesirable school changes, compared to desirable changes, are more likely to precipitate undue stress and concomitant behavior problems in students.

Early investigators targeted geographical mobility as a prominent risk factor related to declines in children's school performance (Greene & Daughtry, 1961; Holland et al., 1974; Kantor, 1965; Long, 1975). Studies have demonstrated that children who transfer frequently exhibit academic problems (Bensen et al., 1979; Brockman & Reeves, 1967; Schaller, 1976). Levine, Wesolowski, and Corbett's data (1966) showed that the more frequently an inner-city elementary student changed schools, the poorer his or her grades were. Although moves often took place when there was some family distress, the authors concluded that the students' poorer school performance was associated with frequent transfers primarily because of the many adaptations the change in school required.

Other studies, however, have demonstrated that the number of school moves may not affect academic achievement (Cramer & Dorsey, 1970; Marchant & Medway, 1987; Perrodin & Snipes, 1966). Some have suggested that in certain cases mobility may actually enhance achievement. Goebel (1981) reported that mobility during the preschool years may improve cognitive development by exposing children to new learning experiences and promote educational achievement later (during adolescence) for boys. The validity of these findings, however, is compromised by the lack of control for possibly confounding variables such as socioeconomic status (SES) of families. In another school transition study that controlled for SES, transfer-student adjustment differed according to children's intelligence (Whalen & Fried, 1973). Students of high intelligence who transferred frequently displayed higher achievement scores than nontransfer students of high intelligence, whereas high-mobility students of low intelligence showed poorer achievement than their nontransfer counterparts (Whalen & Fried, 1973).

Such equivocal findings have led investigators to question the assumption that mobility alone leads to academic or mental health problems (Lacey & Blane, 1979; Long, 1975). Families and children may vary widely in their reasons for and response to moving; this variance likely introduces different levels of complexity to the problem of transition and adjustment (Lacey & Blane, 1979).

Life stress researchers have been criticized by reviewers for being able to account consistently for only about 10 percent of the variance in children's behavior problems with measures of major life stress events (Kessler, Price, & Wortman, 1985; Wertlieb et al., 1987). For example, using a multiple regression analysis and controlling for the stressful processes (for example, punitive parenting, welfare status) in children's and adolescents' social and family networks, Gersten and colleagues (1977) found that life event scores did not make a significant contribution to prediction of children's behavioral disturbance. Instead, they determined that many social and family variables used to characterize youngsters' life situations were significantly correlated with the later occurrence of life stress events. Thus, ecological sources of stress, perhaps indirectly associated with negative life events, may largely contribute to psychological deterioration. What may be critical to the stress resistance process is the match or congruence between an individual's internal resources and ecological sources of stress (Hobfoll, 1988).

In addition to major life events, researchers have recently differentiated several other categories of stress, including enduring life strains, developmental transitions, induced transitions, and daily hassles (Tolan, Miller, & Thomas, 1988). Enduring life strains (for example, poor housing, few material resources) are likely to provoke chronic stress; such strains are often associated with lower SES. Developmental transitions (for example, entering puberty) require adaptation and are associated with stress. Transferring to a new school is an example of an induced transition; such changes may be stressful when support systems and routines are interrupted (Jason et al., 1989). Daily hassles consist of minor day-to-day stresses such as poor school performance and teasing from peers and are thought to contribute to cumulative stress demands on individuals (Gersten et al., 1977; Murrell & Norris, 1983; Tolan et al., 1988).

Wagner, Compas, and Howell (1988) did not find a causal path between major life events and psychopathological symptoms; rather, they determined that daily events have a central mediating role. However, they added the qualification that daily stress leading to symptoms is partly caused by major life events. The authors concluded that both major and daily stressful events play a role in the etiology and maintenance of psychological symptoms. In the case of school transitions, students may be simultaneously trying to adjust to such multiple levels of stress.

Studying the impact of stress on children, Rutter (1979) uncovered possible interactive effects among multiple risk factors. He discovered that children with a single risk factor were no more likely to develop psychiatric disorders than children with no risk factors. However, combinations of chronic stressors exponentially multiplied the likelihood of maladjustment. Rutter believed these results demonstrated the greatly increased adverse effects of an accumulation of stresses. For instance, the combination of a stressful school transition and multiple risk factors (for example, evidence of academic delays and additional stressful life events) might heighten a child's chances for poor school adjustment (Jason et al., 1990). At least among adolescents, findings support the possibility of negative consequences for students who must adjust to school transitions and other stressors at once (Simmons, Burgeson, Carlton-Ford, & Blyth, 1987).

In summary, recent research suggests that major life events such as school transitions may not directly cause psychopathology among children; rather, these events are mediated by other sources of chronic stress. Transfer students exposed to multiple stressors are probably at greater risk for maladjustment. In particular, children from low-SES households are thought to be more exposed to multiple, chronic stressors than are their peers from higher-SES backgrounds.

Socioeconomic Status and Stress

Dohrenwend (1973) proposed that persons in lower social status groups are disproportionately exposed to stressful life events, and that this exposure explains linkages between lower social status and higher individual psychological distress. Hence, children of lower-SES parents are thought to be exposed to a disproportionate number of stressful life events and enduring life strains. Moreover, caretaking by deprived, stressed, or poorly educated parents reportedly exacerbates children's difficulties (Sameroff, 1975). Numerous investigations have implicated low SES as a significant risk factor for poor school adjustment (Mayer & Jencks, 1989; O'Grady & Metz, 1987; Swift & Spivack, 1968; Zigler & Trickett, 1978). In a recent study of early elementary-school children, SES was the strongest single predictor of social competence and school problems (O'Grady & Metz, 1987). Higher SES was associated with fewer school and behavior problems, greater support, and greater social competence.

Similarly, Swift and Spivack (1968) correlated children's classroom achievement-related behavior with parental educational level and determined that, in general, the higher the parents' level of education, the lower was the children's level of problem classroom behaviors. They concluded that elementary students with better-educated parents tend to be more independent in class, more alert, and more motivated to engage in academic tasks than are children with less-educated parents. Apparently, children from higher-SES backgrounds are more likely to be exposed to greater resources that contribute to school success (e.g., larger vocabularies modeled in the home, more experience with school-like tasks). Thus, the research literature suggests that SES serves as a marker for possible multiple sources of support or stress.

Based on the above conclusions, it seems reasonable for researchers to suspect that transfer children can be influenced by the socioeconomic status of their caretakers (Jason et al., 1989; Jason, Filippelli, Danner, & Bennett, in press). Concerning school transitions, Morris, Pestaner, and Nelson (1967) found that students in upper-SES families continued to show high achievement despite school moves, whereas children from lower socioeconomic groups who had been high achievers tended to fall in achievement following school transitions. Felner, Primavera, and Cauce (1981) cited similar evidence that transfer students' achievement and acceptance by peers may be related to social class. Although the authors found high rates of school mobility to be associated with poor academic performance for high school students, this association was stronger for black and Hispanic students. They suggested that students from lower-SES, minority backgrounds may have considerable difficulty adjusting to school transitions while transfers from more advantaged backgrounds may actually benefit from varied school experiences.

There is evidence, however, that higher SES does not necessarily protect children from school problems following a stressful life event. Studying nontransfer students, Garmezy, Masten, and Tellegen (1984) measured SES and life stress in order to examine two important issues: (1) the relationship of SES and stress to children's school-based competence (academic, behavioral, and social), and (2) the role of SES as a mediator of the extent and impact of stressors on the family. Socioeconomic status was shown to be moderately correlated with students' on-task classroom behavior, school records, and performance on achievement tests, but the researchers found no evidence that SES moderated the effects of stress on children's school competencies. These results suggest that caretakers' educational and financial resources might not directly impact school adjustment during difficult school transitions that are complicated by other life stressors.

In general, although there is evidence that SES and stressful events are linked to students' school performance, these two factors seem to have indirect etiological roles in precipitating school failure and social maladjustment following a school transition. No single transfer necessarily affects academic achievement or school attendance. Students may vary markedly in how well they cope with transitions and other concurrent stressful events in their lives (Felner et al., 1981). Duration and constancy of exposure to stress processes are additional dimensions that may contribute to maladjustment (Gersten et al., 1977). Transitions can also be differentiated by how expected they are (Tolan et al., 1988). Furthermore, mediating influences may exist within schools, families, and neighborhoods that attenuate or worsen the adverse effects of school moves (Levine et al., 1966). Eschewing the simple assumption that "bad experiences may have bad effects," Rutter (1981) challenged researchers to determine "just which features of life events make them liable to predispose to which types of disorder by which processes or mechanism" (p. 327). Determining relationships among separate events, that is, the pattern, sequence, and combinations of life events, remains a complex conceptual and measurement problem (Murrell & Norris, 1983).

Eco-Transactional Processes

A new consensus has evolved that negative life events do not play a direct etiological role in psychological disturbances in youth (Wertlieb et al., 1987). The pathways that link negative events to psychological distress are more complex than previously thought. More recent research has focused on both environmental and personality variables that mediate individual differences in response to life stress (O'Grady & Metz, 1987).

Revising her earlier hypothesis, Dohrenwend (1978) favored a comprehensive model of stress processes that places emphasis not only on stressful life events and potential transient reactions but also on such mediating factors as situational and psychological mediators and long-term adjustment. Situational mediators can include processes within individuals' social environments (Garmezy et al., 1984; Mayer & Jencks, 1989; Rutter, 1979). Examples of psychological mediators are individuals' cognitive appraisals (Gersten et al., 1977) and general intelligence.

Similar to Dohrenwend's framework, several theoretical models have further elaborated person-environment transactions in response to stressful events. Directly applicable to school transition issues, the life transitions model (see Felner, 1984) advocated by Cappas (1989) includes (1) placing equal emphasis on both positive and negative life changes, (2) accounting for adaptation to rather than reduction of stress, and (3) considering potential moderating variables which may influence students' ability to cope with stressful school transitions. The first tenet of the life transition model cautions investigators not to overlook positive changes that often accompany and perhaps counterbalance negative changes. For example, following a school transition, a student may experience disruption in peer relations but later find greater support in the new peer network. The second principle suggests that stress is not necessarily detrimental and that an individual's adaptation to greater demands may enhance his or her competencies; conversely, a reduction in stress (for example, lower academic standards) could lessen a student's opportunities to gain greater skills. The third principle directs attention to the combination of personal and external resources that determine students' adaptation to stressful transitions.

Examining the transactions between individuals and their multidimensional environments offers a viable approach to conceptualizing developmental psychopathology and competence among youth (Moos, 1984; Sameroff, 1975). An example of transactional processes is represented by Sameroff's inquiry (1975) into infant development and child abuse issues. He viewed maladaptive developmental outcomes in children as resulting from a continuous malfunction in the child-environment transaction across time. In his transactional model, Sameroff avoided a simple linear causality explanation for children's development (e.g., the contention that poor caretaking causes children's behavior problems). Rather, he claimed that there is a reciprocity in child-caretaker relations resulting in a transaction between such elements as the temperament of the child and the child-rearing attitudes of caretakers. The notion of bidirectional transactions seems to illuminate more complex relationships between individuals and their varied social environments.

Elaborating on prior theory concerning adaptation to stress, Moos (1984) presented a nonrecursive model depicting the transactional, bidirectional linkages between the individual, stressful life circumstances, and the physical and social environment. His framework provides an inclusive strategy for conceptualizing school transitions. He posited that a person's adaptation is affected by the environmental system composed of physical, policy, and social climate factors. The environment transacts with an individual's personal system, which includes demographic, self-concept, health, and functional factors. These first two dimensions theoretically interact with social network resources, an individual's cognitive appraisals, and coping responses toward stressful life circumstances. All of the elements in the adaptive system exert reciprocal feedback on the other elements to collectively determine adjustment outcome.

Moos's model encompasses "multiple environmental microsystems" in order to explain personal maturation. He suggested that nonschool settings such as the family or neighborhood can positively or adversely influence school and classroom settings. Overall, Moos contended that these interactive systems influence the exposure to stressors, individuals' ongoing appraisals, and adaptive or maladaptive coping. From this perspective, transactions between transfer students and their home and school environments are seen as reciprocal and contributing to systemic and individual change over time.

In Chapter Five, we discuss more fully a theoretical framework to guide research in transactional and ecological processes, using behavioral methodology. Such a framework borrows from transactional theory, which focuses on reciprocal effects. According to this theory people are influenced by each other and in turn influence others. We adhere to an ecological perspective, which is valuable in fostering our understanding of children's behavior in relation to their social and cultural settings as well as in identifying interrelationships between different systems or ecologies, such as home and school. Transactional and ecological perspectives contrast, for while the ecological model applies mostly to systems-level interrelationships, the transactional model focuses more on dyadic person-environment relationships.

We believe behavioral methodology can be usefully applied to analyze transactional and ecological processes. For example, repeated measures of a transfer student's academic performance and peer social acceptance could be helpful in assessing transactions influencing behavioral change in both the child and classmates. Measurement can be as rigorous as behavioral observations made every few seconds or as global as behavioral assessments made at the beginning and end of a school year. Herein lies the comprehensiveness of the eco-transactional behavioral perspective: the behavioral approach could accommodate the transactional and ecological models by measuring behavior as influenced by multiple contingencies and setting features.

The theoretical models described here and elaborated in Chapter Five share the common premise that multiple individual and environmental variables moderate individuals' adaptation to stressful life changes. Simple linear causal models focusing on individual adaptive capacities alone may need to be abandoned in favor of more comprehensive bidirectional, nonrecursive models. The concept of reciprocal person-environment transactions adds another important dimension; that is, individuals and their multidimensional environments are interactively evolving over time. Studying ongoing adaptive transactions could illuminate interactive attributes and processes of individuals, schools, and families that influence school transitions. Educational consultants have recommended that interventions to resolve student problems or system-level difficulties (e.g., school, family) should be aimed simultaneously at both the individual and the system levels and not directed at either alone (Zins, Curtis, Graden, & Ponti, 1988). We integrated and applied this multilevel perspective through our individual tutoring and ongoing consultation with teachers and administrators.

Overview of School Transition Project

The remainder of the book describes the guiding theories and applied program elements of the School Transition Project (STP). In this section we present an overview of the project, including a description of program goals, participating schools and students, and estimated project costs.

The School Transition Project sought to offer a cost-effective secondary prevention program for high-risk elementary transfer students. Our primary goal was to boost high-risk transfers' academic achievement to at least the average achievement level of nontransfer students and also to promote transfer students' social adjustment in the classroom. Toward this aim we worked with urban, parochial, elementary schools with diverse ethnic populations across four years. During the first year of the project, twenty of the thirty-one schools selected for the study were randomly assigned to either control or child-focused tutoring conditions. During the third year of the project, additional schools were added in order to have enough schools for two separate interventions. The original group of schools was divided into either a parent or child component. At the beginning of each school year of the program, three hundred to four hundred transfer students in third through fifth grades were tested and screened. Through this procedure high-risk students were selected and assigned to either an experimental or a control condition. Both the child- and parent-focused studies involved individualized tutoring in the school throughout the year. In the parent component the project staff taught tutoring methods to be used at home. Thus, children in the parent-focused study received home tutoring as well as school tutoring.

In an era when school budgets are often shrinking, we believe that school systems can implement cost-effective school transfer programs. Even considering the added costs to research and develop the project, our yearly budget did not exceed $280,000 in direct expenditure. The largest part of the budget went to pay reasonable salaries for research staff and consultants: approximately seventeen part- and full-time paraprofessional tutors, three supervisors, the project director, and the principal investigator. Many school systems could reduce development and operating costs below our research project budget. The budget could be reduced by using parents and volunteers as tutors, involving teachers in the initial screening of transfer students, using in-school materials, and implementing programs in the school district to pool resources. School systems could also use existing school resources such as classroom learning materials and space for tutoring without adding undue indirect costs. Certainly, one goal of a secondary prevention project such as ours is to encourage the greatest possible initial investment of community resources to help prevent academic and social problems from becoming entrenched. Once these difficulties are well established, the cost of remedying them far exceeds the costs of preventive programs.

Summary

In our review of studies on school transition and related phenomena, we have seen that one can view school transition with many different lenses and from various angles. We conceptualize school transitions within an eco-transactional framework. We do so because research findings support the proposition that stressful life processes, children's coping abilities, and social support *transact* to determine the course of individual and system adaptation. This perspective has important implications for researching and intervening in children's academic and social adjustment. For the researcher, rather than merely examining linear, unidirectional relationships between variables, it may be more productive to consider adjustment in terms of nonrecursive, bidirectional transactions among children, stressful situations, and environmental resources.

The school transition literature is mixed regarding transfer-student adjustment. Notably, it does *not* present a general agreement on "(1) the relationship of positive to negative transitional effects; (2) the duration and intensity of these effects; and (3) factors which mediate the impact of transitions" (Jones & Thornburg, 1985, pp. 230–231). Some investigators have suggested that unscheduled school transitions may result in academic, social, and emotional difficulties for students. Apparently, repeated school transfers are associated with school failure for some students. In contrast, other researchers have concluded that no problems should be expected provided transfer students show stable, competent functioning prior to the transition and have adequate support. However, children may be at high risk for school difficulties when they do not possess adequate personal and external resources to cope with multiple transition demands.

School transitions are viewed as stressful life events and have been categorized as one type of induced transition. Yet other categories of stress also may impact transfer students; these include enduring life strains, developmental transitions, and daily hassles. Both major and daily stressful events play roles in the etiology and maintenance of psychological symptoms. Combinations of chronic negative stressors seem to multiply the risk of maladjustment. The studies we have reviewed indicate that transfer students may suffer negative consequences when they must simultaneously adjust to school transitions and other stressors.

Children from low-SES households experiencing significant life stressors may be at particular risk for maladjustment following school transitions. In general, studies indicate that such children have greater school problems. Caretaking by lower-income, stressed, and poorly educated parents may heighten children's behavioral difficulties, but inadequate caretaker support at any socioeconomic level likely places a child at risk. High SES does not necessarily buffer children from school problems following a stressful event. Many researchers now believe that stressful life events may not play a direct etiological role with respect to children's maladjustment but that events are probably mediated by individuals' coping resources and social support.

School transition researchers have been criticized for not adequately integrating theory and research on stress and coping into their theoretical orientations and research designs (Fenzel, 1989). By studying the interrelationships of stress, children's coping, and social support over time, researchers may be able to discover the developmental processes of competent functioning or maladjustment during school transitions. Thus, we have aimed to examine more closely the connections among stress, home, and school ecologies and transfer-student coping. In the next chapter, we explore interrelationships among transfer students' coping styles, academic and social adjustment, and self-esteem.

2

The Problems
and Risks

In this chapter, we address several important questions concerning school transitions: What are the problems and risks of school transfer children? How do students differ in their coping with school moves? In what ways are transfer children's academic achievement, social competence, and self-esteem related? How much does a school transfer disrupt a child's life?

Answering the last question, Blyth, Simmons, and Carlton-Ford (1983) suggested one possibility: the more discontinuous or different the two schools are, the greater is the psychological, academic, and social disruption for newcomers. For example, a child could move from a supportive, progressive school to one that is characterized by low teacher morale and few academic and extracurricular enrichment opportunities. Such discontinuity between old and new schools could influence student adjustment. A second possibility concerns the relative academic and social status of students before and after the transition. A student who may have been generally liked by former classmates could be rejected by new peers perhaps because his social behaviors are different from those of the new group. Thus, transfer students are likely to experience a range of coping demands depending on the degree of incongruity between their old and new schools and between their social and academic standing in each.

Elias, Gara, and Ubriaco (1985) enumerated the challenges of school transitions, which encompass not only students' psychological coping (such as cognitive self-appraisal and problem

18

solving) but also their social and academic adaptation. These demands include the following:

(1) shifts in role definition and expected behaviors;
(2) changes in membership in and position within social networks;
(3) reorganization of personal and social support resources;
(4) restructuring the way one perceives one's world; and
(5) management of stress resulting from uncertainty about expectations and goals and one's ability to accomplish the transition tasks (pp. 112-113; see also Felner et al., 1981).

The coping literature provides clues to the ways a child negotiates the social and academic terrain of new schools. It is reviewed in the next section.

How Children Cope with School Transitions

Coping is an umbrella term that encompasses many facets of our psychology. In general, it can include all individual responses to stressful life events or episodes (Compas, 1987). Personal characteristics likely to be important in coping are age, sex, genetic factors, temperament, intelligence, and other problem-solving skills (Rutter, 1981). In his review of research on children's responses to stress, Compas (1987) differentiated three dimensions of coping: (1) whether it is effortful or noneffortful, (2) what its function is, and (3) what resources, styles, and specific responses it requires. For the first category, Compas assumed that *effortful* coping includes both successful and maladaptive attempts to manage stress. Regarding the *function* of coping, Compas proposed that it can be either actively problem focused or directed toward regulation of emotional states resulting from the stressor. Considering the third aspect, children's coping resources are defined in terms of *personal abilities* (for example, academic aptitude, problem-solving skills, self-esteem) and the *social environment* (for example, supportive social networks within a school and family). *Coping style* refers to an individual's characteristic strategies for managing stress. Specific coping efforts are cognitive and behavioral responses to stressful life events such as a school transition. Compas concluded that supportive relationships within the family and in support networks outside the home are important resources for managing stress. Moreover, personal resources that enhance this ability include good problem-solving skills, internal locus of control, high self-esteem, and autonomy.

Other researchers have posed additional models of coping. Garmezy and colleagues (1984) proposed three generic models to describe the interplay of stress and individual attributes on adaptation. First, the *compensatory model* predicts that severe stress can be counteracted by personal qualities of strength and competent coping. For example, a resourceful student might succeed in a new school despite stresses in the family. Second, in the *challenge model,* stress has the potential to enhance competence, provided the stress is not excessive. In this case, a child might transfer into an academically more demanding school, yet with support, make marked scholastic gains.

The third model, the *protective model,* postulates a conditional relationship between stress and the individual with regard to adaptation. Certain personal qualities promote an immunity to stress while other attributes may contribute to a vulnerability. This concept converges with Rutter's comparison (1981) of vulnerability versus protective factors in children's response to psychosocial adversities. One strength of this model is its emphasis on resilient qualities of individuals and support networks, that is, qualities that contribute to individuals' overcoming stress and disadvantage (Garmezy et al., 1984; O'Grady & Metz, 1987; Rutter, 1981). Based on the models of adaptation developed by Garmezy and others (1984), a child undergoing a school transition may experience psychological growth, no change, or psychopathological development (Dohrenwend, 1978).

Applied research helps illustrate how these models and ideas are translated into action. Garmezy and his associates conducted a series of studies exploring the effects of stressful life events on the functional competence of children and the protective/competence factors that influence their resistance to stress. The researchers predicted that the competence level of a child, even if he or she is at risk, might serve as a protective factor against behavior maladjustment. They discovered that under stressful home situations the academic achievement of children with a high intelligence quotient (IQ) was maintained, but low-IQ children's relative performance declined. Other studies have demonstrated that good intelligence and good academic achievement may exert a protective effect in times of psychosocial stress (Rutter, 1981). These results convince us that personal resources that exist prior to the stressful event can moderate the impact of stressful circumstances. For practitioners, such research implies that intervention efforts should be directed partly toward bolstering the resilient qualities of students (O'Grady & Metz, 1987).

Each child copes differently, and both research and practice must take children's individuality into account. In studying children's coping responses to school transitions, researchers were better able to assess students' risk by recognizing that children, who may differ in their exposure to life-change events, also differ in their psychological functioning prior to the event (Gersten et al., 1977). Clearly, school transition researchers have recognized the need to assess students' previous achievement history (Holland-Jacobsen, Holland, & Cook, 1984) and behavior problems (Cappas, 1989). Additionally, one must consider how a student adjusts emotionally relative to other children (Turner & McClatchey, 1978). Holland and colleagues (1974) found that those transfer students who had demonstrated academic, behavioral, or social problems in their previous school were particularly vulnerable to the risks of school transitions. Thus, an important question asks how well the student was coping before he or she transferred.

In asking this we assume that there is some continuity and connection between earlier and later behavior. Some authorities contend that children's behavior and abilities are indeed stable across time and setting (Baker, Hughes, Street, & Sweetnam, 1983; Dodge, Pettit, McClaskey, & Brown, 1986).

Baker and his associates found that children with behavior problems at an early age (that is, preschool) were more likely to have
behavior problems during elementary-school years. These researchers concluded that behavior problems in young children
can persist and may be linked with educational disadvantage.
Dodge and his colleagues (1986) discovered that elementary boys
exhibited similar social competencies in different peer groups.
Thus, boys who showed poor social skills were repeatedly rejected despite being placed in new peer groups. Learning disabled (LD) children have been observed to maintain either adaptive or maladaptive classroom behavior over a three-year period
(McKinney & Speece, 1986). This evidence points to the possibility that many children transfer into new classrooms with
previously established social behavior problems or assets. Such
entrenched behavior poses challenges to us when we intervene
with transfer children.

It is possible, though, that our assumptions of continuity
of behavior are not correct; some researchers dispute these ideas.
Social learning theory suggests that individuals often behave
differently in different settings across time rather than express
static traits (Mischel, 1971). Obviously, developmental research
has shown that children's behavior changes over time. Sameroff
(1975) is among the researchers who have criticized the assumption of continuity of behavior in child development. He states:
"(1) Transitions from one stage to another with a qualitatively
different level of organization may make many of the adaptations and maladaptation of the earlier stage obsolete; (2) Individuals with completely different experiential histories can not
only achieve these transitions, but also after reaching the new
stage show little evidence of past diversity of functioning" (p.
268).

Cautioning future investigators, Sameroff (1975) expressed
doubt about the validity of broad predictions based on the initial characteristics of the child and environment. This advice
seems especially relevant when one considers the malleable pathways of person-environment transactions that arise during school
transitions. For instance, two transfer students who differed considerably from each other in their prior school performance may
have similar experiences on entering a new school.

Do children progressively learn better coping skills as they are faced with repeated school transitions? Addressing this question, Crockett and her colleagues proposed two hypotheses about students' coping capacities (Crockett, Petersen, Graber, Schulenberg, & Ebata, 1989). First, the *inoculation effect* predicts that students who have already transferred once will cope better during the second transition because they are familiar with the necessary coping skills. In contrast, the second hypothesis predicts that two moves are worse than one because of multiple academic and social disruptions.

The investigators found evidence supporting the second hypothesis: students who underwent multiple school transitions seemed to cope less well in general than students who had experienced fewer transfers. One explanation for this finding is that although some individuals might show gains as a result of coping with new challenges, with increased demands, their coping abilities deteriorate. Thus there may be a critical level of demands for children under stress: under the level, they flourish and grow; above it, they suffer. Such findings may imply that school transfer sometimes exceeds students' critical tolerance levels and we must help them strengthen their coping mechanisms to equilibrate stress.

In broad terms, transfer students have been categorized as *successful copers* and *poor copers* (Holland et al., 1974). Successful copers are transfer students who make rapid and successful adaptations to new schools. Holland and his colleagues observed that these students were average or above average in intellectual ability and were interested in school work and achievement. Moreover, teachers did not see successful transfer children as discipline problems. Conversely, poor copers failed to create good relations with peers and teachers or to meet behavior and achievement expectations.

Our review of the coping literature illustrates how children vary in their coping. During school transitions, students who demonstrate competent coping are likely to counteract stress; for some, adverse conditions may even enhance coping up to a certain level. Competencies such as good intelligence, high motivation, and disciplined behavior likely serve to protect transfer students from maladjustment. However, these students may not necessarily learn better coping skills as the result of repeated school moves; that is, frequent transfers may not inoculate them against stress. Investigators have sought to predict the performance of transfer students based on their previous adjustment history. There is evidence that children's behavior and achievement often remain stable across settings, but not always. Prediction efforts can be complicated; in their adaptation to a new school, transfer students may display coping strengths or weaknesses that are quite different from their prior functioning.

Importance of Social Adjustment

Another lens through which to view transfer is social networks. School social networks play a central role in shaping children's behavioral, emotional, and academic development (Rutter, 1979). When children transfer to a new school, established social support networks are disrupted and they must adapt to new peer groups and different teacher expectations (Holland et al., 1974). As a consequence, many transfer children manifest at least short-term ill effects such as unhappiness, increased need for attention, nervousness, aggression (especially among boys), and social withdrawal (Turner & McClatchey, 1978).

Several studies suggest that transfer students tend to be most concerned about their social adjustment, that is, making new friends and leaving old ones (Schaller, 1975; Snow, Gilchrist, Schilling, Schinke, & Kelso, 1986). Indeed, it seems critical for transfer students to establish positive peer relationships quickly. In one study, newcomers' popularity during the first day in the classroom was substantially correlated with their popularity eleven weeks later; the classroom social structure seemed to crystallize after three to five weeks (Ziller & Behringer, 1961). Successful entry into new peer groups is largely dependent on adaptive social skills (Dodge et al., 1986); at least for third and fourth graders, popular children appear to be more socially skilled than unpopular children (Gottman, Gonso, & Rasmussen, 1975).

Here, it may be helpful to clarify two terms that will be used interchangeably throughout this book: *social skills* and *social competence.* Investigators studying children's social skills continue to debate the criteria for competent social behavior (for example, Curran, Farrell, & Grunberger, 1984), and no broad consensus has been reached. Numerous definitions and heuristic models have been proposed. LeCroy (1982) defined social skills as "a complex set of skills which allow the child the ability to successfully mediate interactions between peers, parents, teachers, and other adults" (p. 92). Gresham (1988) suggested that social skills seen in school settings encompass academic performance, cooperative behaviors, social initiation behaviors, assertive behaviors, peer reinforcement behaviors, communication skills, problem-solving skills, and social self-efficacy. Additionally, he identified four types of social skill deficiencies: social skill deficits, self-control deficits, social performance deficits, and self-control performance deficits. In regard to the performance deficits, the author assumed that children have the requisite social or self-control skills but do not exhibit them. Transfer students who manifest deficits in any one of these categories are likely to experience social adjustment problems.

In general, social competence can be defined as the successful or unsuccessful enactment of social skills. Moreover, adaptive social competence entails an adequate fit between an individual's social skills and his or her social environment. Social competence also implies a child's social status, that is, how well he or she is accepted by peers and adults.

Dodge (1985) presented a five-faceted scheme of children's social interaction that elucidates different levels of assessment and intervention. In brief, Dodge's model includes (1) the judgments of social competence by peers and authority figures, (2) observable social behaviors, (3) social tasks or domains of interaction, (4) unconscious influences (for example, social self-concept), and (5) social information processing. Dodge (1985) concluded that a "profile approach" might be best in describing social competence. An individual profile might be based on selected combinations of Dodge's five proposed social competence dimensions. For example, investigation of transfer students' social competence across different social domains could integrate assessments of peers and teachers as well as individuals' self-concepts. Examination of several assessment approaches illustrates how children's social competence in the classroom can be measured.

In school settings, students' social competence can be assessed from three perspectives: (1) by an adult such as the classroom teacher or independent observer, (2) by peers, and (3) from the individual student's point of view. Teacher ratings have proven to be valid and reliable in identifying students' social adaptation (Achenbach & Edelbrock, 1986). Three popular methods of peer assessment are peer nominations, peer ratings, and peer rankings (Kane & Lawler, 1978). Overall, peer assessments have proven to be highly predictive of children's social adaptation in school. Kane and Lawler concluded that among the peer assessment strategies, peer nominations have the highest validity and reliability.

In the peer nominating method, the shortened version of the Pupil Evaluation Inventory, called the Peer Assessment Inventory, is a useful measure of students' social competence in class (Lardon & Jason, in press; see also Pekarik, Prinz, Liebert, Weintraub, & Neale, 1976). The instrument provides an assessment of children's aggression, withdrawal, and likability in the school setting. Another sociometric assessment framework for targeting children in need of social skills interventions asks students to nominate three classmates they like most and three they like least (Coie, 1985). Coie and his colleagues identified five types of children's social status: popular, average, rejected, controversial, and neglected (Coie, Dodge, & Coppotelli, 1982).

Other investigators have also studied the characteristics of neglected and rejected children (Asher & Wheeler, 1985; Dubow & Cappas, 1988). Neglected children lack friends but are not disliked; they tend to be shy and isolated in school. The rejected students also lack friends in school but are disliked by many peers; they are seen as disruptive, often aggressive, and deficient in social skills appropriate to academic settings. Rejected boys have been further differentiated into subtypes: (1) rejected children who exhibit high aggression, low self-control, behavior problems, and withdrawn behavior; and (2) rejected children who withdraw but do not show aggression, behavior problems, or poor self-control (French, 1988).

Student transfers who are rejected by new peers may be at special risk for school maladjustment. Findings indicate that rejected children tend to be a more isolated and lonely group than neglected children, a condition that makes them more at risk than other social-status groups.

Dubow and Cappas (1988) investigated the peer social status of third- through fifth-grade students. Students were classified into one of five social-status types according to the previously mentioned scheme of Coie and his colleagues (Coie, Dodge, & Coppotelli, 1982). Consistent with previous studies, rejected students were perceived as demonstrating more classroom and peer-related behavior problems. Popular children were seen as well adjusted. Controversial children tended to perform well academically and possessed both positive and negative interpersonal skills. Neglected children reportedly lacked group cooperation skills. These patterns were demonstrated across gender, race, and grade level.

In addition, Dubow and Cappas (1988) reported that teachers rated rejected children as having the fewest friends, the poorest grades, and the greatest number of behavior problems. Teachers viewed popular and controversial students as the best adjusted. Based on peer reports, rejected and neglected children were viewed as the least competent, and popular and controversial children as the most competent. Rejected and controversial children exhibited the most behavior problems, and popular and neglected students showed the fewest behavior problems. An interesting result is that controversial children exhibited both prosocial and aggressive behavior, tended to have the most friends, and showed high academic achievement.

In summary, transfer students need to adapt to new peers and social expectations. Following school moves, one can expect children to display mild symptoms such as nervousness or unhappiness for a brief time. However, more persistent social difficulties can result in transfer children becoming rejected or neglected by peers and teachers. Furthermore, social competence in the classroom is often associated with academic performance. Thus, it is important to assess social competence. Social skills can be measured with several different assessment tools and from various perspectives, including those of peers, parents, teachers, and the transfer children themselves.

Relationships Between Social
and Academic Competence

Academic performance is the main criterion for determining school success. It has also been viewed as one marker of social competence (Green, Forehand, Beck, & Vosk, 1980). However, social competence indices may be an equally important measure of school adjustment (Zigler & Trickett, 1978). Educational research reveals considerable overlap between students' social and academic competence. All educators would agree that systematic learning of basic skills such as reading and arithmetic requires the cooperation and concentrated efforts of students (Feldhusen, Thurston, & Benning, 1967). Thus, certain social behaviors are "important prerequisites for competent academic performance — these can be considered academically-relevant social behaviors" (Cartledge & Milburn, 1978, p. 131). Cartledge and Milburn defined "classroom survival skills" as those social behaviors, interpersonal and task related, that produce positive consequences in the classroom setting.

Classroom Academic Behaviors

Teachers tend to favor most highly those social skills ensuring adherence to order, rule, obedience, and responsibility. Many may place less value on social skills involving peer interaction such as playing (Cartledge & Milburn, 1978). Adaptive classroom behaviors include self-direction, personal responsibility, and functional academic skills (Gresham, 1988). Also, social behaviors such as independence, attention, persistence, self-control, and compliance are strongly associated with academic achievement (Cartledge & Milburn, 1978). Students who are attentive, independent, and task oriented during academic activities with peers are more likely to demonstrate higher achievement than children who are distractible, dependent, and passive in similar group activities (McKinney, Mason, Perkerson, & Clifford, 1975). Attending behaviors appear to be most important for classroom success (Cartledge & Milburn, 1978).

Several studies have demonstrated strong links between classroom behavior, scholastic aptitude, and academic achieve-

ment. Feldhusen and his colleagues (Feldhusen et al., 1967) concluded that the more important determinant of students' daily
success in the classroom is probably their educational status relative to their class rather than to national norms. Similarly, Swift
and Spivack (1969) recommended placing more emphasis on
teacher-assigned grades and teachers' descriptions of classroom
behaviors relevant to those grades. They considered these a more
precise measurement of students' classroom functioning than
standardized test performance alone. Weine, Kurasaki, and Jason (1990) provided data showing that parent reports of children's grades correspond well to actual grades. McKinney and
his associates (1975) demonstrated that combining measures of
children's aptitude and classroom behaviors can significantly enhance the prediction of long-term achievement. Combining
twelve observational indices of second graders' classroom behavior taken in the fall of the school year, the researchers were
able to predict springtime achievement, with a significant multiple R equaling .60. In comparison, the correlation between
pupils' IQ and springtime achievement was .70. When the behavioral measures and IQ were combined for prediction of
springtime academic achievement, the multiple R rose to .87.
Based on this study, the combination of children's aptitude and
classroom behavior appears to predict academic achievement
better than either alone.

Swift and Spivack (1969) explored the classroom behaviors
of achievers and underachievers in the fifth grade. When IQ
was controlled in the analysis, achieving students were defined
as those children scoring above the 85th percentile on the Iowa
Test of Basic Skills in both language and nonlanguage areas.
Underachievers were children whose scores fell below the 30th
percentile in at least one area on the Iowa test and below the
45th percentile in both. A second criterion was teacher grades.
Achievers were defined as students receiving an A or B, and
underachievers as those receiving a D or F. Classroom behavior
was measured by teachers using the Devereux Elementary School
Behavior Rating Scale. The underachievers displayed significantly more maladaptive behavior than their achieving peers.
In fact, at any IQ level, a D or F report card grade was accompanied by classroom behavioral difficulties. Specifically, 69 per-

cent of the underachieving children were rated as inattentive and 45 percent required frequent reprimands from the teacher for disruptive behavior.

Another investigation focused on high-ability fifth-grade students who were underachieving in the classroom (Perkins, 1965). Pupils were considered underachievers if their average IQ was 114 or above and if the point corresponding to their average IQ and grade point average (GPA) fell at least one standard error of the estimate below the regression line for their classroom. Conversely, high achievers demonstrated an average IQ and GPA that was above the regression line but within one standard error of the estimate. Thirty-six underachievers were matched with same-gender high achievers based on IQ and reading score on the California Achievement Test. Weekly observations of classroom behavior and learning activities were made across the major subject areas. Results indicated that, compared with achievers, underachivers spent more time engaged in an academic area other than the one assigned or in nonacademic activities; they were also more frequently withdrawn. Surprisingly, both achievers and underachievers spent equal amounts of time listening, watching the teacher, and reading; however, achievers participated more in social, work-oriented activities with peers than did underachievers. The last finding highlights the potential contribution of cooperative peer relations to improved academic performance for underachievers.

The above two studies differentiated characteristics of high and low achievers. Supporting these earlier findings, Garmezy and associates (1984) did a factor analysis of measures of students' academic achievement, classroom behavior competence, and social competence. From the results they derived bipolar competence factors. The first factor, labeled "engaged-disengaged," reflected children's sociability-leadership, sensitive-isolated, cooperative-initiating, and comprehension-inattention behaviors. Not surprisingly, academic achievement scores also loaded on this factor. The second factor, "classroom disruptiveness," targeted disruptive or negative social behavior. The disruptiveness factor was based on peer reports of aggressive-disruptive behavior and teacher reports of disruptive-oppositional behavior.

The authors' findings revealed a small inverse relationship between stress and the engaged aspect of school competence, and a stronger positive relationship between stress and the disruptive dimension. These results support the popular assumption that stress originating in the home and school precipitates disruptive behavior among students.

Some children's socially maladaptive class behavior may result from repeated frustrations during attempts to learn (Feldhusen et al., 1967). Blai (1985) stated that most students' school failures can be traced to early frustrating school experiences. Certainly, few children can accept school failure without suffering serious consequences such as loss of motivation and emotional instability (Blai, 1985). Ingraham (1985) cited study results showing that only one serious failure experience can have the same behavioral and emotional impact as repeated failures. However, not all children respond to failure in a similar manner.

Transfer students have been identified as successful or poor copers (Holland et al., 1974). More specifically, children have been distinguished as effective or ineffective copers by failure on academic tasks (Compas, 1987). Mastery-oriented students persist at problem solving and increase their concentration. In contrast, helpless children demonstrate ineffective coping by reducing their effort, becoming discouraged, and performing more poorly. The behavior of the two groups may be similar before the failure experience but becomes markedly different following the setback. These differences in coping styles provide one explanation for persistence versus failure on difficult school tasks. Comparison of children possessing different aptitude levels might further illuminate reasons for loss of motivation.

Rutter (1979) studied ten-year-old children, measuring their reading achievement, degree of behavior problems, and level of family adversity. It was clear that highly intelligent children were less likely to display behavior problems than were average children. Corroborating other research findings, Rutter found that students of average intelligence with reading disabilities showed greater conduct problems than peers. One of the most notable discoveries was that students of low reading ability exhibited significantly greater behavior problems, regardless of high- or low-risk family background. Thus, children's academic performance and behavioral competence were strongly related and the interaction between the two appeared to be independent from stressful circumstances outside of class.

In a study of third and sixth graders, teachers nominated children who consistently displayed socially approved or disapproved behavior (Feldhusen et al., 1967). Disapproved behavior consisted of aggressive and disruptive actions whereas approved behavior was cooperative and productive. Not surprisingly, when students' scores on standardized achievement tests were compared, the approved children demonstrated significantly higher reading and arithmetic performance than the disapproved children, even with intelligence as a covariate. The difference was greater at the sixth-grade level than the third-grade level. The investigators' explanation of this finding was that by the time a child reaches the sixth grade, handicaps in basic skills become increasingly more troublesome.

Overall, the above studies indicate that task-focused classroom behavior is strongly associated with academic achievement. Children who have difficulty learning may tend to become disruptive or disengaged from classroom activities. Increasing pupils' academic engaged time is a major problem for teachers in structuring classes to ensure optimal student performance. However, students' academic achievement appears to be related not only to time spent learning but also to time needed for learning (Gettinger, 1984). Gettinger suggested that outcomes of additional instructional time may not be the same for all students because they have individual differences in the amount of exposure required for mastery. Teachers typically allot uniform periods of time for instruction in different subjects, assuming the "time spent learning" is adequate for the majority of students; however, such set time periods often do not accommodate those students who might require longer or more elaborate presentations and practice. At special risk may be transfer students who show gaps in academic skills and need to catch up with nontransfer classmates (Jason et al., 1989; Jason et al., 1992).

Academic Achievement and Peer Relationships

The studies reviewed to this point have shown that social competence and achievement success are linked. We have hinted that peer social relations are an important part of classroom behavior and in the following discussion we consider how they relate to achievement and school transfer.

Students' academic achievement has been associated with social competence (Gresham, 1988; Zigler & Trickett, 1978). Some research findings suggest that children with high academic achievement tend to be better liked and to interact more positively with peers than do low achievers (Green et al., 1980). One explanation for differences in popularity based on achievement is that high achievers are better esteemed by their classmates than are low achievers. Perhaps because of frustration and a sense of inefficacy, lower achievers may be more prone to withdraw or become disruptive. Also, there appears to be some general overlap between the cognitive and social domains of functioning (Cauce, 1987; Ford, 1982). For example, as an underlying factor, general intelligence probably influences social information processing, which largely determines social behavior (Dodge, 1985). Conversely, peer relations may impact academic achievement. Studies have shown that transfer students often are more concerned about peer relations than any other aspect of the transition (Schaller, 1975; Snow et al., 1986). Any problems making friends in a new school are likely to affect a child's academic performance adversely (Long, 1975).

Several studies support a link between peer relations and academic performance. Green and associates (1980) discovered that third-grade children who were high achievers were better liked and interacted more positively with peers than did low achievers. Among mildly retarded seven- to fourteen-year-old students, academic competence was associated most highly with peer acceptance while misbehavior was associated with rejection (Morrison & Borthwick, 1983). Vosk and her colleagues made classroom observations of third and fourth graders who had been identified by teachers as unpopular (Vosk, Forehand,

Parker, & Rickard, 1982). Unpopular pupils spent less time on task than popular children and engaged in more negative interactions with peers. These students can be further distinguished as neglected or rejected (Coie, 1985). One investigation demonstrated that accepted children displayed significantly higher achievement and better behavior than rejected students, but did not differ from neglected children in achievement (Green, Vosk, Forehand, & Beck, 1981). Neglected children performed better than rejected children only in math. Teachers rated rejected children as more inattentive-passive and hyperactive than their peers. These findings imply that neglected children do not differ substantially in achievement from their popular and rejected peers. The noticeable demarcation in achievement occurs between popular and rejected children.

In another study that explored academic and social links, the best behavior predictors of third- and fourth-grade students' achievement included positive peer interaction, initiating activity with the teacher, inattention, and self-stimulation (Soli & Devine, 1978). Similarly, Cobb (1972) hypothesized that a combination of specific task-oriented and non-task-oriented behaviors observed during fourth graders' arithmetic classes would predict achievement. He found that work-oriented peer interactions (such as discussing academic material) ensured greater achievement by students than merely attending to teachers and not interacting with peers. Apparently, successful students receive more practice in scholastic skills through academically focused social interaction than do students whose social contact is less concerned with assignments. Cobb predicted that teaching children to attend and talk to peers about academic material would increase their achievement level.

A recent investigation evaluated the extent to which academic tutoring for high-risk students promoted classroom social competence. Neither study applied interventions directly aimed at improving children's interpersonal social skills. One project selected socially rejected nontransfer children having significant academic delays and provided them with a tutoring intervention. Not only their academic achievement but also their social status rose, as most of the children moved from the rejected to the average social category (Coie & Krehbiel, 1984).

In general, the literature we have reviewed suggests that students' academic achievement and classroom social adjustment are related. However, Kicklighter, Bailey, and Richmond (1980) argued that there is sometimes little compatibility between a child's scholastic achievement and his or her social competence outside the classroom. The authors observed that many incompetent students are failures only in the classroom setting; at home and in the community they are seen as knowledgeable, socially adept, and independent. In other words, children's academic success may not be related to their successful adaptation to nonacademic settings. Still, academic and social connections are strong and well researched. Preventive programs for transfer students must take into account these connections. Later, in Chapters Five and Ten, we discuss how these connections manifest themselves in our research program.

Self-Concept and School Competence

As self-concept is a critical part of anyone's psychology, it is no surprise to find that self-concept matters for transfer students. Changes in transfer students' self-concept may be another important indication of their adjustment to new schools (Crockett et al., 1989). Research evidence suggests that elementary students can make discriminations about their global self-worth (Cauce, 1987; Harter, 1988; Piers & Harris, 1964). Harter (1985, 1988) identified five distinct domains of self-worth for children from eight to twelve years old: scholastic competence, athletic competence, peer social acceptance, behavioral conduct, and physical appearance. Although these competence domains appear to be distinct, they are often closely associated.

Several school transition studies have targeted students' self-concept as the primary indicator of social adjustment. Examining a number of variables thought to be predictive of fifth and sixth graders' adjustment to school transitions, Jones and Thornburg (1985) found that pretransition global self-esteem was the only predictor of later self-esteem. Moreover, students' pretransition perceived anonymity was the strongest predictor of posttransition anonymity.

How a transfer student's peers accept him or her likely impacts the child's self-esteem. Fenzel and Blyth (1986) used self-esteem as the primary adjustment measure for students' transition from sixth grade to junior high school. They predicted a strong association between self-esteem and the quality of peer relationships, which were viewed as mediators of stress. To test for relationships between school adjustment and social relations, the researchers examined only two extreme groups: good adjusters (gainers) and poor adjusters (decliners). Adjustment was operationalized in terms of self-esteem, participation in extracurricular activities, and perceived integration into the school environment. The researchers discovered that males who gained in self-esteem had more frequent and positive peer contacts. In contrast, females who gained in self-esteem demonstrated lower or equal levels of peer intimacy compared to decliners. The authors acknowledged that the direction of change for males was anticipated but the results for females were confusing. They surmised that female adolescents may seek more effective support from family than from peers in times of great stress.

Transfer students who are rejected by peers may show differences in self-concept. In a sample of nine- and eleven-year-old children, rejected children could be assigned to one of two categories (Boivin & Begin, 1989). One rejected group displayed high self-concepts compared to another group who showed low self-concepts. The researchers concluded that, potentially, rejected children who show high self-concepts might be immune to academic declines associated with peer rejection.

Scholastic and behavioral self-concepts may be linked to adjustment during school transitions. Researchers generally agree that underachievers tend to have poorer self-concepts than normal achievers. When exposed to considerable negative feedback, even a child who had a stable, positive self-concept prior to a failure experience may respond with marked decreases in motivation and achievement (Ingraham, 1985). Transfer students who have academic skill gaps and consequently experience lower achievement at a new school may be especially vulnerable to decreases in self-esteem. In one study those who perceived themselves in negative terms in regard to their new school scored significantly lower on math, spelling, and reading achievement tests during the school year in relation to other transfer students (Jason & Bogat, 1983).

Emotional and behavioral difficulties are often associated with learning delays, seen sometimes as the primary causes of the learning problem and sometimes as secondary to the frustrations of repeated school failure (Black, 1974). In his study, Black found that learning disabled (LD) students had significantly lower global self-concepts than normal readers of similar age, sex, grade level, and intellect. In contrast to most reported correlations of self-concept and achievement test performance, which are typically in the .30 range, Black found a closer relationship between these two variables among the LD students, with correlations ranging from .46 to .58. Another finding that emerged was that older LD pupils tended to view themselves more negatively than did younger LD students.

It is apparent that learning difficulties and concomitant low scholastic and social self-concept contribute to depression among children; studies also indicate that depression impairs learning (Colbert, Newman, Ney, & Young, 1982; Cullinan, Schloss, & Epstein, 1987), creating what can become a downward spiral. Symptoms of depression that may hinder school performance include low self-esteem, sadness, decreased concentration, aggressive behavior, and general social, family, and school disturbance. Learning retardation may often result from lessened energy and attention available to depressed children. Colbert and others (1982) demonstrated that depression precipitated poor school performance among six- to fourteen-year-old psychiatric patients who were intellectually capable and without a learning disability. Cullinan and associates (1987) determined that regular classroom students who were depressed tended to achieve less adequately overall compared to nondepressed peers. In neither of these studies, however, was low self-esteem necessarily identified as the primary cause of depression. Depression could have arisen from other sources such as family disruption.

The above research points to the importance and usefulness of assessing different domains of transfer students' self-concepts. By examining changes in their self-concepts, researchers may better be able to determine how transfer students perceive their own adjustment. In particular, learning difficulties and poor peer relations likely contribute to decreases in self-concept, especially among older transfer students. In a synergistic fashion, lower self-concept could potentially lead to and be worsened by behavioral conduct problems and childhood depression. Therefore, researchers, practitioners, and parents need to consider self-concept when intervening with transfer children.

Differences in Individual
Transfer Student Adjustments

We have discussed many common dimensions of the transfer phenomenon, such as social competence, peer relations, and self-esteem. The existence of common aspects, however, does not mean that all children experience transition in the same fashion — far from it. Transfer students may undergo dissimilar school transition experiences depending upon differences in grade level, gender, and exceptional student status (that is, learning disabilities). In this section, we examine these school adjustment differences among both transfer and nontransfer students. We find that these distinctions interact with transfer experience to shape unique outcomes for children.

Grade-Level Differences

School transition researchers should be wary of the "developmental level uniformity myth," which is the assumption that children at various ages or abilities, but with the same behavior problems, are alike (Kendall, 1984). During school transitions, students may experience different degrees of stress depending on grade level (Jones & Thornburg, 1985). Moreover, times of transition coinciding with certain developmental periods (for example, entering puberty) may place children at particular risk for school failure and social maladjustment (Crockett et al., 1989; Felner et al., 1981).

Frequent school transitions during the primary grades (kindergarten through third grade [K–3]) have been suspected to impair mobile students' ability to cope with future academic tasks and adversely affect their later achievement (Black & Bargar, 1975). Black and Bargar reasoned that social and academic adjustment factors during school transitions may interfere with students' learning of basic skills, especially reading, which may negatively impact their achievement in other content areas. Unexpectedly, the investigators found no differences in reading achievement between highly mobile, low-income children and matched control, low-mobility sixth-grade pupils. However, the authors admitted that there was no attempt to control for students who had received special remedial reading services.

Other research indicates that transfer students in the primary grades are less likely than older children to develop academic and social problems (Barrett & Noble, 1973; Ziller & Behringer, 1961). Upper-elementary children or adolescents may experience more difficulties than preschoolers or primary-grade students in making adjustments to school moves because of the greater complexity of social networks and academic expectations in later years. Supporting this hypothesis, an early school transition study examined the social acceptance of 32 newcomers among 720 regular students in grades one through six over a six-month period (Ziller & Behringer, 1961). The primary measure of assimilation was derived from the sociometric question: "Which five children in this classroom do you like best?" Results indicated that first-, second-, and third-grade transfers were accepted more readily than upper-elementary transfers.

More recent findings also indicate that many older youth find it difficult to manage stress associated with demanding social and academic tasks confronted in a new school (Barone, Aquirre-Deandreis, & Trickett, 1991; Gilchrist, Schinke, Snow, Schilling, & Senechal, 1988; Snow et al., 1986). One survey of sixth graders' transition to junior high school revealed that the students' greatest concern involved fear of physical intimidation and fighting (Snow et al., 1986). Worries about school work and grades and meeting new children ranked lower in their perceptions of the school transition. Additional findings demonstrated that young adolescents may experience considerable anxiety concerning not only anticipated transitions to junior high

school but also dissatisfaction with themselves and peer relationships (Gilchrist et al., 1988). Such pervasive worries and
low self-esteem can influence achievement; for example, Ingraham (1985) has shown that low self-concept can contribute to
deterioration in a child's academic achievement beginning around
ten years of age.

These findings suggest that older transfer students who
manifest delays in academic and social competence appear to
be at a greater disadvantage than younger children. In particular, older transfers may experience difficulty assimilating into
new peer networks. Additionally, teachers' grading standards
become more stringent for older transfer students and this may
translate into lower academic scores (Simmons, 1987). Overall, the increased pace and complexity of curricula in the upper
grades likely make it hard for older transfer students to do well,
particularly if they suffer from academic deficits. These academic
problems often begin early in their school years. Hess (1987)
found that for the subjects of his study the roots of school failure
and later dropout could be traced to third grade. Hess's research
strongly suggests that third through fifth grade are critical years
to begin a successful intervention.

Gender Differences

Boys tend to have more behavior problems than girls
throughout the elementary grades (i.e., kindergarten through
sixth grade) (Swift & Spivack, 1968). During the norming procedures on their twelve-factor child behavior scale, Swift and Spivack found that boys were rated as more problematic on nine
factors. For example, in achievement-related behaviors, the
results indicated that boys were more disruptive, less willing
to wait for instructions, more disrespectful, and more anxious
about classroom demands. Another group of investigators reported that eight-year-old boys were more likely to manifest anti-
social rather than neurotic problems as compared to girls (Baker
et al., 1983). In connection with learning problems, Bryan (1978)
found that LD boys (K–6) spent significantly less time on task
in the regular classroom and were twice as likely as comparison children to be ignored by classmates and teachers.

Among other elementary-school transfer studies, findings have pointed toward gender differences in social adjustment. Transfer girls appear to be more readily assimilated into peer groups than boys (Ziller & Behringer, 1961). Schaller (1975) discovered that fourth- and fifth-grade nontransfer boys were more negative than girls toward transfer children, particularly new boys. In a recent study, elementary transfer boys were rated by peers as more aggressive and less likable than girls (Orosan, Jason, & Weine, 1991). These studies, however, do not indicate how soon after transfer the negative perceptions were measured or how long they lasted.

Vernberg and Wilcox (1984) investigated the social competence and social acceptance of third-, fourth-, and seventh-grade transfer and nontransfer students. Seventh-grade transfer boys were the only group who displayed significant behavioral problems and lack of social involvement throughout the school year. Although mobile boys in elementary school exhibited more maladjustment than nonmobile boys at the beginning of the year, these differences disappeared by the end of the year. Transfer and nontransfer girls appeared similar at both testing points. These findings point to a possible age-by-gender interaction; that is, gender distinctions among transfer students may manifest at different ages. There may be a time when social assimilation versus academic achievement is more or less important, in part, based on gender differences.

Drawing on correlational analyses, Pillen, Jason, and Olson (1988) reported transfer girls' academic ability appeared to be linked to social status whereas boys' peer popularity and academic achievement were not significantly related. In a later study, transfer boys reported significantly higher scholastic and social self-concepts than transfer girls (Orosan et al., 1991). Similarly, Crockett and others (1989) found that girls who had experienced two school transitions tended to show poorer self-image than male transfers and nontransfers.

Two investigations indicated that transiency may have a greater negative effect on achievement for girls than boys (Brockman & Reeves, 1967; Levine et al., 1966). Nonetheless, Brockman and Reeves found the overall number of school transitions was not very significant in relation to achievement of

girls. In contrast, although boys were not affected as m~~ch~~ ~
the initial transfer, increasing number of transfers w?
with lower achievement. Despite this evidence, mo
not found significant gender differences in transfe
demic achievement; Crockett and others (1989) c
gender differences in the impact of timing and nur
transitions are sparse and, considering the possibi
effects, should be viewed with caution.

To review, there are indications that boys
perience transfer differently, though no overwhelm
exists. Overall, research findings on gender diffes
transfer students reveal several trends. Transfe. boys appear
to display more disruptive behavior problems than girls during
the elementary grades, and transfer girls may be more readily
assimilated by peers than boys. Nonetheless, transfer boys may
display higher self-concept than girls. Possibly, gender is an important distinction only for certain age groups. Finally, there
is no strong evidence indicating gender differences in transfer
students' academic achievement. These questions need further
study.

Differences for Exceptional Students

School transition research has targeted low-achieving children, some of whom are likely to have undiagnosed learning
disabilities. Besides academic delays, it has long been recognized
that learning disabled (LD) students tend to manifest a broad
array of behavioral and social difficulties (Bryan, 1978). Bryan
described such children as often being hyperactive, distractible, inattentive, aggressive, emotionally labile, and unable to
delay gratification. There is evidence that a significant number
of LD students experience difficulty establishing friendships and
eliciting positive responses from others (Bryan, 1978). Compared to average students, LD students are often at a disadvantage in socialization because they may have fewer initial social
skills, may learn new skills more slowly, and may be less sensitive to the many subtleties in social interaction (Hazel, Schumaker, Sherman, & Sheldon-Wildgen, 1982).

In particular, children who demonstrate learning disabilities may be more likely to display difficulty in verbal and non-verbal social skills than their non-LD peers (Minskoff, 1982). For example, impairments in children's receptive and/or expressive cognitive processes can impact their mastery of language which, in turn, influences their verbal communication with peers (Bryan, 1978). Moreover, LD pupils may sometimes be less accurate than their non-LD counterparts in comprehending non-verbal communication. Findings from a series of Bryan's studies suggest that LD students experience difficulties in social development as well as perceiving and understanding others' affective states. Based on Bryan's results, it is also clear that teachers and peers make negative evaluations of these children: LD children experienced significantly more social rejection than their comparison peers.

Richmond and Blagg (1985) compared the adaptive behavior, social adjustment, and academic achievement of learning disabled (LD), behavior disordered (BD), educable mentally retarded (EMR), and regular classroom six- to nine-year-old students. The Children's Adaptive Behavior Scale (CABS) and Wide Range Achievement Test (WRAT) were administered to the 120 participants; in addition, a behavior problem checklist for each child was completed by teachers. Social adjustment constructs distinguished the BD children from the others. On the WRAT and CABS, regular classroom students scored highest, followed by LD, BD, and EMR students in that order. Surprisingly, the differences between the LD and BD children were not significant and suggest that these identified students may not be dissimilar in terms of academic and social performance.

Overall, the literature indicates that LD students often experience academic problems in conjunction with social and behavioral difficulties. It is likely that, in one or several subject areas, some transfer students have actual learning disabilities that are undiagnosed. Furthermore, academically able transfer students, who have skill deficits relative to new classroom academic expectations, may experience social and behavioral adjustment problems similar to those of LD students. Transfer thus represents a key gateway at which a child's competencies weaken and problems emerge. Certainly, it is a timely opportunity for educators to identify and aid such high-risk candidates.

School transition researchers have attempted to identify children at risk for school failure in order to provide them with specialized school services. However, predictions of poor outcome have tended to be overinclusive; that is, many more children are labeled high risk than actually develop problems (O'Grady & Metz, 1987). Few school transition studies have endeavored to classify academically and socially distinct subgroups of transfer students and to study their year-long adjustment. Examining homogeneous groups of transfer students (e.g., low achievers, unpopular children, and students displaying behavior problems) could reveal different patterns of school adjustment. By more accurately classifying transfer students and exploring their varied paths of adjustment, educators might be able to identify subgroups of high-risk children with greater precision and tailor intervention efforts specific to their academic and social adjustment needs. In Chapter Ten we discuss our recent attempt to achieve such an accurate classification of high-risk transfer students.

Summary

In coping with school transitions, transfer students must adapt to new peers, meet new academic and behavioral standards, and be accepted by teachers. These students vary in their coping resources and styles, which can include both successful and maladaptive attempts to manage stress. Transfer students' coping can be further characterized as directed toward problem resolution or regulation of emotions. In general, children and their support networks may possess attributes that promote immunity to stress; other coping characteristics, however, may make them more vulnerable to maladjustment. Some transfer students may be able to counteract transition difficulties and actually gain from the challenge of switching schools. A number of studies have indicated that good coping resources such as high intelligence and adept social skills may help children deal with adverse conditions more successfully. In order to predict school transition outcomes, it seems important to assess the relative adaptability and previous emotional and academic adjustment of transfer students. However, despite prior performance, a transfer student may display quite different coping strategies and capabilities following a school transition.

We explored relationships among students' academic achievement, social competence, and self-concept. Transfer students who display academic and social skills deficits as well as low self-concepts are prone to ongoing adjustment problems. It appears that academic performance and social/behavioral competence are closely related. School failure has been implicated as a primary source of children's frustration and consequent behavior problems. Research findings suggest that underachieving students tend to display more maladaptive behavior than their achieving peers. However, not all students respond similarly to failure experiences; mastery-oriented students maintain motivation and persistence whereas helpless children reduce their coping efforts. Students who remain task focused, even during social exchanges with peers, tend to achieve better than disengaged or disruptive children.

Regarding social acceptance in the classroom, one helpful classification categorizes children as average, popular, neglected, rejected, and controversial. In addition, investigators have identified aggressive-disruptive, withdrawn, and likable characteristics of students that are related to social status and academic achievement. Children with high academic achievement tend to be liked by peers, whereas those who perform poorly on academic tasks often can be classified as rejected. Children's self-concept is also associated with social and academic competence. Researchers agree that underachievers tend to have poor self-concepts. Children experiencing poor self-concepts may manifest other depressive symptoms such as reduced effort and lack of concentration, which impair learning.

Transfer students may differ in their adjustment depending on grade level, gender, and academic aptitude. Upper-elementary transfer children may tend to experience more school difficulties than preschool or primary grade pupils because of the more demanding social and academic tasks in later grades.

Although school problems may not be apparent during the primary grades, school moves during this period may cause academic delays and lead to problems in later grades.

Concerning gender differences, transfer boys appear to display more disruptive behavior problems than girls. One study suggests that transfer girls' academic ability is associated with their social status, but in general, underachieving boys may be at greater risk for peer problems than underachieving girls. Nonetheless, transfer boys seem to display higher self-concepts than girls. There is no strong evidence indicating gender differences in transfer students' academic achievement. Overall, research findings on gender differences among transfer students have not been consistently replicated.

Finally, transfer students who exhibit marked learning delays or disabilities are likely to be at risk for maladjustment. In addition to academic disadvantages, students with serious learning problems often exhibit social and behavioral problems as well as low self-concept.

In the next chapter, we explore ways that transfer children can be supported by teachers, peers, and parents during school transitions. In particular, past school-based intervention programs for transfer students are described.

3

The Need
for Social Support

The quality of social support children receive appears to be directly related to their success in coping with stressful life transitions (Compas, 1987). Social support in all spheres of children's lives presumably contributes to their successful adaptation. In contrast, the absence of social support in any important area may precipitate poor adjustment. Supportive interpersonal relationships, both formal and informal, have been shown to buffer individuals from stress and to enhance their coping abilities (Hirsch, 1985; Kessler et al., 1985; Moos, 1984). Observing six- to nine-year-olds' adjustment to recent parental divorce, Wertlieb and colleagues (1987) found a strong inverse relationship between a family's social support and their children's behavior symptomatology. Social systems such as social service networks, schools, and neighborhood groups can also provide support for a child coping with a stressful situation (Caplan, 1974). Because of the importance of social support in stressful experiences such as school transfer, we next consider how other scientists have viewed and categorized support.

Barrera (1986) organized social support into three broad categories. First, *social embeddedness* refers to the connections that individuals have to important others in their social environment. For school transfers, this first dimension of social support may be seen, for example, in students' entry into new peer networks. Second, *perceived social support* involves the cognitive appraisal of being connected to others. Transfer students form perceptions of their social acceptance among new classmates that can in-

47

fluence their willingness and confidence to work and play with peers (Cappas, 1989; Dubow & Ullman, 1989; Fenzel & Blyth, 1986). The third category, *enacted support,* involves the actions taken by others to assist another person. This third dimension may be demonstrated in the supportive acts of transfer students' teachers, parents, and peers.

Social support has been further categorized along the dimensions of formal, informal, and family support (Cauce, Felner, & Primavera, 1982). *Formal support* can be gained from counselors and teachers. *Informal support* networks are formed by other adults and friends. Cauce and others (1982) reported that family support, often associated with informal support, fell into a separate dimension when factor analyzed. *Family support* consisted of parents and other relatives. People can experience various combinations and levels of these types of support. Moreover, some sources of support likely play a more important role and are more effective than others (Murrell & Norris, 1983). Adolescents, for instance, might gain more support from informal peer networks than from teachers, counselors, and parents.

Social support has usually been viewed as having a positive impact on individuals struggling with adverse circumstances although different sources of support may have a positive or negative impact on an individual (Barrera, 1986). Barrera argued that the global concept of social support should be abandoned in favor of more precise definitions that fit specific stress-distress relationships, that is, the specific form of stress and the type of distress displayed by an individual. In his review of the literature, Barrera extrapolated four simple relationships between support and stress or distress. In Barrera's usage, stress refers to external stress factors such as major life events; distress means negative feelings such as anxiety and sense of failure or helplessness. Social support is (1) positively related to stress, (2) negatively related to stress, (3) positively related to an individual's distress, and (4) negatively related to an individual's distress.

An examination of one of the least obvious of these relationships is informative. A positive relationship between support and distress would indicate that increases in support are associated with increases in a person's experience of distress in the face of stressful circumstances. In the case of a transfer student who shows academic delays, a teacher might attempt to help the student catch up with the rest of the class; but in doing so, the teacher might create a distressful, failing situation for the student. Thus, social support may not always be beneficial nor serve to decrease stress and a person's experience of distress. Barrera's scheme highlights the importance of determining the specific relationships among social support, stress, and manifestations of distress.

Student roles for transfer children are defined in part by teachers, parents, and peers, all of whom may have different expectations for behavior and performance. While these three groups may be a potential source of support, they may also be a source of strain because of their demands for students to fill conflicting or ambiguous roles (Fenzel, 1989). For example, peers may ostracize students with good grades while parents reward these same high-achieving students. Role conflict and low social support may be especially daunting hurdles for transfer students. Helping a child negotiate roles and get appropriate social support is a challenging task for educators, parents, psychologists, and everyone involved with helping children. If we are to help, we must first identify the various sources of social support, beginning in the school.

Social Support in the School

Discussing interventions for dropouts, Ginzberg, Berliner, and Ostow (1988) alluded to the complex multidimensional problems associated with promoting pupils' social competence, especially in many faltering inner-city school systems. Schools are increasingly being called on to provide students not only traditional academic resources but also direction and guidance in their socialization (Durlak & Jason, 1984; Elias & Clabby, 1989; Hawkins & Weis, 1985). Nevertheless, parent involvement with schools continues to be important in ensuring children's successful academic and social adaptation (Dolan, 1978; Epstein, 1983; Walberg, Paschal, & Weinstein, 1985). The combination of various sources of support aimed at promoting both social and academic competence might have additive benefits for students confronting school transitions.

School-related social support depends on daily interactions between students and their supportive networks, which include teachers, peers, and parents (Dubow & Ullman, 1989; Jason, Kurasaki, Neuson, & Garcia, in press). Helpful interactions seem to be influenced by the characteristics of both children and their supporters. For example, an important social skill needed to cope effectively in a learning situation involves help-seeking behavior. One team of researchers found that first, third, and fifth graders differed in their help seeking according to achievement level (Nelson-Le Gall & Glor-Scheib, 1985). High- and low-ability students were relatively successful in their bids to seek help from peers and teachers whereas average students were often rejected or ignored. The authors suggested that many average children may experience academic and social isolation from instructional exchanges. This study exemplifies the potential variance in support opportunities, such as those offered by teachers, that may be influenced by children's academic and social competencies.

Cowen, Lotyczewski, and Weissberg (1984) examined the relationship between identified risk and resource indicators for elementary children's adjustment to school. The authors were interested in the extent to which the presence of resources moderated the effects of risks. They considered four areas for assessing risks and resources: (1) the physical and health characteristics of the child, (2) recent critical life events, (3) special school services and activities, and (4) family background. The authors found the expected negative correlation between scores on the composite risk and resource indices. In the sample, high-risk children with moderate resources were significantly better adjusted than high-risk children with few or no resources. Other research studies document similar findings. Rutter (1979) concluded that favorable home environments tend to protect children from developing disturbances in the face of stressors; conversely, children raised in chaotic and negative family circumstances do not seem to experience support in the home and consequently are more prone to manifest psychopathology. Another investigation found that third- and fifth-grade children reported feeling more lonely when they experienced fewer supportive behaviors from family, peers, and teachers during stressful times (Dubow & Ullman, 1989). These findings emphasize the supportive roles of families as well as special school services, teachers, and peers in counterattacking risks and ensuring transfer students' adjustment to a new school.

Teacher Support

Remedial services provided by teachers or other educational paraprofessionals probably lessen the adverse effects of school transitions; however, only a minority of transfer children actually receive such attention (Panagos et al., 1981; Turner & McClatchey, 1978). Perhaps too often newcomers are seen as presenting unwanted problems for teachers (Bensen et al., 1979). Teachers must accommodate the abilities of new students or deal with their potentially disrupting effects on classroom routines. One investigation revealed that teachers tend to hold stereotyped views of transfer children with regard to attendance, ability, attitude, and academic attainment (Warner, 1969, cited in Turner & McClatchey, 1978).

In recent decades numerous researchers have investigated the influence of teacher attitudes and expectations on students' academic progress. The relationship a teacher has with a student can potentially affect the child's classroom performance. Good and Brophy (1972) identified four types of relationships students have with teachers: attachment, concern, indifference, and rejection. For example, in an attachment relationship students present as highly competent and have qualities valued by the teacher; in contrast, in a rejection relationship students are held in disfavor by the teacher. Teachers may show special concern for some students while remaining indifferent toward others. Good and Brophy (1972) found that teacher attitudes correlate with differential teacher behavior toward pupils. Another study showed that teacher criticism and student withdrawal were related to decreased academic achievement (Perkins, 1965). These findings imply that transfer children who are either ignored or rejected by teachers may receive less positive academic and emotional support in the new classroom.

The effects of teacher attitudes and biases toward students can sometimes be seen in academic grades. Gregory (1984) found that low teacher expectations are followed by poor student progress. Kim, Anderson, and Bashaw (1968) described a teacher-rated scale that measures three dimensions of students' social maturity: academic, interpersonal, and emotional. The strongest relationship emerged between the grades teachers assigned and their ratings of students' academic maturity. It would seem that children's interpersonal and emotional maturity also influence academic functioning, such as staying on task. Nonetheless, Kim and his associates did not find strong correlations between the measures of interpersonal/emotional maturity and grades. These results suggest that teachers may attempt to separate their perceptions of students' academic and social competence in evaluating scholastic achievement.

In a more recent literature review on self-fulfilling prophecy and teacher expectations, Brophy (1983) concluded that a minority of teachers have major expectation effects on students' achievement. He suggests that teachers' expectations have minimal influence because these are generally accurate and open to corrective feedback. Other investigators discount the power of self-fulfilling prophecy or bias and credit social perception as mostly accurate (e.g., Jussim, 1991). Brophy infers from his review that teachers need not maintain equally high expectations for all students; rather, they should individualize their instruction for each student's particular needs.

For successful transition, transfer students must be accepted by teachers as appropriate classroom members. Part of the student's difficulty in transferring may evolve from changes in teachers' perception of his or her ability. Thus, teachers may accurately assess a given transfer student's performance as being below the class level. In some cases, teachers may reject or ignore newcomers, who subsequently may feel less motivated and suffer a drop in achievement. In particular, disruptive students attract the most teacher disapproval and censure; such students are at high risk for failure. Nevertheless, evidence exists that teachers tend to evaluate students' achievement independent of their social and emotional maturity and that these perceptions of student ability are largely accurate. For transfer students who are behind new peers and are struggling to succeed in new classrooms, positive support, encouragement, and individualized instruction from tutors and teachers may boost their academic performance and self-concept.

Overall, teachers and other school support personnel such as teacher aides, counselors, and school psychologists play a central role in helping new students to succeed in school. Educators not only can provide academic support but also can influence student adjustment in other important ways — through classroom management, contact with parents, and informal emotional support for the student. In the rest of this chapter and the ones that follow we discuss how administrators, teachers, and tutors can help transfers.

Peer Support

Friendships appear to buffer the adverse effects of stress (Price & Ladd, 1986). Research on adolescents indicates that peer support is positively related to school competence (Cauce & Schrebnic, 1989). In reference to students' middle school transitions, Elias and others (1985) underscored the potential importance of out-of-school and peer contacts as critical sources of support and continuity during the stressful transition period. Hartup (1983) reiterated the possibility that children's social experiences through friendships may be just as or more important in their development than family interactions. Price and Ladd (1986) concluded that the potential contributions of friendship to the development of social competence in school-age children are considerable. Alternatively, the social development of children who fail to form friendships may suffer. The authors claim that students develop a greater need for peer intimacy and acceptance as they near pre-adolescence (around nine years of age). Friendships help children acquire certain social skills. Peers can serve as role models, demonstrating prosocial behaviors, reinforcing norms for acceptable behavior, and promoting alternatives to deviant behaviors (Jason & Rhodes, 1989).

One way to capitalize on positive social factors in schools is to implement peer tutoring or encourage cooperative learning efforts among students. The advantages of peer tutoring have been well documented (see, for example, Jason, Ferone, & Soucy, 1979). Peer tutoring is a promising approach that allows teachers to program academic and social benefits simultaneously (Algozzine & Maheady, 1986; Jason, Christensen, & Carl, 1982). In basic subject areas, classwide peer tutoring as opposed to teacher instruction has been shown to produce more academic responding and higher achievement among students (Greenwood et al., 1984).

Similar to paired peer tutoring, student team learning is another educational approach that groups students to complete class assignments; with this strategy, individual student achievement depends on the cooperation and success of the group (Hawkins & Weis, 1985). Both disabled and nondisabled students have benefited from such programs (Maheady, Sacca, & Harper, 1987). Once supportive peer interactions have been established in the classroom, there is evidence that children carry these supportive tutoring behaviors into other settings and with other children (Jason et al., 1979).

Studies examining the effectiveness of orientation programs for transfer students document the importance of peer social support during school transitions, especially in providing helpful information and expectations about the new school (Sloan, Jason, & Bogat, 1984). During orientation programs, the coupling of nontransfer "buddies" with newcomers has been shown to establish immediate social networks within the school for transfer students, thereby potentially contributing to successful transition adjustment (Jason & Bogat, 1983). Collectively, the above studies indicate that supportive peer interactions can positively impact children's social and academic performance.

Of course, peers do not always help. Peer influence sometimes can lead to poor classroom behavior and decreased achievement (Fenzel, 1989). A study of inner-city, lower-SES adolescents showed informal peer support to be correlated to better self-concept but lower academic achievement (Cauce et al., 1982). The investigators conjectured that informal support from peers may bolster the student's self-concept in the social realm but have a negative effect in the academic realm if these peers do not value academic success. Hence, school transition research should distinguish ways that peers may positively or negatively influence the transfer student's academic achievement.

Parent Support

Both parents and teachers can play significant roles in promoting social competence in children. Adults can provide a role model for competent functioning, give children opportunities to become independent and to make decisions, and combine firm discipline with reaffirming affection (Sharma, Saraswathi, & Gir, 1981). Galejs and Stockdale (1982) hypothesized that both teachers and parents recognize children's social competency behaviors, and that home and school behaviors are interdependent. The authors' correlational findings from a sample of fifth- and sixth-grade children suggest that competent or incompetent behaviors carry over from home to school. Thus, teachers and parents seemed to be observing similar behaviors in different settings. Both home and school behaviors predict competence and skill mastery in school.

The competence of the primary caregiver affects the coping skill of the child (Garmezy et al., 1984). Sines (1987) found evidence that levels of parental warmth, affection, and acceptance of children correlate significantly with aggressive behaviors among both boys and girls. In particular, low-income parents who have been described as insular (that is, parents who have few positive contacts outside the family) tend to be ineffective and harsh in communicating and managing their children (Wahler, 1980). Blechman (1984) described such parents as lacking a repertoire of problem-solving skills and not accessing or interacting with other parents who model more functional problem-solving skills. Feldhusen and others (1967) proposed that such family and other background factors are frustrating influences that precipitate children's aggressive and disruptive behavior, which in turn decreases their opportunities to learn in the classroom. As a consequence, such children do not achieve as well as might be expected based on their intelligence.

Citing the continued pervasive, poor achievement of urban children compared to their suburban counterparts, McKinney (1975) suggested that a major reason for this failure is the small degree of support and reinforcement lower-income, urban children receive in often single-parent homes. In her review of the literature, Shinn (1978) identified high levels of anxiety, financial hardship, and in particular, low levels of parent-child interaction as important causes of poor academic performance among children in single-parent families. Other studies suggest that living in a one-parent family can have a negative impact on a child's school adjustment (Sandler, 1980) and academic achievement (Milne, Ginsburg, Myers, & Rosenthal, 1986), but these effects have been shown to differ by age, race, and family structure. The negative total effect of having only one parent was reduced in smaller families (Milne et al., 1986). Milne concluded that the amount of time a working parent has to spend with each child is directly related to the number of children in the family. We present these findings on single-parent households with caution. The majority of single parents are likely competent caregivers.

In contrast to these studies, Rutter (1979) examined the protective influence of at least one good relationship with one parent in both harmonious and discordant families. For children living in discordant households, a stable relationship significantly decreased their likelihood of conduct disorders compared to children who did not have a close bond with one parent. These findings are encouraging and indicate that parents can often provide guidance and support to their children even when they themselves are experiencing difficulties.

Other studies have shown the importance of psychosocial factors that may mediate the association between compounded stressful life events, such as divorce and subsequent school transfer of a child. Levine and others (1966) suggested that there may be positive mediating influences in some families that attenuate adverse effects of moves following stressful life events. Research also indicates that an adequate home support system may offset the negative effects of single-parent family status on children's academic performance and emotional health (Roy & Fuqua,

1983). Morris and colleagues acknowledged (1967) that one weakness of their study of transfer students was that they did not consider the personality variables of students and parents and how those variables moderated the effect of the school transition. Therefore, to assess a child's risk of maladjustment more accurately we need to take into account the adaptive capacities of the individual child and family. In Chapter Eight we examine more closely how parents can help children.

Overall, various sources of social support can enhance transfer students' social and academic adjustment. Transfer children who are rejected or neglected by peers, parents, and teachers are at risk for poor school performance. The support process can be examined from an eco-transactional, behavioral viewpoint showing that transfer children and people in their social networks reciprocally influence each others' behavior, attitudes, and adaptive competencies during school transitions.

Interventions for Transfer Students

Many school systems offer brief orientation programs for newcomers but few schools offer comprehensive preventive interventions for high-risk transfer children. A national survey concerning innovative programs for U.S. transfer students sampled school counselors in public middle schools (Cornille et al., 1983). The results showed that the most common type of orientation program offered to newcomers consisted of nothing more than documenting immunization histories and collecting records of achievement. Orienting transfer students to the new school's structure — providing a handbook, giving a guided tour, introducing teachers — was provided less often. The authors reported that in some schools, when the number of newcomers was low, school counselors scheduled one or two interviews with the transfer students at which time parents were sometimes consulted. Throughout the country, social integration of transfer children and families into the school community through such strategies as parent orientation or use of name tags appeared to be a low priority. A few of the surveyed schools offered parents lists of community resources or a packet of information regarding the school. An open house for newcomers and their parents was another vehicle for integrating the new family into the school system. As might be expected, the survey revealed that school systems assimilating relatively large numbers of transfer students tended to provide more services.

While many school systems have been concerned about the needs of transfer students and have developed generic orientation programs, few have evaluated the success of these programs (Cornille et al., 1983). Details of several programs for transfer students have been published, however. Hirschowitz (1976) described a project in which volunteer mothers served as small group discussion leaders for school newcomers. No data were collected to evaluate this program. In another project, Levine (1966) trained upper-grade children to serve as guides for transfer children, giving them tours of the building, instructions about general rules, and information about facilities in the school and neighborhood. This innovative program also was not evaluated. Finally, in a comprehensive program developed by Donohue and Gullotta (1981), families moving into a community were visited by a volunteer from the parent-teacher association and were provided booklets about the school and local resources. In addition, transfer students were provided an in-school buddy during the first week of school. Once again, a formal evaluation has not been conducted for this promising preventive program.

There are a few programs for which evaluations were made. In one of these, the Summer Visitation Program developed by Keats, Crabbs, and Crabbs (1981), families of new students were targeted. Through home visits by the school counselor, newcomers' picnics, and an orientation program, students who moved to the community in the summer were invited into close contact with the school. Evaluation results indicate that the program was effective in reducing the number of school absences for the experimental group compared to the new students from the year before for whom the program had not been available. In addition, parents and children felt more familiar with the new school and less anxious about the beginning of the school year.

Several studies have focused on children's transitions to junior high school. While not an intervention study, Hirsch and

Rapkin's longitudinal work (1987) with students transferring to junior high school offers important clues that interventionists need to consider. Their findings showed complex and differentiated patterns; for instance, girls, more than boys, reported an increase in depressive and other symptoms over time. Also, perceived quality of school life declined dramatically for all groups. For blacks of high academic competence, peer social support increased. Black students reported greater distrust of the environment than did white students, but white students reported more negative internal states than did blacks. The authors concluded that adjustment varies considerably depending on the domain, and that future research should consider subgroups of children who may be at risk for decline in certain areas.

Other studies have been designed to provide students with skill-building interventions prior to their entering junior high school (Snow et al., 1986), but formal evaluations of these have not been conducted. Elias and others (1986) succeeded in enhancing ways of coping with middle school stressors among fifth-grade students prior to their advancement into a middle school. Finally, Hellem (1990) used three sessions of role-playing involving problem situations to help sixth graders before their transition to a junior high school. After the children had practiced using coping skills in the problem-solving situations, they began to view stressful situations as challenges that could be overcome.

Jason and his colleagues were among the first to formally evaluate orientation programs for unscheduled school transfers (Bogat, Jones, & Jason, 1980; Jason & Bogat, 1983; Sloan et al., 1984). The first study (Bogat et al., 1980) divided transfer students into two groups: (1) an experimental group (E) who were provided a peer-led preventive orientation program prior to the start of the new school year, and (2) a control group (C_1) who received no such program. A second control group (C_2) consisted of matched children already in attendance at the school. The E transfer students were provided booklets containing school information, given a tour of the school, and included in a peer-led discussion session. In the discussion group, students introduced themselves and described in two or three words their feelings about transferring into new schools. Peer guides expressed support, empathy, and concern for the feelings that the new students experienced. The intervention produced positive effects. The E group experienced significantly greater increases in peer-related self-esteem than either the C_1 or C_2 groups. Moreover, the E group knew more school rules and had better first quarter conduct ratings than either control group.

Seeking to improve transfer orientation programs, Jason and his associates tested new components for these (see, for example, Sloan et al., 1984); the four groups included discussion only, slide presentation only, discussion and slide presentation, and a no-treatment control. For the slide presentation groups, the transfer children observed thirty-five slides that depicted various school locations and important school personnel. At the end of the first quarter, youngsters in the slide-discussion group knew significantly more information about the school than the controls, and only the slide-discussion group members evidenced significantly lower anxiety than controls. The discussion and slide-discussion group members also showed significantly positive changes in their attitudes toward school.

A later study incorporated the ideas of the previous orientation programs (that is, provision of school information, peer-led discussion group, and a tour) and in addition, assigned a buddy to children in the participant group (Jason & Bogat, 1983). Similar to the previous studies, after the orientation program the E transfer students knew more school information than did the C group. As an indicator of the program's success in fostering friendships, during the latter part of the year 90 percent of the E children described their buddy as a good or a very good friend. Although these youngsters responded positively to the orientation program, some of their group could have benefited from tutoring aimed at helping them master new academic expectations (Jason et al., 1989).

Another preventive intervention demonstrates how changing the ecology of a school system can potentially impact transfer students' academic and social competency. Felner and others (1982) developed a successful intervention for students undergoing a scheduled transition to high school. The first component of the transition project redefined the role of homeroom teachers. They assumed additional administrative and guidance responsibilities, their goal being to increase teacher support, student accountability, and student access to important school-related information. The second component of the project involved restructuring the social environment by establishing a stable peer-support system. Rather than being scattered into many different classes, as would have occurred in a typical high school, all project students remained together throughout four major subject periods during the school day. This change was made to promote peer support, enhance students' sense of belonging, and increase their perceptions of the school as a stable place. At the end of their ninth-grade year, project students showed significantly better grades and attendance and more stable self-concepts than did controls. Project participants viewed the school as having greater clarity of organization and expectations and higher teacher support and involvement than did nonparticipants.

This program shows that schools can be restructured to accommodate the needs of transfer students. In Chapter Nine we discuss this important study in greater depth, examining its organizational implications for both scheduled and unscheduled transfers.

Reyes and Jason (1991) evaluated a similar program to ease the transition from middle to high school but found no significant effects on academic measures. This school, however, was nearly twice the size of the one studied by Felner and colleagues. Moreover, it had considerable drug and gang problems. These studies suggest that the success of preventive interventions may be strongly influenced by the environmental context.

Weinstein and others (1991) designed an intervention for at-risk ninth graders during their first year of high school. The multifaceted design attempted to help establish more positive expectations for the low-achieving adolescents by making the curriculum more participatory, placing students in more heterogeneous groups, recognizing multiple abilities, introducing cooperative learning strategies, and establishing ongoing communication and shared expectations between teachers and parents. The intervention helped the program children improve their grades and decrease disciplinary referrals, but at a one-year follow-up the improved performance was not maintained.

One of the few evaluated programs for transfer children and one that attempted to address the issue of enhancing resources in all spheres of at-risk students' lives was Operation SAIL (Students Assimilated into Learning) (Panagos et al., 1981). The program was located in a small suburban school district where 20 percent of the students transferred each year; 70 percent of the transfer students had significant cognitive and affective deficits. The program's goal was to enhance the academic and social competence of at-risk transfer students through triangular educational involvement of students, parents, and teachers.

Students selected for participation in SAIL scored at least one year below grade level on a standardized test of academic achievement. In addition to children with academic difficulties, children with behavior control and motivational problems were included. The small groups were instructed by specially trained teachers and college volunteers five days a week, forty minutes per day. Units in academic subjects and on self-concept and behavior control techniques were incorporated into remedial sessions. Each high-risk transfer student participated for a twelve-week instructional cycle; at the end of the cycle, school personnel reviewed student progress to determine whether SAIL services should be extended or the student was ready to be integrated full time into the regular classroom. Parents received a written plan of instruction for their child at the beginning of each month and a graded copy of the plan at the end. Also, parents received informal phone calls and progress reports. Nevertheless, there was no systematic attempt to assess or enhance the parents' skills to teach or counsel their own children; rather, the goal was merely to keep parents informed and involved in the educational process.

The SAIL program evaluation employed pre- and post-testing but did not include a control group, limiting the validity of the findings; with this qualification, significant gains were made by SAIL participants in all six grades for academic areas such as reading comprehension and vocabulary. However, only the third and fifth graders showed significant improvement in their motivation. These findings suggest the efficacy of providing similar programs to aid transfer children and also point to the need for further program development.

The school transition interventions cited above encompass schoolwide and individually focused efforts to integrate transfer students into new schools. These past interventions offer promise that school-based efforts can promote positive academic and social adjustment for all transfer students, especially those who are at highest risk for school failure. To help you make better decisions about what interventions work best for which transfer students, Chapter Ten describes important findings from the four-year evaluation of our own School Transition Project for high-risk elementary transfer students. The upcoming chapters in this book offer recommendations for further program development.

Summary

We believe that school-related social support, arising from formal, informal, and family sources, influences transfer student adjustment. Support from teachers, peers, and parents, in both academic and social domains, might bolster children's adjustment. However, investigators should differentiate the positive and negative impacts of different sources of support. In particular, transfer students may often experience role strain in trying to meet conflicting expectations of teachers, parents, and peers. Teachers can offer positive support through providing remedial services and shaping the social climates of classrooms. Alternatively, by rejecting or ignoring transfers, teachers can have a detrimental impact on student motivation and performance.

Friendships promote social skill development, and peer support seems to function as a buffer against stress. Positive peer support can contribute to students' academic success, but negative peer influence can disrupt student motivation and performance.

Few school transition studies have examined the influence of family support on transfer students' adjustment (Kroger,

1980). Parental support and involvement in children's schools may also promote students' school competence. A unique aim of this book is to describe and evaluate the help families can give to their children who are transfer students. Overall, different sources of social support can potentially promote or hinder transfer student adjustment.

We view our study as a significant contribution to school transition research for several reasons. Although past investigations on school transitions have examined separate factors contributing to transfer students' academic achievement and peer acceptance, no study has fully integrated the various factors in an empirically based model of transfer students' adjustment. The School Transition Project uses a much more comprehensive model of transfer students' adjustment, accounting for eco-transactions of key individual and systemic factors that potentially contribute to academic, social, and psychological adaptation. In Chapter Ten we describe these key transactions as they emerged in our results.

The School Transition Project described in this book combined both practical service to a school system and ongoing research to guide program changes. Our preventive intervention is characterized by a number of factors common to the interests of school systems throughout the nation. First, the year-long intervention has been successfully implemented in four cohorts: academic years 1986–87, 1987–88, 1988–89, and 1989–90. During the first two years, we offered a child-tutoring program to a group of elementary schools. During the third and fourth years, we expanded our project with some schools receiving a child-tutoring program and other schools receiving child tutoring plus a parent training and home visiting program. Additional schools served as control groups within each of the four cohorts. The broad scope of our project points to the feasibility of such a systemwide intervention.

Our project employed paraprofessionals to tutor children and also to train caretakers in homework tutoring; thus, schools could utilize teacher aides and other paraprofessionals to conduct the intervention, which extends teaching resources in a cost-effective manner. Finally, the schools, transfer students, and families with whom we have worked represent a broad spectrum of multicultural, multilingual, and socioeconomic backgrounds.

The following chapters describe how we analyzed and met the diverse needs of high-risk transfer students in different school settings. We begin, appropriately, at the beginning, examining the reasons that cause children to change schools.

4

Why Kids Transfer Schools

To understand school transfer fully, it is not enough to gather information that begins when a child arrives at a new school. We must reach further back and explore why children transfer in the first place. Will a child whose parents transfer her or him for religious reasons perform better than one whose family moved because the parents divorced? Does it matter whether a child transfers because his or her parents change jobs, move to a new neighborhood, or want a school that challenges children?

Exploring the reasons for school transfer may provide insight into the different kinds of adjustment a student must make or the levels of performance he or she demonstrates. The family's intentions and history may distinguish transfer children. Our inquiry into reasons for moving also illuminates the nature of our very mobile society and how it affects children.

Findings from the Literature

Unfortunately, researchers have not yet described in detail why children move, nor have they empirically explored whether the reasons for the school transfer relate to subsequent school adjustment. Marchant and Medway (1987) wrote that one of the serious methodological flaws of research on residential mobility is that the authors typically fail to differentiate the reasons for moving. Instead, they found researchers grouping together families who may have moved because of job transfer, financial difficulties, marital disruption, or desire to change neighborhoods.

Studying the reasons for school transfer should help explain the unique difficulties children may have in adjustment. For instance, issues of loss (that is, grieving the loss of old friends and familiar neighborhoods) may be abundant for transferring children (Freeman, 1984). Some suggest that a change in residence is analogous to a change in a parent (Holland et al., 1974). Freeman wrote that students who relocate while suffering multiple losses outside of school may have problems exacerbated by the new school staff's inadequate knowledge of their circumstances.

Holland and others (1974) reasoned that children whose families move as a result of financial problems may be less likely to adjust quickly because of stresses outside of school and because the entire family feels that they are not in control of the transition. Whatever the reasons for moving, children usually have the least control over the decision, and they may have great misunderstandings about the process. Beem and Prah (1984) found the following: "From the child's point of view, the family's decision to move is an arbitrary one. Adults may discuss with each other the pros and cons of a move but the child is expected to accept the parents' decision. At the time of relocation, a child's sense of control is threatened. The child is asked to leave a style of living which has provided a much-needed sense of security. The familiar suddenly becomes the unfamiliar" (p. 310).

One exception to the trend of clustering all reasons for moving is a study by McAllister, Kaiser, and Butler (1971). These authors examined a sample of 1,561 adults for racial differences in reasons for their residential relocation. They found that black families moved most frequently because they were forced out of their homes and least frequently because of job transfers and a need for more space. White families, in contrast, reported moving most often because of job transfers and the desire for a larger home.

The literature on job transfers as a specified reason for moving is extensive. Williams, Jobes, and Gilchrist (1986) found that, among 390 people who migrated to rural areas, 61 percent moved for job-related reasons. They compared this figure to one in a study by Sell (1983), in which approximately two-thirds moved for a job- or employment-related reason. Gaylord and Symons (1986) estimated that in all, twenty-two million workers move for job-related reasons each year. An interesting finding is that female heads of households moved more often for quality of life considerations while male heads of households cited job considerations as their reason for relocation (Williams et al., 1986).

Most researchers have assumed that children change schools because their families move. However, Cornille and others (1983) listed several reasons for transferring that do not include residential relocation. They hypothesized that school closings, transferring from public to private schools, and busing to achieve a racial balance should all have unique implications for students' experience of school transfer.

The number of children transferring to new schools varies with the socioeconomic status of the families in the community. Sexton (1961) reported that schools serving higher-income families had a 16 percent turnover each year whereas schools serving lower-income families showed a 49 percent turnover. Levine and colleagues (1966) found that 85 percent of sixth graders had not attended the same inner-city elementary school since the first grade. Thus, as income decreases, mobility from school to school seems to increase. Perhaps, then, the reasons for school transfer are different for low-income, nonwhite groups versus upwardly mobile, Caucasian samples. Lower-income, minority families suffer an extraordinarily high rate of school transfer.

To review, the research literature on reasons for moving poses several questions: Do families indeed move or change schools for different reasons? Do those distinctions significantly matter for children? Do race, SES, and other variables distinguish reasons for moving?

Complexity of Reasons for Transfer

Our research tells of increasing complexity in why children transfer between schools. We are beginning to learn what effects the various reasons have on children's subsequent adjustment. To begin to understand the possible impact of the reasons for moving, we offer examples of two children with whom we worked.

Gerardo was the youngest of several children and the only child still living with his parents in a rural Mexican community. Gerardo's parents sent him to the United States when he was eleven to live with his sister in order for him to receive a good education. He had not had any formal education in Mexico. Gerardo's sister lived with her husband — neither spoke English — and their teenaged daughter, who was fully bilingual. Speaking no English, separated from his parents and friends, and learning a new culture, Gerardo entered the fifth grade at the neighborhood Catholic school.

The second transfer child, Nina, was the fifth of seven siblings from a Mexican-American family that has lived in the United States for two generations. Her parents were factory workers in Chicago, taking different shifts so that one of them would always be with the children. Nina attended Catholic school from kindergarten through third grade, when her father was laid off from his job for eight months and the family could not afford private school tuition. She attended fourth grade at the local public school and transferred back to the Catholic school for fifth grade when her father was working again.

Obviously, Gerardo's transfer poses many more potential difficulties than Nina's. He has to grapple with the challenges of language, culture, and social adaptation, which Nina has probably already mastered to some degree. As these children have such different needs — based on the reason for the transfer — it seems logical that schools need to tailor services to each child's unique situation. Children with distinct experiences in transfer also have distinct needs. These cases provoke us to think that the reason for moving does indeed matter and deserves investigation, but to generalize further, we describe the larger population of kids with whom we worked.

As explained in Chapter One, we chose to work with transfer children because they face a number of difficult hurdles that may impair their ability to succeed. In our study, for each of the four years, we worked for one year with a new cohort of the third, fourth, and fifth grades. Thus, we had four separate cohorts. For a full description of our prevention intervention, see Chapters Six and Eight.

Our sample consists of families whose children attended Catholic elementary schools in the inner city of Chicago. As part of the School Transition Project, we asked parents of all third- through fifth-grade transfer students at these schools why their children changed schools. For parents of the first- and second-year cohorts, twelve options were available for the question, and they could choose only one option. Their responses were grouped into five categories: personal decision to change schools to give child a "fresh start," transfer from public school, household considerations (space/cost considerations; forced out of last home), sought better place to live, and old school closed.

Findings from the First Two Years of the School Transition Project

Our analyses for the first two cohorts revealed two distinct groups (Warren-Sohlberg & Jason, 1992). First, the students who transferred because of *school closing* (n = 44) were primarily from one or two schools. Thus, this group was fairly homogeneous. They were mostly black and they attended school in poor, violent neighborhoods. However, their families had a relatively high socioeconomic status compared to families transferring for other reasons, and the children performed better than other groups academically.

Further, although the socioeconomic status of these families was fairly low compared to national samples, their status relative to other families in the school and neighborhood may have afforded them a privileged status within which their children flourished (Mayer & Jencks, 1989). Another reason for the high academic performance of these children may be that teachers and administrators who know their school will close prepare their students more effectively for the transition to a new school. All the students undergo the transfer, not just one or two. A supportive milieu may embolden students for the move and thus buffer the stressful effects of the transition.

The second group that is notable in our analyses was composed of families moving because of *household considerations:* space and cost considerations, being forced out of their home, and forming a new household (n = 70). This group reported distinctly higher numbers of undesirable events occurring within the past year, and their children suffered decreased academic achievement. It is likely that the double burdens of adjusting to household changes plus the stress of acclimating to a new school overwhelmed the students' coping abilities, as in the case of Keith. Keith's father decided he could not adequately care for him alone, so the boy moved in with his aunt, uncle, and two cousins. Adjusting to the new school, in addition to adjusting to his home changes, was very difficult for Keith. He often seemed distracted by emotional issues and his school achievement suffered from his lack of concentration. Tutoring provided Keith with emotional support and a sympathetic ear as well as academic assistance.

Finally, the other reasons for moving did not readily distinguish groups of families from one another. These categories could have meant different things to different respondents. For example, changing schools for a *fresh start* could mean leaving a school to avoid being held back to repeat a grade or it could mean entering a school to be with a new group of children.

Finding from the Revised Project Questionnaire

We revised and expanded our questionnaire to capture more precisely the reasons families transfer their children into new schools (see Resource A). The reasons cited by parents in our third year of interviews are shown in Table 4.1. The frequency totals for year 4 are comparable. We invited parents to indicate as many reasons for moving as were relevant.

The frequencies are a combination of data from those families who actually moved into different homes and those whose children only transferred to another school. Many families reported a number of school-related reasons in addition to changing residences. Therefore, we decided that reasons from these two groups overlap enough to warrant combining them in the analyses.

Table 4.1. Frequencies of Reasons
for School Transfer: Data from Cohort 3.

Reason for School Transfer	Frequency
FINANCES	55
New job (7)	
Lost job (2)	
Promotion (1)	
Demotion (0)	
Other financial reason (45)	
PEERS	49
Trouble with kids from old school (29)	
Wish to be with kids at new school (2)	
Other reason involving peers (18)	
ACADEMICS	131
Problems with old school (44)	
Avoiding retention in grade (7)	
Wanted more of a challenge (50)	
Other academic reason (30)	
RELIGION	87
Wanted religious training (29)	
Wanted the structure of a Catholic school (46)	
Other religious reason (12)	
SCHOOLS THEMSELVES	394
Old school closed (17)	
Problems with teacher at old school (44)	
Problems with principal at old school (23)	
Problems with policy at old school (43)	
Location of old school (39)	
Attracted to personnel at new school (31)	
Location of new school (45)	
Wanted a private school (77)	
Other school reason (75)	
FAMILY	34
Divorce (3)	
Remarriage (6)	
Other breakup of household (5)	
Other joining of households (3)	
Other reason involving family (17)	
APARTMENT/HOUSE	84
Needed more space (27)	
Needed less space (2)	
Could afford a better place (4)	
Old place too costly (8)	
Forced to move (3)	
Wanted a better neighborhood (9)	
Other reason involving a home (31)	

The results show that approximately one-third of the sample changed residences whereas the remaining children changed schools without a residence move. Of those families who relocated, 71 percent moved from within Chicago and 29 percent moved from outside the city. Clearly the current literature on school transfer that assumes cross-country residential relocation is not pertinent to the majority of these families.

The data in Table 4.1 show that only ten families in our sample moved because of employment. Therefore, the job relocation literature also does not seem to be relevant for this group of families. Part of the discrepancy may be that job transfers pertain mostly to white-collar workers; the majority of our sample are families from low socioeconomic backgrounds who move primarily within the city. Contrary to expectations that many of the children's families had been disrupted, only three parents mentioned that divorce was a reason for school transfer. Much of the past literature has assumed that divorce is a prominent reason for school transfer. Realizing the church's attitude toward divorce, the parents enrolling their children in Catholic schools in this study may have decided not to mention divorce and instead cited other plausible reasons for transferring their children.

Relocation because of household considerations was another of our hypotheses that the data did not confirm. Being "forced out of the house" (for example, because of increased rent) was the number one reason for moving cited by blacks in one study (McAllister et al., 1971). Although half our sample were African-American families, only three respondents in total mentioned being forced to move from their residences.

Taken together, reasons for relocation and subsequent school transfer in the third year of our program did not meet our expectations from the literature. Specifically, we were led to believe that families moved and changed schools because of job, household, or family considerations. Yet for the families we interviewed, these reasons were seldom chosen. Instead, parents decided to place their children in different schools most often because of reasons related to the schools themselves.

Transfer Because of Dissatisfaction with Public School

In the first year of our program, more than forty youngsters transferred because their old school closed. However, only seventeen children were in that situation in the third cohort of children, transferring in the fall of 1989. This number will certainly vary from year to year, depending upon demographic shifts in neighborhoods. The "graying" of some residential areas may force school closure while other cities or neighborhoods may experience a large influx of new families with school-age children. From our talks with school personnel, school closings seem to involve a variety of circumstances, from financial problems to decreased enrollment due to gentrification of the school's neighborhood.

Probably the most telling statistic of our sample is that, immediately prior to this transfer, 64 percent of the children were enrolled in a public school. That such a large percentage of families would choose to take their children out of the public school system is somewhat emblematic of Chicago but also representative of the rest of the country. The Chicago public school system has been described both as "a case of institutionalized neglect" and "the worst in America" by the former United States Secretary of Education, William Bennett (Thomas, 1988). Nearly half (48%) of its students drop out before finishing high school, and one-fourth of those who finish graduate at a sixth-grade reading level (Thomas, 1988). Finally, 67 percent of Chicago public school students come from families below the poverty level (City of Chicago Education Summit, 1988). Thus, our families' reasons for transfer probably reflect the larger movement from public to private schools that has been occurring in Chicago for some time.

An example of dissatisfaction with the public schools was given by one of the students in our study. Paul lived with his mother, who was struggling through a number of unsatisfactory jobs. She was a college graduate raised in an upper-middle-class home. When our staff first met with Paul and his mother, they told us many stories that led to their dissatisfaction with the public school Paul previously attended. They said Paul's teacher had little control over her class, rarely assigned homework, and was often absent herself. Further, there was a notable lack of supervision of students during recess. The school administrators also seemed to be unreceptive to meeting with Paul's mother.

On entering the new schools, the public and private transfer students in our sample showed no significant differences in achievement test scores in spite of the supposed contrast between the quality of public and private schools. This is a surprising finding that cannot easily be explained.

One hypothesis is that, at least in the elementary grades, public and private schools actually prepare their students equally well — or equally poorly — and the public school system has been singled out for criticism while private schools have escaped notice. Another possibility is that children from families who would transfer their children from public schools are actually higher-achieving students than those who remain in public schools. Perhaps their good performance in school motivated the parents to seek better training for them.

Based on our informal conversations with Catholic school personnel, we found among them a widespread belief that the public school transfers will be academically handicapped in their new educational environment. According to one principal, about 95 percent of students who transfer from public to private schools are "deficient." He explained: "There is better communication in the private schools. In the public schools if a parent is not notified by the school, a parent assumes that everything is okay. Notification of parents is nonexistent at the public schools. Some teachers assume that it is better to give a student a C than to hassle with the parent." This perception, however, is not supported by the findings from our project. It is not clear from these data that, in the academic arena, children transferring from private schools will necessarily outperform those from public schools. On the contrary, our data discount the notion that private school students outperform public school students.

Other Reasons to Transfer

Racial differences in reports of reason for school transfer were notable in only a few instances. For example, Hispanic families more often reported transferring to Catholic schools because of the religious aspects of the schools. There were no significant differences in academic scores for children from these families compared to children who transferred for nonreligious reasons. In addition, African-American parents reported more often than parents of other races that they chose a new school for their child because it would provide an increased challenge. Later in this chapter, we elaborate possible implications of these findings, including the need for schools to challenge students, involve parents, and instill a sense of community.

From the entire sample, those students transferring because they were avoiding retention in a grade or having academic problems at the old school did, in fact, enter the school scoring significantly lower on achievement tests in reading and spelling as compared to children transferring for other reasons. Also, the families reporting a large number of complaints with their old schools were of generally higher socioeconomic status than the rest of the sample.

Some of the most interesting differences we found came from analyses of groups according to the distance of the residential move and the number of school transfers children had experienced. The data suggest that, generally, multiple moves impair children's academic success, confirming the literature on this point (e.g., Holland et al., 1974). In addition, the distance of the move may affect a child's academic performance, although these data may be confounded by the fact that moving from another country involves enormous adjustment. Children from these families, such as Gerardo mentioned previously, are required to make a transition not only to the unfamiliar physical surroundings in their home, school, and community but to differences in language, culture, values, and life-styles. It should be noted that while we found differences in test scores along distance and number of moves, such effects did not carry over to teacher grades. Still, the findings are an important confirmation that moving great distances and frequently can hinder children's learning.

Implications for Schools

Our findings have several implications for future interventions. First, we have seen that the children who undergo transfer due to *school closing* adjust better than other transfer children. We can conjecture that these youngsters benefit from the supportive camaraderie of a large group of children who experience together the shock, mourning, anger, sadness, and uncertainty of school transfer. Therefore, it seems reasonable to conclude that all children who transfer need such support to cushion their arrival. If support does not occur naturally (as with the large group that moves together from a closed school), educators should provide such support artificially through orientation programs, buddy systems, tutors, and the like.

Second, the large number of children in our first years who changed schools for *family or household considerations* confirms the need to address such issues in working with transfer children and in schools in general. If large numbers of children cannot learn because they are reeling from the personal shock of divorce, new homes, or otherwise disrupted families, educators and mental health workers would do well to address such issues. The question is how to accomplish this.

First, school personnel who conduct interviews with families in order to register children for school could ask about the reason for school transfer. From the information gained in these interviews, individualized programs may be set up with teachers to address the specific needs of the transfer student. A child who transferred because of academic difficulties would be assigned to a tutor; a child whose family transferred him or her in order to get more religious training would be linked with religious activities, as in the case of Stephan. Stephan entered the fifth grade at one Catholic school after transferring from the local public school where he had been enrolled in a bilingual program. At his new school, he spent one or two afternoons a week in catechism (Catholic preparation to receive Communion). This special program helped him to make friends, encouraged him to continue learning in Spanish and English, and also gave him the opportunity to learn about his religion. Thus, registration is a key time to query the reason for the move and to refer the transfer child to appropriate services.

Second, reducing the stigma that may be associated with family disruption and household changes could significantly help the many children who suffer the ill effects of these changes.

Programs could be initiated to gather together children of divorce in group activities after or during school. Such referral should be part of the routine enrollment procedure.

Finally, the large number of children transferring because of family and household changes raises the need for educators and mental health professionals to design preventive interventions for these children and their families. Possible interventions include the following:

1. *Designing orientation programs.* For new students and their "buddies," school administrators should design orientation programs (described in Chapter Six) that are sensitive to family and household changes. That is, in addition to exploring children's feelings about the new school, orientation leaders and materials should help children sort out their reactions to changes in family structure or residences. Several questions could be discussed: What does it feel like to move to a different house? What's different about the new house? How is your new family different from your old one? What will be the best and worst things about your new family or house? Such questions should be discussed in a similar manner to other issues, such as how your old and new school differ.

2. *Having an open school day.* The personnel from one school with whom we worked set up an "open school day" toward the end of the school year, when many families had already decided to enroll their children in that school the coming fall. Regular classes were held on one Sunday afternoon in order for prospective students and their families to visit the classrooms, meet the teachers, and get a feel for the school. Such school open houses would be particularly helpful to students who transferred due to family or household changes. These newly moved or newly structured families, which may bear more stress and uncertainty than other intact and nonmoving families, may have a correspondingly greater need to get acquainted with the new school. They have a need for less uncertainty and more communication.

Benefits of an open school day included a reduction of anxiety among prospective transfer students who gained information about what to expect in the coming year. Such encounters help families to become informed consumers of education and may result in their having more positive feelings about their choice.

3. *Tapping community resources.* Clearly, there are many limitations placed on school personnel in addressing the needs of families in transition. Collaborating with other resources in the area such as the community mental health center, day-care facilities, and other social services may play a central role in early referral and intervention for these families.

An example of appropriate referral to community resources is Craig's family. Craig lived with his mother, sister, and his mother's boyfriend on the southwest side of Chicago. His mother was hesitant to talk to us at first, but over time, she came to trust Craig's tutor. On a number of occasions, she would call our staff to talk, and eventually she revealed the physical violence she had been suffering at the hands of her boyfriend. With familiarity of the services available through the community mental health center, we were able to refer the family for help.

Importance of Religious, Family, Community, and Ethnic Values

We also have seen in our analyses that there are the phenomena of intracity moving and public to private school transfers that have not been captured in other research, which emphasized job relocation. To some degree, this shifting may be peculiar to Chicago, where the public schools have been spotlighted as deficient. However, it seems reasonable to suspect that most major cities suffer similar dynamics. Apparently, public schools are not meeting important needs of parents. This is not at all a new occurrence in American education but it is one on which our perspective of school transfer and "reason for the move" can shed some new light.

It is important to understand what it means for parents to transfer their children to new schools. Because most of the families with whom we worked had access to few financial resources, we were continually impressed by their sacrifices in order to pay the school tuition. Transferring from a public school to a private one that charges annual tuition of $1,000 is a dramatic move. Clearly, the education of their children is important to these families. Because of this motivation, school personnel should provide opportunities for parents to volunteer in the school.

In this way, whole families can make the transition to a new situation quickly and successfully.

As reported, our data showed a great number of families moving for religious reasons. To us, religious reasons meant the parents wanted their children to have religious instruction and participation integrated in their school curriculum. Thus, we assumed that religiosity meant going to church regularly, as a part of school; being taught by nuns and priests; learning religious history; and so on. However, we saw in such schools two additional factors that may be subsumed under "religious reasons": a potent sense of family and community involvement and a strong sense of racial and ethnic identity.

Parents were encouraged (and sometimes required) to attend Mass; they often volunteered in the school or church to pay off tuition debt; parents were known as parish members, not just as parents of students; in short, parent participation was often sought. In many of these schools, too, there was a sense of community and a very positive school climate (elaborated in Chapter Nine). Finally, many schools vigorously promoted ethnic and racial pride, whether through Black History Month, teaching Hispanic heritage, or constant messages in hallways and classes about prominent blacks and the importance of uplifting oneself. Such messages were integrated into the religious curriculum, too. How well or how much public schools convey ethnic and racial pride, we cannot be sure, but such teaching may be part of what lures parents away from public schools to private ones under the guise of religious reasons.

One school with which we worked, on the west side of Chicago, excelled in providing a base for children to build a strong cultural identity. They taught and celebrated Quansa, and they decorated the walls with African cultural materials and pictures of famous African Americans. In addition, teachers served as positive role models and incorporated black history and culture into their curriculum. Schools with such cultural missions and confidence-enhancing environments seemed very appealing to parents with whom we worked.

The message for private schools, then, is that much of what attracts families for religious reasons may not be, as widely thought, religious training and higher academic standards, but family involvement, a sense of community, and racial pride. The message for public schools is that while they cannot, by constitution, provide religious training, they do need to address forcefully the possibly unmet needs of family, community, morality, and ethnicity. These needs may be partially met by what is widely known as the Inclusion Movement, which currently challenges public schools to teach the history and culture of various races, groups, and countries. Further ideas for involving parents and instilling a sense of community are badly needed. All schools could strengthen their role in providing a setting around which a stronger sense of community may be built for individuals and families.

Summary

To conclude, one key implication of the information provided in this chapter is that school personnel should ask the reason for school transfer at the first contact with the family. In addition, because distance of the move and number of prior school moves seem to be important in predicting ease of adjustment, these questions should also be included in the initial interview with the family. Children who have moved far and often might be a special focus of intervention, along with children who move for other particular reasons, such as household changes. Orientation programs can help address reasons for moving. Referral to appropriate groups or services should be commonplace. Finally, it would be ideal if school personnel could emphasize their expectation that they and the family can work together effectively to accommodate children and families into the life of the school and community. There is much that schools can do to match the incoming needs of transfer students.

Part Two

Effective Intervention Strategies

5

The School Transition Project: Putting Theory into Practice

In designing and implementing the School Transition Project, we based our work on ideas from several major areas including developmental, behavioral, and community psychology. In this chapter, we elaborate how theory in these fields informed our intervention. In addition, we review other critical antecedents and foundations for our work, including the ecotransactional and psychoeducational models.

By articulating theory, we are better able to establish goals as well as develop and implement new portions of the program. Theory also guides our evaluation. Without a foundation in theory, our work would be a patchwork assembly of program activities lacking a comprehensive pattern. All of these theories are essential to understanding school children in transition, and we strongly encourage that any school-based intervention similarly anchor itself firmly on theory from the start.

Foundation in Community Psychology and Prevention

The theoretical and practical beginnings of our effort lie in community psychology (Tolan, Keys, Chertok, & Jason, 1990). Community psychology is concerned with serving populations that are typically inadequately served: ethnic and racial minorities, children, adolescents, the handicapped, and the poor (Levine & Perkins, 1987). Community psychology is interested in changes not only within the individual that lead to positive mental health but also in societal changes, since social and individual factors influence psychological well-being (Felner, Jason, Moritsugu, & Farber, 1983).

We believe that schools offer prime opportunities for community psychologists interested in preventing illness among large, poorly served populations (Jason, Hess, Felner, & Moritsugu, 1987). Child and adolescent educational programs do not receive enough funding from state and federal resources. By working within schools, community psychologists can reach many children in need of psychological services who would otherwise slip through the cracks.

Primary and secondary prevention are of central concern to community psychology. Secondary preventive interventions attempt to correct early signs of disorder and prevent these from becoming serious. Jason and Glenwick (1984) discuss three specific types of primary prevention interventions: interventions addressing the needs of at-risk youth, programs that enhance competencies, and projects concerned with milestone transitions.

High-risk populations can be characterized as children and adults who are at risk for later psychological problems (Jason & Rhodes, 1989). These individuals are vulnerable but do not exhibit any problematic overt behaviors. As an example, children living in inner cities where there is considerable gang activity are at risk for becoming gang members. Thompson and Jason (1988) provided elementary-school children with a two-month classroom program informing children of gang characteristics, gang violence, and recruiting strategies used by gang members. In addition, children who were at risk of becoming gang members were given a year-long after-school sports program. The comprehensive program was effective in decreasing gang recruitment among the high-risk children.

Other programs are designed to promote skills and competencies in children to prevent the occurrence of later maladaptive behaviors. As an example, children might be provided skills and information about countering offers to begin experimenting with cigarettes or other drugs; such programs have been effective (Rhodes & Jason, 1988).

Another type of primary prevention involves helping youngsters through milestone transitions. Transitions can be very stressful but individuals can be provided support and taught certain skills that can better equip them to handle the transition. These transitions can involve changes in school (such as entering a new school), family (such as parenthood), and work (such as a first job). As an example of this type of intervention, Jason and Burrows (1983) provided students with skills training and support before they made the transition from high school to college or work.

The School Transition Project constitutes a combination of the above approaches. The children are undergoing a transition into a new setting. In addition, those selected are at risk, as they evidence early academic and social adjustment problems. It could be argued that this is really a secondary prevention program because many of the children already have some early academic and social difficulties. However, many children were functioning well in their previous schools, and their difficulties occurred only after they entered a new setting. Some children do not overtly display academic or social problems but are vulnerable to having difficulties by exhibiting lower than average scores on achievement tests and experiencing some risk factors at home. For these children, the intervention can be considered primary prevention.

We hypothesized that children transferring to a new school who suffer stressful life events, come from lower-socioeconomic-status families, and have lower than average scores on achievement tests are not as well equipped to adjust to the new school as transfer students without these risk factors. Therefore, these children, whether they show early signs of overt difficulties (requiring secondary prevention) or are evidencing vulnerabilities but no overt signs of difficulties (requiring primary prevention) probably need an intervention to help, boost, or maintain their academic performance during this unstable period.

Behavioral Perspective

The School Transition Project relies heavily on theory developed from the behavioral model. We believe that children's behaviors are strongly influenced by the type of reinforcement they receive from others. It is a common notion that children may persistently act out because they like the attention they receive. If tutors and parents can learn to ignore negative behavior and reinforce favorable behavior, the favorable behavior will occur more frequently. To improve a child's academic and social skills, we actively employ this behavioral model in a variety of techniques.

Although many behaviors are affected by reinforcement, not all learning is contingent upon direct reinforcement. Social learning theory, an expansion of behaviorism, states that many of us learn by watching others and imitating their actions (Bandura, 1971). Many children in a classroom environment learn by imitating their teachers and especially other children. Most likely, a child will not repeat a behavior that previously resulted in scolding from the teacher. However, there are some children who would rather receive negative attention than no attention at all. In this case, a child may deliberately imitate a classmate's undesirable behaviors in order to receive negative attention.

Direct reinforcement for the imitated behavior does not always need to occur. The individual who imitates others does not receive direct reinforcement but is vicariously reinforced by observing the reinforcement given to the model.

Behaviorists typically keep track of specific behaviors by using graphs, charts, and other behavioral tools to measure changes in behavior. The behavior tools we utilized in this school transition project included the Direct Instruction method of teaching, rigorous collection of academic data, and computer-generated graphs.

The teaching techniques we use, which are further explained in Chapter Six, involve frequent use of reinforcement, rapid rate of presentation, and the model-lead-test correction procedure (Rosenshine & Berliner, 1978). These techniques exemplify behaviorism.

Bogat and Jason (in press) have argued that the power of the behavioral approach is that it translates problems into a schema where solutions are possible, even if they are in the "small win" category. Behaviorists are increasingly adopting a more systems approach in their work. For example, it is possible to understand behavior as influenced by multiple contingencies and setting features (Patterson, 1982). Willems (1964) has suggested that behaviorists need to examine second- and third-order consequences of interventions in order to understand system-like principles that permeate behavior and the environment. Other behaviorists have advocated adopting an ecological or systems perspective into behavioral interventions (Fawcett, Matthews, & Fletcher, 1980; Kranser, 1980; Rogers-Warren & Warren, 1977; Winett, 1985).

The most sophisticated writings in the behavioral field have come from Evans and colleagues (Evans, Meyer, Kurkjian, & Kishi, 1988). They state that positive generalization effects can happen when snowballing occurs, where change produces ripple effects on interactions with others. In fact, a goal of interventions might be for these ripple effects to occur, so that natural environmental contingencies can take over to sustain the behavioral changes (Stokes & Baer, 1977). To illustrate such behavioral methods, we examine one child's experience.

Terri was a fourth-grade Hispanic student who was performing two years below her grade level in reading, spelling, and math. Her mother spoke only Spanish and her father was bilingual but usually spoke Spanish at home. Terri's tutor trained her father in teaching techniques to help improve Terri's reading by using Science Research Associates (SRA) reading cards. Terri's father recorded on a family assistance calendar the amount of time he spent teaching his daughter.

Terri was asked to bring certain materials to her tutoring sessions with the DePaul University tutor: paper and pencil, spelling book, SRA cards, the family assistance calendar, and her glasses. During the baseline phase (see Figure 5.1), Terri brought 0–20 percent of her materials to the tutoring session.

Her tutor designed a responsibility chart indicating what materials Terri remembered each tutoring session. For every item she returned, Terri received praise and a sticker. The responsibility chart helped Terri return her required materials. She usually would bring her classroom materials (paper, pencils, and spelling book), but she did not bring her materials from home (family assistance calendar, SRA cards, and glasses). Her

Figure 5.1. Terri's Responsibility over Time:
Bringing in Materials as a Function of Reinforcement.

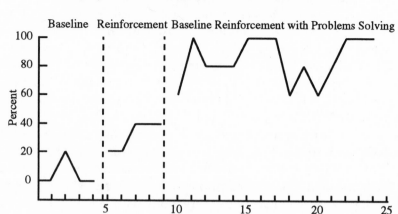

tutor tried phoning Terri the night before her tutoring sessions to remind her to bring her materials from home. However, even with this prompt, Terri continued to forget (or claimed to have misplaced) her glasses, SRA cards, and family assistance calendar. The tutor asked Terri how much help she was receiving at home. Terri admitted that she was not receiving any tutoring at home because her father had little time to help her. Terri and the tutor discussed other resources in the environment. Together they discovered an aunt and two teenage cousins in the neighborhood who could tutor Terri three times a week.

At the next tutoring session, Terri proudly brought 80 percent of her required materials. Terri worked with her cousin over the weekend. Her family assistance calendar and SRA cards were completed, but she continued to forget her glasses. For the next few weeks, she maintained this pattern of returning materials. To encourage a 100 percent return rate, her tutor proposed that she wear her glasses contingent upon Terri wearing hers. This agreement proved to be successful. Terri began to attend tutoring sessions with all her materials. Thus, the behavioral approach was multidimensional, and it involved a variety of strategies to change Terri's behaviors. As a result of this intervention, her classroom performance and attitude toward learning improved.

Transactional Model

Although there are many developmental theories and principles used often by community psychologists, few have received the attention of the transactional model. In an influential review article, Sameroff and Chandler (1975) found that infants with pregnancy or perinatal complications had few if any negative long-term effects if they came from high-SES, intact families. The same complications often lead to later retardation or personality problems if the parents come from low-SES and unstable environments. These findings point to inadequacies in the main effect model (that is, the child's constitution or environment exert independent influences) or the interactional model (that is, the combination of the environment and the constitution are considered, but this model does not include the possibility that the characteristics of each might change over time).

With a transactional model, reciprocal changes are proposed, so that as a parent begins to change a child, changes in the child begin to bring about changes in the parent. The transactional model focuses on breakdowns in continuous organism-environment transactions over time, which prevent children from organizing their worlds adaptively (Sameroff & Chandler, 1975). A transactional approach points us toward focusing not just on children or parents but on the transactions of both over time (Sameroff, 1987).

For instance, a child who is withdrawn due to feelings of inferiority is not accepted by peers. Because of peer rejection, the child feels even more inferior and continues to withdraw. As a result, the child is further rejected by peers. The pain of rejection eventually reaches other areas of the child's life and can interfere with the academic progress and family relations. This cyclic pattern continues unless there is a change in one of the cyclical forces (Zins et al., 1988). The following example shows how the transactional model helped one child's adjustment in our project.

Mike was a ten-year-old transfer student who was academically behind his third-grade classmates. Mike's opportunity to learn was limited because he was frequently late or absent from school (see Figure 5.2). Mike's frustration over his poor school performance made him dread school and attend as little as possible. His tutor developed an intervention within the tutoring sessions and the classroom. First, she spoke to Mike about his absences and tardiness and suggested ways to help him arrive on time. Second, she encouraged Mike's teacher to praise him in front of his classmates each day he arrived on time. The teacher agreed to give Mike positive reinforcement for on-task behavior rather than focusing on his deficits.

Mike's teacher noticed improvements in his attendance and praised him in front of his classmates. His teacher felt that his progress and attitude toward learning had improved. His tutor also noticed that Mike was much more excited about learning. During tutoring sessions, Mike enjoyed showing his tutor all the stories he had completed. His attendance improved from an average of 60 percent to 100 percent. In addition, his on-time arrival increased from an average of 20 percent to 100 percent (see Figure 5.2). As Mike's attendance improved, he began to feel better about himself. As indicated by achievement

Figure 5.2. Mike's Attendance and On-Time Arrival.

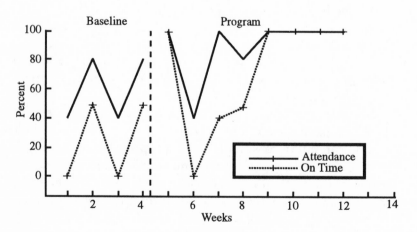

scores, he improved a year and a half in reading and spelling, and a half-year in math — all in a period of about eight months.

This improvement was a function of changing two systems that affected Mike's attendance behavior: the classroom and tutor environments. His tutor discussed with Mike ways to improve his attendance and on-time arrival. The classroom environment behavior changed because his teacher began to reinforce on-time arrivals. Both classroom and tutor environments encouraged Mike to attend school, and once he arrived, he was further rewarded for attempting to do his work.

Here, transactional change can be viewed in this way: both his teacher and tutor changed their communication toward Mike and Mike in turn began to attend school. Because of his success in attendance, his teacher and tutor began to further reward Mike in academics. As a result, both his attitude toward learning and his academic performance improved.

Ecological Psychological Model

A competing paradigm, which has captured the attention of many community theorists, is the ecological model. Kelly and colleagues have been the leading theorists to pursue this line of research (Kelly, 1968, 1987; Kelly, Snowden, & Munoz, 1977; Kelly, Munoz, & Snowden, 1979). Kelly's goal has been to develop propositions of how people become effective and adaptive in varied social environments.

In brief, Kelly has proposed several ecological principles that can serve as a conceptual framework for examining settings and behavior; each is described below.

Succession

Succession is an ecological principle that refers to the changing demands of adaptive capacities over time. Communities and organisms are in a constant process of change, and this process causes changing requirements for adaptation. What is true about a person or setting today may not be true tomorrow.

The behavioral time-series methods for collecting data

provide investigators an excellent technique for capturing the process of learning or adaptation over time. If a child is not making adequate progress, this is evident immediately, as opposed to the end of a posttest assessment phase. Early identification allows an investigator to respond to changes in the person and the setting. For example, Figure 5.3 shows that a tutored child's progress on a phonetic ladder had slowed. Because this leveling off of progress was immediately evident to the tutor and supervisor, the intervention techniques were modified, with positive results.

Time-series data are typically collected by behaviorists for relatively short periods of time. The principle of succession would suggest that behavior should be collected over longer periods in order to reflect the inevitable changes that occur in person-setting transactions. In order to maintain intervention effects, programs need to adapt to changes persons and settings will inevitably manifest over time.

Interdependence

The principle of interdependence helps us understand that changes in any part of an interrelated system will affect changes

Figure 5.3. Child's Phonics Level over Time.

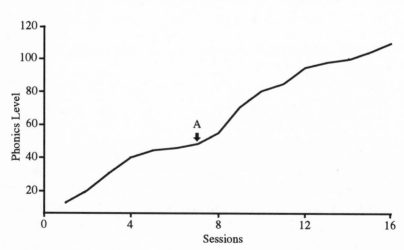

in other parts of the system. Borrowing principles from inter-dependence, if parents become more active in the school or more involved as advocates of their children as a function of participating in the program, intervention in one system has influenced another powerful system. Regardless of whether these do occur, the principles of interdependence would help investigators begin seriously to look at these second-order effects.

As a second example of this principle, in the third wave of our program (1988–1989) we compared the effects of providing preventive intervention to the children alone versus providing the intervention to children and parents. We reasoned that if changes in both the child and parent might be needed, then an approach that focused on both parties might be more effective than one that focused on only one of the groups. Figure 5.4 illustrates the benefit of increasing involvement of a parent in the program. During the first six weeks, the child completed 58 percent of the SRA cards and homework calendars. After week 7, the child's parent became more involved in tutoring, and the rate of returning homework items rose to 87 percent.

Figure 5.4. Percent of SRA Cards and Homework Calendars Returned over Time.

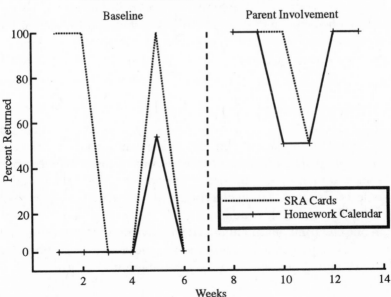

Cycling of Resources

The third ecological principle refers to how resources are used and created in a setting to cope with identified problems. By understanding this principle, we can often identify untapped resources and employ them in our efforts to assess and possibly change people and settings. Resources can be skills and expertise, information, networks of social support, access to supplies or equipment, and socialization processes that either deter bias (that is, gender or racial) or provide events (for example, celebrations) for social and cultural cohesion. Using this principle, we might either uncover existing competencies in a setting or match individuals with the settings that provide the resources they need.

The principle of cycling of resources might alert us to untapped resources within the school. Such resources could help make the intervention more effective and the school system better at solving problems. As an example, in our third wave of the School Transition Project we noticed that several parents volunteering in the schools had begun observing some of our tutoring sessions. They had expressed interest in our work and the techniques that we regularly use. Is it not possible that there are volunteers in most schools who could be properly trained and supervised to implement our program for at-risk youngsters? Focusing on existent resources in the school broadens our perspective on how our programs might be adopted and implemented without excessive reliance on outside financial resources.

Adaptation

Individuals must constantly revise their coping behavior in response to concurrent and competing contingencies. Behavior is a result of a continual process of accommodation between persons and their environments. Behavior observed in one setting reflects one's negotiation of a combination of environmental pressures. The principle of adaptation suggests that behavior adaptive in one environment might not be adaptive in other environments.

The principle of adaptation suggests that transition children might function differently in different settings. We have recently begun clustering children into different subtypes and have found that some children have academic problems, others have academic and behavioral problems, and others have only behavioral problems. These different types of children seem to function differently in a variety of school and home settings. As we look at these different clusters of children, we see that some youngsters who do poorly in the classroom on academic tasks are also aggressive and rejected by their peers. In a variety of settings, these children are perceived as being a problem. These types of children might need the most intensive interventions to overcome their multiple problems. On the other hand, some children evidence difficulties only in the classroom, where they do not meet their teacher's expectations; however, they are popular with peers and otherwise well adjusted. What we are finding is that there are very different groupings of children, and their behavior in different settings is remarkably variable. The principle of adaptation helps us to begin understanding the variability of children's behavior in different settings.

Kelly (1985, 1987) maintains that ecological principles should be used by professionals who join in long-term collaborative relationships with persons and settings. By being involved actively in the planning of interventions, the recipients of the programs receive support, learn to identify resources, and become better problem solvers who are more likely to be effective with future problems and issues. Change efforts that are not well integrated into the setting are unlikely to produce lasting effects. Interventions that have been generated by collaborating to define, produce, and implement change are most apt to endure.

Psychoeducational Model

The psychoeducational model utilizes psychological techniques such as counseling, consulting, and programming services to initiate change at a school. This change may take place on an individual level (with a child, teacher, or principal) or an organizational level (with school policy and administration, or the entire school district).

Typically, when a child encounters academic difficulties or behavioral problems in school, he or she is referred to a social agency. Sarason, Levine, Goldenberg, Cherlin, and Bennett (1966) state several reasons a mental health referral may not be the most effective route for a child who is in need of mental health services.

First, the referral process takes an extended period of time since most clients are put on waiting lists. The referral process may be halted even further if parents are not willing initially to contact the clinic and/or bring their children to the clinic for appointments. Within the psychoeducational model, children receive consistent service directly from their school. Consequently, parents do not bear the burden of contacting the mental health center and taking their child to the clinic.

Second, rarely is a relationship established between teachers and the psychologist when a child is referred to a mental health clinic. Without this connection it is especially difficult for teachers to be fully aware of the problem and supportive of an intervention suggested by the psychologist.

A psychologist may suggest that an aggressive child use a particular relaxation technique to calm himself or herself when provoked. The child's teacher, not aware of the psychologist's intervention, could not prompt the child to use this technique or praise the child for appropriately performing it. As a result, the intervention takes longer to produce a positive effect, and in the meantime the child continues to fight with other children.

This situation would be remedied if the psychological services were available at the school. In this case, a psychologist would observe the child in the classroom and consult with the teacher: together they would devise an intervention that the teacher could monitor and assess within the classroom. More generally, the psychoeducational model encourages the use of psychological techniques by all school professionals in consultation with psychologically knowledgeable practitioners.

Thus we arrive at an appealing solution that the psychoeducational approach suggests for transfer students: What if each child had a personal agent to advocate his or her well-being?

What if this agent, almost like a coach, consulted with teachers regularly on fostering the child's adjustment?

The School Transition Project was in part an opportunity to advocate well-being and provide counseling for kids. As stated previously, we tutored children directly in the school setting. Because the tutoring program existed within the schools, the teacher and tutor interacted on a regular basis and also devised programs that helped boost the child's academics, self-esteem, and peer relations. Teacher-tutor communication was one of our top priorities. Tutors communicated with teachers either by note or orally at least once a week and shared observations about the child's progress and difficulties; they also planned further strategies. Such communication is integral to a psychoeducational approach.

Another type of communication manifested by the psychoeducational model is among school personnel, tutors, and families. Because the children and parents we worked with were new to their school and neighborhood, they often were in need of a variety of resources. Many parents inquired at their child's school about services that might be available to their families. Although the school often had a list of available resources for reference, some parents were in need of special services unfamiliar to school personnel. Principals and teachers often utilized our staff to locate resources to help parents. These resources included psychological services, bilingual services, educational testing, tutoring for siblings, and low-cost health services. One of our tutors accompanied an apprehensive parent and her child to some necessary test administrations. Over the four years of the project, we became familiar with a variety of services offered throughout the Chicago area and shared our knowledge with school personnel and parents.

Through frequent communication we developed a close professional relationship with teachers and principals. Some teachers felt comfortable asking tutors for advice and opinions concerning the children in our tutoring program. In this situation, we served the school in a capacity similar to that of a consultant. Therefore, traditional consulting services are very much in line with the psychoeducational perspective.

Summary

In this chapter we have argued for an appreciation of the useful role that behavioral time-series data might play in better documenting some of the rich theoretical perspectives of transactional and ecological investigators. Similarly, the reciprocal system's orientations can provide us new perspective for understanding the behavioral influences that contribute to the long-term success of their interventions. One might even argue that without an appreciation of these transactional and ecological factors it will be difficult to understand the reasons certain interventions maintain their effects whereas others seem to dissipate over time.

To review, the drawing board of the School Transition Project details elements of community, behavioral, developmental, and ecological psychology as contributing to our theoretical foundation. More specifically, to conceptualize behavioral flux and change, we rely on transactional models; to understand our role in school settings, we refer to ecological theory and the psychoeducational model. These theories have been more fully discussed in a paper that uses the term *eco-transactional behavioral* model to describe the confluence of these different approaches (Jason, in press). All of these ingredients have helped us to lay the groundwork. The next chapter describes the program itself.

6

Developing an Intervention Program

The School Transition Project is our attempt to help transfer students. As explained in Chapter Five, the program is based on eco-transactional theory. This theory holds that an intervention that interrupts and alters a dynamic between people will set into motion a cascade of change among other interactions and behaviors as well. Our interaction with participants stimulates a momentum of change that, we hope, ultimately stays in motion independent of our initial intervention.

The goal of the School Transition Project was to teach students skills they needed to succeed at their new schools. At the same time we sought to increase their teachers' awareness both of what it means for a child to be new at a school and of these students' special needs. We also attempted to involve parents in their children's transfer experience by training them to tutor. (Parent training is discussed in detail in Chapter Eight.) Thus, the success of our program depended on building resources and support for the transfer students during our one-year intervention so that children would continue learning and progressing on their own.

We offer our program as an example of what schools and communities can do to help transfer students. This program is described more as a helpful and flexible guideline than a rigid plan to which schools must adhere. Before the details of the School Transition Project are described, we look briefly at our general approach and rationale.

An Integrative Approach

In designing our program, we took an integrated, community-based approach that stresses collaboration between tutors, the intervention team, principals, parents, and same-age as well as older peers. This multifaceted, multiperson approach promotes flexibility in the program to allow individualized interventions designed for each child's needs.

Getting teachers and principals involved seemed to heighten the school's awareness and competence in helping transfer students. Thus, in quite informal and subtle ways, our intervention could be considered an organizational intervention. While we did not formally evaluate the organizational implications of our intervention, it seems clear that when you work with all the people in a child's environment, you probably are affecting how that environment is organized, the way it attends to a child's needs.

The School Transition Project was a data-based intervention. In addition to collecting standardized pre-intervention, post-intervention, and follow-up data, we collected behavioral and academic data throughout the year. Continuous data collection was essential in developing and evaluating the program. For us, the combination of evaluation and implementation harkens back to models of the scientist-practitioner and action researcher. We attempted simultaneously to implement and study the intervention, remaining open to new avenues of research and practice. As shown later, we closely monitored students' progress and used that information to bolster their improvement. We collected consumer satisfaction data, which pointed out the successful aspects of the program. We queried parents about their willingness to be trained as tutors and then designed a home-tutoring program. We became interested in students' reasons for transferring, which seemed to affect adjustment, so we designed a questionnaire assessing why transfer occurred; we refined and expanded this measure over several years. All of these are examples of how we attempted to blend our interest in scientific study with our desire to help transfer children.

Prevention: Our Raison D'Être

The primary concern of the School Transition Project was prevention. Several studies reviewed earlier have shown that increased school mobility is associated not only with problems in academic areas (Bensen et al., 1979; Brockman & Reeves, 1967; Schaller, 1974) but also with psychopathological disorders (Millet, Pon, Guibaud, & Auriol, 1980; Stubblefield, 1955). Our goal was to help the children academically and, at the same time, support them socially and emotionally. There is growing awareness that emotional and social development are as important as academic development in determining educational success. We wanted to motivate our children to learn and to equip them with the skills that accelerate learning.

Studies on transfer children raise two key questions: how to prevent the negative consequences of school transfer, and how to identify those transfer students with increased risk of becoming disorganized and demoralized following the transfer (Freedman, 1964). In addition to being in a low-SES family, youngsters may inadequately handle the challenge of coping with a school transfer if they are also confronted with multiple stressors (Shaw & Pangman, 1975) and lack requisite personal and social resources (Gilliland, 1958; Goebel, 1981; Holland et al., 1974; Jason, Thompson & Rose, 1986; Turner & McClatchey, 1978; Whalen & Fried, 1973).

The research reviewed earlier also strongly indicates that children at high risk for school difficulties and failure are from lower-SES backgrounds and are exposed to multiple life stressors. If such children received the necessary resources and support to navigate this transition successfully, patterns of long-term poor achievement and school failure might be averted.

Helpers for Transfer Students

Paraprofessionals — in psychology, education, social work, and other fields — have emerged as a new, important, and effective resource as change agents. Research has shown that paraprofessionals can be as effective as professionals in many areas (Durlak, 1979, 1982). The School Transition Project used paraprofessionals who were undergraduate students, graduate students, graduates, part-time workers, full-time workers, people native to Chicago, and nonresidents. They had various career interests including teaching, school psychology, counseling, clinical psychology, and community empowerment. This diversity only helped the project, and we suggest that an intervention like ours engage similarly diverse personnel. The diversity of personnel reflected the range of the project itself: from basic research, to service and education, to community enhancement. Using only one type of intervention employee may limit the scope of the intervention.

Training Paraprofessionals

Training is a critical part of any intervention. Our tutors, who were either DePaul University undergraduates or graduates applying to graduate programs, were trained for two weeks at the end of a summer. The main purpose of the training was to familiarize the tutors with the philosophy of the program and to instruct them in how to use the Direct Instruction Technique (Englemann et al., 1975; Rosenshine & Berliner, 1978). Other parts of the training focused on how to use reinforcement, introduce material in an interesting way, and pace the sequence of material, as well as how to help youngsters relax and feel comfortable being tutored. The following are some of the main topics covered in tutor training.

Instruction. Our project used special methods of instruction. Direct Instruction is a well-researched teaching method that utilizes careful organization of materials, high level of student involvement, rapid rate of teacher presentation, immediate effective feedback, positive reinforcement, and teaching to criterion level (Rosenshine & Berliner, 1978). This technique was used to tutor children in four subject areas: math, phonics, reading, and spelling.

One frequently used technique of Direct Instruction is the model-lead-test, in which the tutor first demonstrates the correct response (model), then tutor and student say the response together (lead), and then the student says the correct response alone (test). Model-lead-test can be used with any type of material, from reading to math facts. For example, suppose the tutor were correcting a word the student mispronounced. The sequence might look like this:

Tutor: "The word is extreme. My turn: extreme. Our turn . . ."

Tutor and student: "Extreme."

Tutor: "Your turn."

Student: "Extreme."

Tutor: "All right! Good job!"

We also discussed with tutors five types of teaching goals identified by Hatoff, Byran, and Hyson (1981): instructing, setting problems, providing experiences, helping children with feeling and behavior, and helping children manage routines and rules. We showed tutors how to administer various measures and to calculate reading accuracy, rate, and comprehension.

Communication. Tutors also were advised to communicate with teachers by (1) talking with teachers in person, (2) sharing with teachers one weekly sheet per student summarizing that student's performance in each tutoring subject, and (3) sharing a notebook with teachers to exchange private information on students (the notebooks were stored in a mutually accessible place, such as the teachers' mailbox).

With students, tutors were told to introduce themselves, discuss what tutoring involves, and to explain that they were chosen for the project because they are transfer students and that "sometimes new students need a little extra help and attention." Tutors would say, "I am here to help you get used to the new school"; further, they would let students know that, in the future, it would be okay for them to discuss feelings or things on their minds. To develop a closer relationship, tutors were encouraged to discuss students' interests, family, and hobbies. At the end of the academic year, tutors were advised to have a goodbye party, with games, music, and talk about whatever topic the student might choose.

Other effective ways to communicate with students were discussed, such as proper eye contact, speaking courteously, and addressing current behavior. Tutors were instructed to give specific, descriptive, nonevaluative feedback; to make statements rather than ask questions; and to have a high ratio of positive to negative statements (Curwin & Fuhrman, 1975). Active listening was taught, including the use of paraphrasing (Johnson & Johnson, 1975).

Reinforcement. A significant part of training was devoted to discussing ways to reinforce children positively (Hofmeister, Atkinson, & Henterson, 1978). These suggestions were offered: (1) notice when children are behaving; (2) be specific in your praise; (3) reinforce immediately; (4) reinforce small steps; (5) follow the three steps for teaching; (6) be consistent; (7) ignore misbehavior; (8) create a "quiet area" and use it when necessary; (9) set conditions; (10) make effective demands; and (11) reason with a child only when he or she is behaving. Trainers discussed tangible rewards (stars, pencils, a book), social rewards (verbal expressions, facial expressions, physical nearness or appropriate touching), and using preferred activities as rewards.

Other Issues. Finally, tutor training also covered such issues as keeping safe in the schools' neighborhoods, dressing properly, and reporting child sexual abuse.

Using Tutors as Advocates for Transfer Students

Besides academic tutoring, tutors had an important advocate role for the child. As an advocate, a tutor serves as a link between the child and teacher or principal, and between the child's parents and the school. Students might be afraid to talk with teachers about certain adjustment problems they may be having, but may feel more comfortable talking and working it out with a tutor, as in the following example.

Joel, a nine-year-old fourth grader, frequently acted out in class, but not during tutoring. In a conversation with the tutor, the teacher admitted that she did not like this student because he was disruptive and difficult to handle. The tutor designed a brief behavior checklist that the teacher filled out every day. The checklist included items such as staying in his seat, completing his work, and not talking to his neighbors. The tutor discussed the teacher's feedback with Joel during tutoring. Together they developed alternative strategies for Joel to use in the classroom, such as ignoring his classmates' provocations, telling the teacher when he was done with assignments, and being prepared each day at the beginning of class (which meant sharpening pencils, getting his books from his locker, having paper ready). Soon, the teacher noticed that Joel was being more attentive and less disruptive, and that his work was improving. She therefore commented to both tutor and student on his progress. The positive feedback encouraged Joel to improve his classroom behavior and performance further, which also strengthened the student-teacher relationship.

In this situation, the tutor had the advantage of being able to work with the student individually. This enabled her to focus on his behavior without having to neglect the rest of the class. She could act as a mediator between the student and the teacher and help facilitate a more positive relationship between the two.

Getting Parents to Help

Tutoring a child can provide some of the individual attention the teacher cannot provide in the class setting. Some children, however, need more than two fifty-minute tutoring sessions each week. Therefore, the parents of a child are key agents for extra help. In Chapters Eight and Ten, we explain how children who received help from their parents did better than those who did not receive help. The tutor has only limited time with the child; parents have much more time as well as a long-lasting and usually stable relationship with the child. Tutoring might even foster stronger relationships between parents and their children.

Two Ways to Help Transfer Students

Any social service must seek lasting change. Social services should attempt to develop the beginnings of empowerment that snowball into self-sustaining, healthier behavior. We were hopeful that our program would have such long-term effects. One strategy for ensuring long-term success was to train parents in tutoring techniques. To assess the interplay between parental support and academic success, we divided the experimental group into two subgroups: one in which the children were being tutored at school by our staff (the School Tutoring Program) and one in which we tutored the children at school and additionally trained parents themselves to tutor (the School and Home Tutoring Program).

The basic School Tutoring Program consisted of three major parts:

- Transfer children received a same-sex, same-grade "buddy" in the new school.
- At the beginning of the year, transfer children and their buddies participated in a one-hour orientation program about the new school. (See Resource B.)
- School Transition Project staff tutored transfer children twice a week and acted as advocates for them.

The School and Home Tutoring Program featured the *same* components as the School Tutoring Program plus these additions:

- School Transition Project staff trained parents to tutor their children twice a week.
- School Transition Project staff acted as a liaison between parents, teachers, principals, and children.

In both components, a telephone interview was conducted with the parent at the beginning of the year. This interview provided information on the reason for the move, the family's socioeconomic background, life stressors they might have experienced during the past year, a measure of family functioning such as Faces III (Olson, 1986), and other information that might be helpful.

Before explaining the two programs in depth, we first discuss the orientation we developed that was used in both programs (see Resource B). This program is a helpful and easy way for a school to begin addressing transfer issues without a large investment of time, resources, or staff. We recommend the program as a minimal step schools can take toward helping transfers.

Orientation Program

The one-hour orientation program occurred at the elementary school following pre-point testing. This session occurred during the first few weeks of the new school year. By linking the student's entry to school with a positive experience (that is, the orientation program), the intervention induced a more relaxed emotional state. Children were placed in groups of fifteen to twenty children. Within these groups, the youngsters were provided a review of school rules, personnel, information, and clubs. Students were encouraged to ask questions about the school and activities. They were prepared cognitively for stressful situations by helping them anticipate and think about the potentially difficult experience of transferring into a new school. By emphasizing the rules and information, the research team familiarized the children with the school. Students then had a fuller appreciation of the school's expectations and were better prepared to function without elevated levels of arousal.

The school information was conveyed by discussions led by a sixth-grade peer leader. A friendly and confident peer guide, who modeled adaptive coping responses and was enthusiastic about school, provided the transfer students a potential model for effective coping in their new setting. In addition, some peer guides were former transfer students who revealed their own positive experiences following their transfer into the school to enhance the transfer children's sense of efficacy in mastering their own transitions.

When the children discussed feelings, the project personnel rather than the peer leaders guided the discussion because they possessed more expertise in encouraging self-disclosure and in validating the emotional responses of the children. The transfer students were asked to think about and discuss how their new school compared to their old one. To help the children feel comfortable talking about feelings, project staff conducted a matching game that required the students to match differently named feelings. The transfer students were asked next to write down and discuss two feelings they had about entering their new school.

The orientation program also facilitated peer relationships. Each transfer child was paired up with a buddy who actively participated in the orientation session. The pairs were involved in various activities that encouraged cooperation and communication. The children interviewed each other about their favorite foods and television shows, and they engaged in the discussions about school personnel, rules, and activities. In regard to school rules, five general good conduct rules (e.g., being on time) were discussed with the assistance of the peer leader, and these rules were written down in an orientation book.

The pairs of children also considered how they could be good friends to one another. The sixth grader and a member of the project staff role-played a situation involving how children could support each other during lunchtime. The pairs of students were then asked to role-play one of a variety of suggested scenes involving a cooperation task leading to the development of trust. At the end of the session, the children were asked to pretend they would get together the next week after school. They were instructed to interview one another and decide (1) where they would meet, (2) what games they would play, (3) what they would have for snacks, (4) what they would do if it was raining, (5) who else might join them, and (6) what they would talk about. The children were given five minutes to discuss these issues and then reported back to the group what occurred.

In addition, the children were provided pictures to color that carried the messages, "Help Out New Students" and "Be a Friend." They were also given a page of riddles that they could complete together. Finally, to promote sharing, each transfer student was given a package of four cartoon pencils, and they were asked to give two of the pencils to their buddies.

In the following sections, each of the two programs is reviewed in detail.

The School Tutoring Program

Our General Approach

Staff tutoring was central to both programs. The tutoring sessions were scheduled twice a week for forty to sixty minutes for each student. In some cases the tutor spent two to four days at the school, depending on how many children were in the program. Tutoring consisted of teaching new skills, practicing recently acquired skills until mastered, and reviewing previously learned skills. The individual format of the session gave the students an opportunity to repeat trials as often as necessary to strengthen areas of weakness before moving on to progressively more difficult skills. The tutor and student also spent several minutes a day talking about any subjects or problems brought up by the student, such as problems with a teacher or difficulties at home. The sessions were scheduled during regular class time, but the tutors were sensitive not to take a student from class when teachers introduced a critical subject or during gym or art class.

Subject Areas for Tutoring

Tutoring covered four subject areas: spelling, reading, math, and phonics. The curriculum was partly taken from the materials the teacher used in class and partly developed by project staff. The following sections briefly describe each of these tutoring areas (see Resource C for full curricula in each of the four areas).

Spelling. Lessons in spelling consisted of the weekly spelling lists used in the classroom. A tutor gave a student the whole list during the first tutoring session of the week; the student then corrected and practiced the words he or she misspelled and was given those words again during the second tutoring session. The weekly score was the percentage of correct words obtained during the second session. The tutors charted and discussed results with the student. In this way, learning in the tutoring session complemented learning in class, and success in tutoring would spill over to success in class.

Reading. The reading materials used were also taken from the class. In most cases, the tutor and student practiced reading the story being covered in class. However, for some students such materials were too difficult. The tutor then would use either a lower-level reading book provided by the school or reading cards. Reading cards are small, four-page booklets with a short reading selection plus questions and exercises about that selection. We used reading cards by SRA (Science Research Associates, 1982). The main advantage of using SRA cards is that the tutor can adjust the level of difficulty to the student's ability. SRA cards also make it easier for tutors to plot a student's progress.

Three criteria were used to document a student's reading progress: accuracy, rate, and comprehension. To obtain these scores, a weekly reading assessment was administered. The students read a 100-word passage from their current reading material. The tutor recorded the percentage of correctly read words and calculated the reading rate using the formula as outlined in Resource C. In addition, the tutor asked five comprehension questions based on the passage. Two of the questions were factual (pertaining to the main facts), two were inferential (information not stated explicitly in the text), and one was sequential (pertaining to the order of events in the passage). Again, tutors recorded the percentage of correct answers.

Math. The math curriculum consisted of five hierarchies: addition, subtraction, multiplication, division, and fractions (see Resource D). At the beginning of the year, the students were given a math placement test containing problems from each step of the five skill hierarchies. The results from this placement test were used to determine the starting point for tutoring. Instruction began on the step corresponding to the first missed item in an area.

Each math hierarchy started out with the most basic concepts of that area. For example, steps 1 and 2 on the addition hierarchy are recognizing inequalities of numbers less than ten and understanding seriation of numbers less than ten. At the highest level of each hierarchy the student has to be able to apply and generalize the concepts learned. Step 18 of the division hierarchy, for example, requires a student to be able to solve mixed addition, subtraction, multiplication, and division word problems. The tutor and the student work on each level until the student can solve all five problems correctly. Typically, much time is spent on practicing basic concepts of math, such as multiplication tables. For some students it was especially helpful to apply the concepts of addition, subtraction, multiplication, and division to real-life situations, such as shopping, ordering in a restaurant, or telling time.

Phonics. The children we tutored often had a deficit in phonics, which carried over into their reading and spelling proficiency. In many schools a phonics curriculum is not taught beyond the second grade. However, the phonics curriculum, developed by the School Transition Project staff, consists of groups of the most commonly used words and rules for reading these words. (See Resource E for an example of the phonics curriculum.) The goal of teaching phonics is to enable the students to recognize similar sounds in different words and to be able to generalize these sounds from one word to another. For this purpose, the phonetic ladder was divided into a series of 170 steps each consisting of ten similar-sounding words. The ladder begins with a "step" of ten one-syllable words featuring short and long vowel sounds, such as *cat, sit,* and *tune.* Words at later steps of the ladder have several syllables and feature complex vowel and consonant combinations such as *geothermal, calligraphy,* and *virulent.* When a student can read nine out of ten words correctly, he or she has mastered the step.

All data collected by the tutors was entered into a computer. The tutors could then print out graphs to show to their students and to discuss their progress with them. Some tutors even created large, colorful charts, embellished with rockets, ladders, and other symbols to help illustrate the students' progress. These graphs well exemplify a behavioral, data-based approach. Children take an active part in assessing and monitoring their development and feel more in control of their behavior. We can illustrate the School Tutoring Program by detailing one child's progress.

Quenton was a white, ten-year-old boy in the fifth grade. His parents had recently separated and Quenton was living with his mother and aunt. His father was living in the southern part of the country. Because of the divorce, the financial status of the family had worsened.

At the beginning of the year, Quenton was given the Wide Range Achievement Test-Revised (WRAT-R). The subtest scores indicated that he was working more than a grade level below the fifth grade in spelling and math. In reading, Quenton received a score equivalent to a third-grade level.

Data were also collected from the individual tutoring sessions. These data gave the tutors and project supervisors an indication of the effectiveness of the tutoring sessions. If Quenton steadily improved in an area, no change in the intervention plan was necessary. But if Quenton was slow in progressing, the content, style, pacing, or presentation of the curriculum was changed to bolster his learning rate.

On the phonetic ladder, Quenton initially began at first-grade level (see Chapter Five, Figure 5.3). At point A on the graph, the tutor and supervisor decided to spend more time on phonics by starting his tutoring sessions with ten minutes of phonics instruction and finishing the session with five to ten additional minutes of phonics. Consequently, Quenton improved, working his way up to the 109th step of the phonetic ladder to achieve at the fourth-grade phonics level.

Quenton's multiplication performance (Figure 6.1) demonstrated a need to review his multiplication facts. After steady review and practice, he completed the multiplication hierarchy and then proceeded to progress well in the division hierarchy.

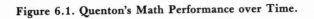

Figure 6.1. Quenton's Math Performance over Time.

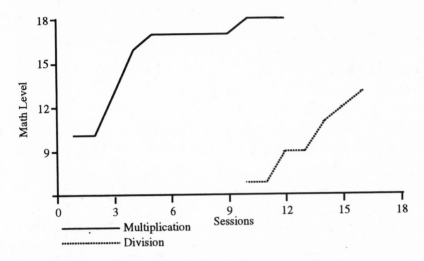

In spelling, if Quenton misspelled a word on Tuesday (pretest), he practiced and was retested on Thursday (posttest). His posttest scores were consistently high (Figure 6.2).

In reading, the tutor used a 100-word assessment to calculate the student's accuracy, comprehension, and rate. Over the course of the year, Quenton maintained a high level of reading accuracy and comprehension while his rate increased (Figure 6.3).

With the tutoring data, the project team could map the student's learning development for the school year. By analyzing the data, project workers targeted areas of special need so the tutors could adjust their focus in these areas. The behavioral utility of these data can be seen in the tutor's strict concentration on Quenton's performance, the high frequency of measurement, and the way Quenton himself could see where he stood and where he needed to be. Along the way, the tutor also used ample and appropriate verbal praise. Quenton made great gains in all academic areas. By standardized achievement tests, his reading level rose between the beginning and end of the year from a third- to fifth-grade level. He also gained one grade level in spelling and two grade levels in math.

Figure 6.2. Quenton's Spelling Performance over Time.

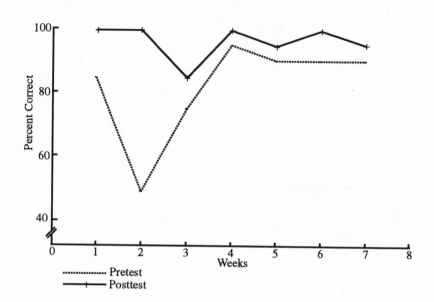

Home Tutoring: A Special Addition
to the School Tutoring Program

In Chapter Eight, we discuss at length how we involved parents. A brief sketch of that work is given here.

First, we obtained permission for testing transfer children and selected those for tutoring according to the criteria discussed earlier. Soon after we selected the children for tutoring, we contacted their parents and asked them to join a meeting with a tutor, a supervisor (someone from our staff who oversaw the tutor's work), and the principal. The purpose of this meeting was to let parents get to know us, to explain our program, and to train them in tutoring techniques. The tutors then established regular biweekly telephone contact with the parents to exchange information and to provide support.

A few weeks after the initial meeting, the tutor and the supervisor visited the student and his or her family in their home.

Figure 6.3. Quenton's Reading Performance:
Percentage Correct in Accuracy and Comprehension.

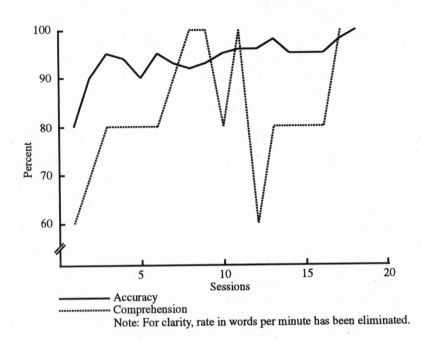

——————— Accuracy
···················· Comprehension
Note: For clarity, rate in words per minute has been eliminated.

This visit provided a more personal atmosphere than the telephone conversations and a more casual setting than the principal's office. It also allowed the tutor to observe the student working with his or her parents and to provide feedback to the parents. Sometimes these home visits were somewhat difficult to arrange around time constraints and work schedules, but when completed they were beneficial to everyone involved. Not only were they a great opportunity for the tutor to get a sense of the student's home life and atmosphere but they also provided the parents with an opportunity to ask questions, talk about their successes and failures, and form a better relationship with the project people. Parents and tutors arranged to have weekly or biweekly telephone contact throughout the year. They also communicated through notes brought to school by the child. Later in the academic year, staff held a second home visit.

Measuring Progress

Evaluating Academic Progress

An essential part of any intervention is program evaluation. In the School Transition Project, a range of measures were used at several time points to assess the effects of the intervention. The most direct and tangible outcome was academic achievement expressed in higher grades and higher scores on the Wide Range Achievement Test-Revised (WRAT-R) (Jastak & Wilkinson, 1984). The WRAT-R was administered during the first three weeks of school and again after the tutoring program had ended in early May. The WRAT-R is a standardized measure that assesses three academic skill areas: spelling, math and reading. While grades are often available, they vary from school to school and are thus not as reliable to use in cross-school comparisons as are WRAT-R scores.

Improving Social Behavior:
Equally Important as Academics

For some students academic tutoring was not enough. These children also had deficits in social skills, manifested in the classroom by aggressive or withdrawn behavior. When considering the tandem of social and academic problems, we find ourselves faced with a chicken-and-egg, cause-and-effect quandary: which comes first? Do social deficits precipitate academic failure, or can academic failure potentially inhibit one's social development? Like most binary controversies in science (e.g., the nature-nurture argument), this question may have no answer. However, the most helpful conceptualization, we think, is a transactional model. Here social and academic behaviors interact and transact, playing off one another as both causes and effects. Moreover, their dynamic relationship becomes a cause itself, spiraling both academic and social problems upward or downward, or maintaining them at the same level. Two examples can illustrate.

Rosa was an eleven-year-old, fifth-grade student who spoke some English but was afraid to use it. Her native language was Spanish. Rosa's difficulty with English led to problems in the academic areas of reading, spelling, and phonics. It also interfered with her ability to form relationships with teachers, peers, and her tutor. However, after several months of tutoring (in which the tutor concentrated on language skills), Rosa was improving in all areas, including socially. By the fall of the following year, Rosa's teachers were amazed at how self-confident and active Rosa had become. With a little support from the tutoring program, Rosa was able to develop into an active, confident, and successful student.

Another child with whom we worked, Carlos, suffered similar problems. An eight-year-old, third-grade Hispanic boy, Carlos was very shy at the beginning of the tutoring program. He was physically a small child and spoke very little to his tutor. He was weak in all academic areas, especially the ones involving the use of English. Carlos came from a Spanish-speaking home so he had little contact with English before school started. Most of Carlos's communication was done nonverbally with nodding and smiling.

Carlos worked very hard. Once he had adjusted to the routine of the tutoring sessions, his performance in class began to improve. With some additional help from his English-speaking cousins, Carlos made the B honor roll in his class, which excited both his tutor and his parents. His communication became increasingly verbal as his knowledge of the English language improved.

Tutoring, combined with family support, seems to have enabled Carlos gain the self-confidence and skills he needed to succeed in school. The tutor's main function for the remainder of the year was to maintain Carlos's high level of learning and self-expression. Although some children do catch up with the rest of the class during the course of the year, others, like Carlos, need continued attention and support.

Measuring Social Behavior

The social life of children is a diverse and complex realm to measure. For this reason, our approach was a multifaceted effort to tap the many dimensions of social behavior. Assessment included a teacher report form, sociometric measures, and a self-concept scale.

The teachers filled out the *Teacher's Report Form* (Achenbach & Edelbrock, 1986). The scale consists of a 113-item checklist. For each child, the teacher determines whether each behavior description is not true, sometimes true, or always/often true.

Social evaluation of a student by teachers should be complemented by a peer-based evaluation. Sociometrics have emerged recently as an important and promising way to complement more traditional, teacher-based measures. The sociometric assessment we used consisted of a combination of three types of measures. First, peer ratings asked how much children like to work and play with each other (Oden & Asher, 1977). Second, a shortened (9-item) version of the Pupil Evaluation Inventory, the Peer Assessment Inventory, was used (Pekarik et al., 1976; Lardon & Jason, in press) (see Resource F). This measure asks each child to select and rate the other children in the class along various dimensions by indicating, for example, which children are worried a lot. The subscales measure aggressiveness, withdrawal, and likability. Third, peer nominations ask which three children they like most and least; calculations then assign each child a social status: popular, rejected, neglected, controversial, or withdrawn (Coie et al., 1982). Each of these measures taps slightly different domains of social functioning and, when combined, form a comprehensive picture of a child's social life. Caution must be taken to discourage and prevent children from finding out how they rate each other; all ratings should be confidential. Overall, sociometrics should be used sensitively, in a way that upholds privacy and avoids stigmatizing anyone. With adequate care taken, these measures can yield valuable information on social standing.

Measuring Self-Esteem

Learning can be a way to help children feel good about themselves. Also, children may learn faster when they like themselves more. Thus, in tutoring we sought to enhance children's self-confidence. To assess children's self-confidence, we employed the *Perceived Competence Scale for Children* (Harter, 1982), which asks children to assess how competent they perceive themselves in a number of areas (for example, scholastics, sports, social acceptance). While not a behavioral measure, self-concept remains an important correlate of effective education and a helpful outcome indicator for our intervention.

Measuring Social Support

An intervention also needs to account for external factors that impinge on a child's adjustment, such as social support. *The Survey of Children's Social Support* (Dubow & Ullman, 1989) helps us see how much and what type of external support the child perceives he or she receives. The scale has thirty-one items and addresses four sources for support: friends, family, teachers, and classmates.

Measuring Feelings About the Move

Finally, a questionnaire designed to assess the child's feeling about her or his transfer experience was given (Cappas, 1989). This scale consists of seventeen possible stressors, for each of which the child reports whether that particular item is no problem, a small problem, a medium problem, or a large problem. It also allows children to rate on a five-point scale how happy they are with their new home (when applicable) and with their new school.

Summary

The success of the School Transition Project rested on its multilayered approach. The following is a short summary of its major components:

- The School Transition Project is a preventive program designed to help transfer children adjust to their new school. We utilized staff tutors to tutor and act as an advocate for each student individually. With the home-tutoring program, we trained parents to foster their children's adjustment to the new school.

- The project included a buddy system and an orientation program for the transfer students at the beginning of the school year. The orientation helped students become familiar with the rules and resources of the school. The buddy can make the usually difficult entry into a new social system a little easier.
- The program was theory-based. It incorporated eco-transactional and behavioral principles, maintaining that each part of a system influences all other parts of that system.
- The program was multifaceted, enlisting the support of many people in the child's environment, including parents, teachers, principals, tutors, and peers. Each group of people provided different resources and support to the student, such as social support, personal advocacy, and academic support.
- The School Transition Project also included an ongoing evaluation to assess students' adjustment. Areas of measurement included academic achievement, peer and teacher ratings, self-concept, and social support.

One of the basic premises of the project was the importance of individualized attention within a framework that worked for a large number of children. We used a broad array of measures covering social and academic skills. For tutors and supervisors, it was extremely helpful to have as much information as possible on any individual student.

7

Overcoming Hurdles
to Implementation

No matter how organized and detailed an intervention may seem in theory, there are always problems. We like to think of some of the difficulties we encountered as hurdles that must be leaped over before the race for a successful intervention can be won. Sometimes, this race can last for years and the number and variety of hurdles can seem overwhelming. However, if taken one at a time, these blocks *can* be jumped, or even removed. In this chapter we discuss some implementation hurdles with which we struggled in the School Transition Project. Because a listing of every problem experienced would fill this book, we have limited our discussion to three major areas: staffing a program, relating with the schools, and meeting the individual needs of children. This chapter ends with general suggestions for readers on how to negotiate future hurdles they may find in their interventions and how, with forethought, to avoid such problems altogether.

Of course, not all programs will have available a large pool of undergraduate students and interns, as we did, or the funds to hire tutors. Some educators may design a program using parents who volunteer to tutor and support new children and their families. They may solicit high school children to tutor transfers. Other school administrators may involve staff of the local community mental health center to be available to counsel transfer children. School faculty might implement only the orientation program or just meet regularly to discuss transfer students. Whatever the specific content and structure of your intervention to help transfer students, the organizational issues addressed in this chapter will be of concern. Thus our comments are also meant for the schools and service agencies that, with limited resources, are struggling to address transfer issues.

Consultation has been discussed as an important and relatively recent advance in schools (Zins & Curtis, 1984). There is a great need to further develop ways for a variety of people, from psychologists to teachers to parents, to consult within the educational system. Our work in schools was an attempt to set up a consultation network around transfer students. Such activity involved not only consulting on specific cases of transfer students but also sensitizing teachers to transfer issues and implementing and developing schoolwide programs. Each of these levels of consultation required us to take on different roles, from knowledgeable expert to helpful adviser to friendly staff member to diplomatic observer. These and other roles have been discussed in the consultation literature (for example, Goodstein, 1978; Meyers, Parsons, & Martin, 1979), and assuming multiple roles has often been seen as necessary for school consultants (Hansen, Himes, & Meier, 1990). In this chapter, we discuss the process and content of consultation within these many roles.

A helpful framework for defining our roles in schools is intervention assistance, which means using collaborative consultation to deliver special services (Zins et al., 1988). For further information, the book *Helping Students Succeed in the Regular Classroom* (Zins et al., 1988) provides an excellent overview of how intervention assistance works, including a discussion of ways to resolve resistance to implementation.

Staffing a Program

The demands placed on project workers are usually plentiful. Because of tight budgeting, the pay is almost always low, the hours are long, and the expectations for quality work and dedication are extremely high. Our project is no exception. Effective consultation in schools requires many skills, including effective questioning, listening, and problem solving (Zins & Curtis,

1984). In addition, we needed to find people who could teach a variety of children with a variety of problems, who could think of creative new programming, who could contend with the large amount of paperwork and assessment required for evaluation, and who could work well with school principals, teachers, and other staff—all for about $6 an hour. Luckily, because we are in a university, we found such people. In the first year, our staff of tutors consisted mainly of undergraduate psychology students from our university and other local schools who, for their involvement, received a small hourly wage. These tutors worked part-time, though many did extras for their students on their own time. However, the great number of tutors needed to serve the large number of children caused problems of responsibility and efficiency. This was the project's first managerial bout with productivity. It was necessary to define the various roles of project director, supervisor, and tutor. It quickly became clear that this intervention team was resembling a service corporation more than just a group of researchers.

In the next three years, we gave more attention to how we selected tutors. The application process became more rigorous, and the job specifications became much more refined. Individuals who were looking to further their career in the areas of psychology or education seemed to us to fit the job description. In addition to part-time tutors who either were being paid or were fulfilling an internship requirement with the university as well as being paid, full-time tutors were also hired to enhance efficiency and communication within the agency by offering leadership and commitment. Finally, the project's goals and expectations were more clearly spelled out for potential tutors, as well as for staff so as to prevent misunderstandings concerning each person's responsibilities. This program was definitely more than a research endeavor; it was an educational and psychological service agency.

When any social service project widens in scope and increases the amount of services it offers, new hurdles inevitably arise. Our project increased in the number of personnel, the number of schools and therefore students serviced, the amount of information gathered, and the number of parents involved in the added parent component. With more personnel, we were confronted with the challenge of avoiding an impersonal bureaucracy. Organizational literature suggests that when people are more involved in setting goals, they are more committed to their work (Forman, 1984). In our project, the tutors wanted more in terms of research training and academic guidance. At the same time, they wanted more flexibility than allowed by the established curriculum and behavioral teaching strategies—they wanted to personalize their work. It was clear to the tutors that the tutoring program, as it was originally designed, did not meet all the needs of the children they were trying to help. The tutors asked for more information about social and behavioral problems. They wanted to know about child abuse and child advocacy. They struggled with new teaching strategies to reach the most distant child. The general feeling in the School Transition Project was a combination of excitement and frustration because of the agency's and the children's limitations. The staff soon discovered that the special needs of the children were not the only needs that required attention; the needs of tutors demanded attention as well.

The project attempted to meet these needs on two levels. In group meetings, several specific topics were introduced for discussion. These included tutor safety, tutor burnout, and working with difficult children. One staff supervisor wrote a miniature tutor safety manual that encouraged the tutors to travel in pairs and keep a quarter with them at all times for an emergency phone call. These tips and many others were shared with the tutors in a large group meeting and later incorporated into the tutor training manual we wrote and used.

During these group meetings, tutors also shared some of their feelings toward and experiences in the project. They were able to express to understanding ears their frustrations with the work, their assigned school's staff, and the slow progress of some of their students. The group thus acted as a sounding board and support system. But this kind of help was not always enough. When tutor burnout became clearly problematic, we added project boosters to keep up the spirits of the overworked and the underpaid. We had holiday parties, gift grab bags, and even "earn-a-day-off" programs.

An outside educational consultant was also brought in to help tutors liven up their teaching routines and improve their behavior control skills. After these suggestions were put into use, the tutors became semi-experts on alternative learning strategies and were able to share their ideas with each other. The cycling of information was encouraged so that we could take advantage of every gain in knowledge possible. In fact, our valuable supply of excellent tutors from one year often were recycled the following year as supervisors and tutor trainers.

In an attempt by the supervisors and director to become more sensitive to the individual experiences of each tutor, weekly one-on-one meetings were also arranged. The supervisor-tutor meetings allowed the tutors to share and explore their experiences as well as the progress of the children with whom they worked. Both the group and private meetings cultivated many supportive bonds within the agency. With these ties established, the system ran more smoothly. Enhancing communication among the entire staff has been the key to overcoming many seemingly insurmountable barriers.

Finally, although similarly trained, tutors bring their own styles, personalities, and varying levels of commitment. All tutors received fifteen to twenty hours of training before tutoring, but there were differences in the amount of prior experience working with children, parents, and schools that tutors brought to their work. Also, some tutors were better able than others to build trusting and personal relationships with their students. In general, students with close relationships to their tutors were more motivated to try than students with more formal relationships. These varying levels of relationships may partly be a result of differing degrees of personal investment and time involvement tutors had with the School Transition Project. While some tutors worked full-time tutoring ten students, others only had three to five students, or worked on the project as part of their undergraduate internship. Thus, it was a challenge for us to help everyone to achieve and maintain a similarly high level of involvement and motivation with their assigned children.

The training issues we have been discussing pertain not just to a research-based project such as ours, which employs many tutors, but to any program that attempts to address school transfer. The systems issues of personnel selection, financial compensation, staff communication, training, and balancing individual versus program needs are common concerns for any program. Therefore, some of the solutions we found can be helpful to others. For instance, group meetings for training, feedback, and support can be used by any organization, such as with tutors, principals, teachers, teacher aides, or mental health professionals. One-on-one feedback is beneficial for anyone who volunteers in a classroom, whether that person is a parent, undergraduate, or high school student. And everyone in a program needs to have personal needs addressed and to be rewarded for effort. Rewards may be financial (salary, tuition waiver for children of parents or employees who tutor); in some programs, rewards may be a thank-you certificate or a special end-of-the-year ceremony for tutors. Thus, keeping in mind that even the smallest program constitutes a system, we think the issues we have discussed here can be helpful to a variety of organizations.

Relations with the School: Everyone's Great Expectations

Before our intervention could get off the ground, it was important to have a community that needed our services as much as we needed their support. We wanted to work with a school system that had little in the way of established child tutoring programs that might conflict with our intervention, but we also needed schools that would agree to the additional burdens of much evaluation in exchange for these services. The Catholic school system met these criteria; moreover, the principal investigator had had positive experiences consulting with them in the past. The decision seemed simple enough. Although higher-level administrators decided that the schools would participate, the support of the individual school principals and teachers remained to be won. Thus, the smooth practice of public relations became an emphasis for all those staff members who would ever need to come in contact with the schools.

The School's Expectations

Many times, meetings between program workers and school staff were pleasant, but these conferences were not always easy. The limitations of our project were difficult for some school personnel to accept. This was especially true for the schools who would not receive any tutoring services but were still asked to participate in all the testing sessions (nonprogram schools). After hearing of the tutoring program at other schools, the personnel at nonprogram schools required reassurance from the project director of the importance of their participation. As the project expanded, we later selected some nonprogram schools to become program schools. It seems best if nonprogram schools have the chance later to participate in the program. Whenever possible, we gave these schools testing information and other support, such as counseling referral information, as compensation for their continued involvement. While the basic expectations of nonprogram schools regarding our services seemed fulfilled, this was not always the case for the program schools.

Grappling with schools' expectations usually first meant working with principals. Principals of Chicago Catholic schools are relatively autonomous in their decisions concerning programs at their schools and have very different management styles. We needed to be sensitive to their various approaches. For example, some principals were very involved with all activities at their schools. They planned and participated in activities and therefore had frequent contact with the children and their families as well as School Transition Project staff. Other principals saw themselves mainly as administrators. Their secretaries were responsible for all contacts with outsiders.

Often the principals were aware of the special needs of transfer students but did not have the resources or the time to become involved. Therefore, we discussed with them the resources we could offer and they decided that their investment of time and support would be well worth the benefits to the children.

Teachers' Expectations

As with most hierarchical organizations, the principals' level of involvement and support seemed to have a trickle-down effect in the schools, contributing to teachers' enthusiasm and cooperation. Principals became important allies when we made extra demands on teachers by asking them to fill out forms on their students or letting us conduct testing. The teachers' involvement, in turn, impacted parents' interest in helping their transfer children. An involved teacher was much more likely to help us in forging and maintaining contact with parents.

Every teacher, of course, has unique experiences, style, and opinions on "outside help." Some teachers have been working in the school system for twenty years or more. In order not to offend these professionals — who, after all, were much more experienced in teaching than we were — we had to be extremely sensitive to their views and expectations. This sensitivity meant training tutors to hone their communication skills and to listen actively. Some examples follow.

One of the most common teacher requests was that we tutor a child who had not transferred but nevertheless had academic difficulties. While we were sympathetic to this plea, we were bound by federal funds to tutor only those children who were new students to the school. If a teacher persisted and the tutor had an open session that could not be filled by a transfer student, sometimes we would also help these children. For the most part, however, such an arrangement was not possible. Schools needed to accept this limitation as a condition of the help we were giving to transfer children.

Another frequent request of teachers was that we tutor children in an additional area other than the four subjects of our program. Again, after trying to explain the boundaries of the intervention, we would usually try to meet the teachers' requests by offering additional help in the desired areas during the last ten minutes of the tutoring sessions if the students had been able to complete all other assignments. We also worked out this kind of arrangement when children were missing what the teacher considered to be invaluable time and work by being in the tutoring session instead of the classroom. Some teachers, for example, did not want to have students taken out of their class. Coordinating special and regular education has been identified as an organizational challenge facing schools, one that requires patience, clear rationale, and good communication among all concerned (Driscoll, 1984). Thus, instead of simply insisting on taking the students, the tutor would try to learn why the teacher was opposed to the idea and would then work in collaboration with a teacher toward a solution.

Educators prefer a collaborative model in consultation (Babcock & Pryzwansky, 1983); indeed, collaboration was crucial when we met with resistance. Many times the teacher expected immediate results from the tutoring without any disturbances to the regular classroom schedule and workload. Expectations of this type are unreasonable. It was up to the tutor and the supervisor to help the teacher understand our constraints while the tutor made all possible attempts to help the child keep up in class. Here again, the compromise between teachers' wants and tutors' restrictions was made in order to preserve the working relationship between systems.

Our Expectations

As helpers, we also had expectations for the school and the teachers that were not always easily met. The environmental conditions for tutoring varied greatly across schools. We had hoped that each tutor would be able to work consistently in the same private room each visit, but in some cases this was not possible. While some tutors had the luxury of their own personalized classrooms in which to teach, others were forced to tutor in a corner of the school library or at a table in the hall right outside the open door of the child's classroom. Yet, even though some conditions were less than perfect and other options may have seemed possible, it was important for the project staff members working with their assigned schools to respect the decisions and limitations of that school. As visitors, our staff always needed to be extremely flexible and courteous.

But as specialized educators who taught in a school all

year, were tutors still just "visitors"? The level of each school's personal involvement with the tutor varied. On one end of the continuum, some tutors entered, tutored, and left a school without any school personnel every saying hello to them. Necessary information about the students was passed between teacher and tutor in the form of brief notes or short, sporadic, prearranged meetings. In contrast, some tutors were invited to private birthday parties for other staff members, ate lunch regularly with many of the school personnel, and freely exchanged information regarding the children at any time during the course of the day. Schools seemed initially to set the tone for the working relationships. While it seems that we would have benefited from a personal relationship with each school, such closeness was not always desirable. Problems in collecting information were sometimes caused because of a tutor's difficulty in acting assertively with teachers who were his or her friends. Often the supervisor needed to wield a heavy hand in order not to upset the valued teacher-tutor relationship.

Finally, the project's expectations for consistency were many times unmet because of the school's busy calendar of events. More than once, a tutor was left waiting for a child who was in an unannounced dress rehearsal for the school's Christmas pageant, or left with the single option of tutoring two children at the same time because of parties, holidays, or a shortened school day. We quickly learned that consistency in the elementary-school schedule was sometimes impossible. We adapted by trying to gain as much information as possible about special events beforehand. Once again, our service accommodated the needs of the situation.

To review, relationships with all participants—principals, parents, teachers, students, and tutors—are vital to a community effort to aid transfer students. A good relationship with the principal influences how teachers feel; they, in turn, affect how parents involve themselves. Ultimately, all these relationships affect students; that is why it is so important for us to intervene gently, sensitively, and with great respect for all those involved. If the key figures around them are enthusiastic about tutoring and play active roles, the students receive more support and are more likely to take the initiative in their schoolwork. By the same token, a student who succeeds after a transfer might elicit more supportive behavior from his or her teacher, who could then act as an advocate for the student in encouraging parents to become more involved in their children's education.

In addition to considering the needs of each individual, psychologists intervening in schools must be aware that each school represents a dynamic ecological system, and that overall a program must be flexible and sensitive to the needs of the community. We must continuously evaluate our strategies and be prepared to make changes. Some communities, for example, had more demands for bilingual, Spanish- or Polish-speaking tutors while others required more sensitivity to racial issues. Also, people from different ethnic backgrounds varied in their perception of their role as parents and in their expectations of the schools. As a result, some communities offered us more potential for parent involvement than others. These and other challenges are further elaborated below.

Meeting the Needs of Individual
Children and Their Families

If there was one area in which the most implementation hurdles occurred, it was in working with the special needs of children. We designed the intervention to help an identified high-risk group of third-, fourth-, and fifth-grade transfer students in the academic areas of math, spelling, reading, and phonics. While we expected some variation among children, for the most part we saw these students as a homogeneous group. Later, we discovered that this belief was inaccurate. Every child required a mini-intervention of his or her own, an individualized educational plan.

As most educators and psychologists already know, working in schools requires that you be familiar with a variety of childhood problems and disorders. We have had to develop expertise in the areas of child advocacy, English as a second language, learning disabilities, parenting skills, and psychological referrals. We have accumulated a working resource pool of specialized consultants as well as books, articles, workbooks, and activities on these subjects and more to help us meet the additional needs of our population and community. And of course, we have relied on the talents and past experiences of our staff, which we have readily tapped during group meetings and training sessions. We describe four examples of special needs — children with limited English proficiency, children from violent or impoverished homes, children with behavior problems, and children with special cultural needs.

Children with Limited English Proficiency

Originally, we foresaw that we would need to work with children who did not speak English fluently. Therefore, we hired at least one person on staff who could speak Spanish in addition to being a good tutor. But the demand for Spanish- and Polish-speaking tutors and parent interviewers always seemed to exceeed our resources. We continued to hire qualified bilingual tutors but also looked to the schools for help. Many times we found that a classmate or school staff member could act as a translator until the child was able to speak and comprehend English more fluently. Some tutors began to learn the child's language or at least some important words of the language. Whenever possible, we translated written information we gave to parents, such as permission slips and directions for the children in testing, into their native language. The frustration some of our English-speaking staff experienced when beginning to work with these children helped us to sympathize with the language barrier facing these families.

We also struggled with the issue of correcting a child's cultural dialect. For instance, should a child who says "axe" for the word "ask" be told that the correct pronunciation is indeed "ask"? Many of our staff were divided. It seems that studies in English as a second language have not determined the best method for dealing with a child's dialect, or for teaching subjects not directly related to language, such as math. Should math be taught in English, as it is in the classroom, or should the tutor use the child's native language when working on this topic? Our staff was divided. Many of our tutors concentrated on the concept while overlooking the dialect or language issue; others insisted on the use of standard English at all times. Furthermore, many communities differ on the way they resolve such questions. Until research in this area provides some more definite direction, we think tutors should attempt to follow the policies of the school in which they teach while also considering the needs of the individual child.

Children from Impoverished and Violent Homes

As we worked with children from backgrounds different from those of most staff members, we began to explore, through discussions and readings, new treatment issues demanding our attention. We developed a structured psychological referral and child abuse reporting policy, and among the staff we tried to foster an awareness for social differences. The project has taken on a more active role in child advocacy with the schools themselves and sometimes the parents. The latter is especially true when problems in the home prevent the child from attending school regularly and therefore cause him or her to miss tutoring sessions. In extreme cases, tutors have been known to call students each morning to remind them to get up for school. Other tutors buy books or take a child to the library to encourage the child in reading. Still other tutors work with school personnel to gain a better understanding of the difficulties at home and to explore possible support systems for the children and the parents at the school or in the community. If at any time during this intervention parents objected to our additional support, we had no choice but to respect their wishes and stop. Our attention to social issues has been both an enlightening and discouraging experience, for the more we learned about some children's misfortunes, the more helpless we sometimes felt. For these children especially, we need to realize the limitations of our intervention and then do our best to provide services within these boundaries.

Children with Behavior Problems

Many times teachers identified children as having behavior problems, such as poor attention, not turning in homework, and bullying other students. We have found a behavioral approach is helpful to working with teachers and students on problems in conduct. Curtis and Zins (1981) discovered that, in consultation of this sort, teachers preferred a behavioral approach; the teachers with whom we worked seemed to respond favorably to such an approach as well. When tutors received information about students' behavior problems in class, they usually looked for similar actions within the tutoring session before acting. If the teacher's report was confirmed, tutor and supervisor discussed methods of behavior assessment and modification. In most cases, supervisors observed the child working with the tutor and sometimes observed the child in the classroom. This observation information was shared with the tutor so that an understanding of the problem and a possible treatment plan could be developed.

When the tutor had a clear conceptualization of the problem, he or she would discuss this with the child and talk about the impact of the behavior on the tutoring session and on learning in general. Then the two would work together to establish a plan for change, such as self-monitoring and/or a reinforcement system. In order to ensure that a behavior change plan succeeds, a tutor must discuss with the child his or her problem behavior, along with ways to change it (Amatea, 1989). It was also essential for the tutor to inform if not train the teacher in the new plan so that any progress the child made would generalize to the classroom. To achieve such generalization, a program must be implemented and constantly monitored by the tutor, the supervisor, the teacher, and the child (Zins et al., 1988). This detailed evaluation and feedback procedure for problem identification and treatment attempts to give the child the specialized attention most helpful for behavior change.

While not all the children's behaviors changed in the classroom, most tutors found that their efforts improved students' behavior during tutoring sessions. In fact, this special attention enhanced many tutor-child relationships. Of course, some behavior problems were more severe than others and required an outside referral, such as medical or psychological testing and counseling.

Necessity for Cultural Sensitivity

Hansen and others (1990) have discussed the importance of being sensitive to multicultural influences in school consultation. In a large intervention such as ours, one is likely to encounter different patterns of child raising, definitions of family, and holidays and celebrations. Handled without sensitivity, these issues can block the formation of important working relationships. We found it essential to learn more about all of these differences as we tried to understand the individual needs of our students. Regarding parent tutoring, we needed to know all family members available to provide support. In the Hispanic culture, we were pleasantly surprised by the involvement of the extended family and many times found ourselves connecting with English-speaking cousins for their support of home tutoring. Other alterations to the plan occurred *within* the tutoring sessions. During Black History Month, some tutors found it educational and motivating for both the child and themselves to have the child discuss and write short stories about famous African Americans. While these are only two examples of our attempts to connect with individual children by respecting and appreciating their heritage, we could cite many others. However, this listing would not be as helpful as listening to the needs and unique qualities of the populations with which you work. Being culturally sensitive is the first step in this type of hurdle jumping.

In general, the special needs of the targeted population forced the School Transition Project to expand into new areas, such as behavior management, child advocacy, and cultural education and sensitivity. The development of the project through constant needs assessments and formative goal reaching took a lot of time and resources. However, without this accommodating growth, the project might not have survived. This readjustment of service and program evaluation to the needs of the community is essential for the acceptance and survival of any intervention.

Summary

In this chapter, we have discussed some of the most salient obstacles encountered during the four years of the School Transition Project. We have tried to convey two messages. First, it is important to explore the needs and behaviors of the community which will be subject to the intervention so that possible problems can be prevented. Second, flexible and accommodating intervention strategies seem to work best. Both of these points seem to recur, especially as we move farther from the fixed and controlled regime of the laboratory into the unknown and unpredictable environment. By getting to know the community before an intervention, a team can avoid or reduce many possible hurdles. But of course the unexpected will always happen, and when it does, flexibility and compromise are the keys. After all, one never knows when a child or tutor will be sick, or when the looming school epidemic of head lice will strike! Perhaps this mystery is the beauty of studying real life.

To review, here are the more specific strategies we used to jump our implementation hurdles. Many of these extend or reflect ideas we have discussed from the literature on consulting in schools.

- *Carefully select project personnel* by specifying job expectations and responsibilities.
- *Train well!* Try to anticipate tough situations and prepare staff members with the skills of accessing resources and solving problems.
- *Build strong lines of communication among staff members* through frequent meetings (one-on-one or group).
- *Allow time for frequent brainstorming and feedback sessions* both at the group and individual level.
- *Form relationships with the community.* Get to know the individual systems (schools, classes, neighborhoods, or parent

groups) with which you will be spending the most time and start building relationships with community members.

- *Value the information coming in from all channels:* every opinion must be heard and respected before compromises can be made.
- *Be flexible* enough in all areas to address individual needs and constantly solve problems.
- *Have patience!* Program development takes time and lots of fine tuning.

8

Getting Parents Involved

Both parents and teachers can play significant roles in promoting school competence in children. School competence encompasses children's academic, social, and behavioral performance in school as well as at home; for example, timely completion of homework assignments is considered necessary for students to function competently in school. Adults can provide a role model for competent functioning, give children opportunities to become independent and to make decisions, and combine firm discipline with reaffirming affection (Sharma et al., 1981). Although it is largely the teacher's responsibility to assess the incoming transfer student's academic and social skills and match the new child to the classroom environment (Bensen et al., 1979), parents remain a critical source of support for most transfer students. Therefore, we believe that it is incumbent on staff and volunteers working in schools to foster parents' involvement with their transfer children.

Our own research suggests that parents greatly influence their children's adjustment to school transitions. Johnson and Jason (1992) found that transfers who received strong support from parents in school-related tasks demonstrated higher achievement and better overall social adjustment than transfer students who received low support from their caregivers. Less-supported students had significantly lower reading, spelling, and math grades. Moreover, the less-supported students were rated by peers as being significantly more aggressive, withdrawn, and less likable. Teachers rated the low-support group as more anxious and nervous, withdrawn, unpopular, inattentive, and aggressive. Similarly, other investigations have found that higher levels of family support are associated with better academic self-concept among transfer children (Cauce et al., 1982) as well as non-transfer students (Dolan, 1978). Despite such evidence, there has been little history of parents being included in prevention or remedial programs for transfer children who are at risk for academic, social, and behavioral maladjustment (Cornille et al., 1983; Panagos et al., 1981).

It is instructive here to examine what other researchers have said about parents helping their children. Afterward, we describe in detail how we mobilized parents and the way such parent support can succeed.

The Promise and Potential of Parent Involvement: A Look at the Literature

Parents can greatly influence their children's school achievement and behavior (Gips & Burdin, 1983; Roberts, 1975). For years, competence of the primary caregiver has been targeted as a major factor contributing to the competence and coping of the child (Garmezy et al., 1984). Both positive and negative behaviors and attitudes children learn in the home likely carry over to school and influence classroom performance (Galejs & Stockdale, 1982). For example, one investigation demonstrated that levels of parental warmth, affection, and acceptance of children are correlated significantly with aggressive behaviors among both boys and girls (Sines, 1987).

In particular, mental health and educational researchers have targeted low-income, *insular* parents (that is, parents who have fewer positive extrafamilial contacts); such parents tend to be ineffective and harsh in communicating with and managing their children (Wahler, 1980). Blechman (1984) further described such parents as lacking a repertoire of problem-solving skills and failing to access resources from which they could learn more functional parenting skills. Such disadvantaged family and other background factors have been viewed as frustrating circum-stances that precipitate children's aggressive and disruptive behaviors, which in turn decrease opportunities to learn in the classroom (Feldhusen et al., 1967). As a consequence, such children do not achieve as well as might be expected based on their intelligence.

Children from stressed *single-parent* families have also been identified as being at risk for school problems. Citing the pervasive poor achievement of low-income, urban children as compared to their higher-SES suburban counterparts, McKinney (1975) proposed that a major reason for this failure is the small degree of support and reinforcement the low-income, urban children receive in typically single-parent homes. In her review of the literature, Shinn (1978) concluded that evidence strongly implicates high levels of anxiety, financial hardship, and in particular, low levels of parent-child interaction as important causes of poor academic performance among children in single-parent families. Other studies suggest that living in a one-parent family can have a negative impact on school adjustment (Sandler, 1980) and academic achievement (Milne et al., 1986), but these effects have been shown to differ by age, race, and family structure. For example, the negative total effect of having only a single parent was shown to be reduced in smaller families. Milne and his colleagues suggested that the smaller family may enable the working single parent to spend more of his or her limited time with each of the fewer children.

Other research indicates that an adequate home support system may offset the negative effects of single-parent family status on children's academic performance and emotional health (Roy & Fuqua, 1983). Such a support system may include relatives and friends of a single parent and older siblings as well. Even for children living in discordant families (for example, families characterized by frequent fighting between parents), at least one good relationship with one parent seems to have a protective influence (Rutter, 1979). In Rutter's study, a stable parent-child relationship significantly decreased the likelihood of conduct disorders as compared to children who did not have a close bond with one parent. Regarding school transfers, researchers have speculated that positive forces within families and support networks attenuate the adverse effects of school moves, especially school transitions coinciding with other stressful life events, such as divorce (Levine et al., 1966; Morris et al., 1967). Thus, caregivers may often provide guidance and support to their children even when they themselves are experiencing hardship.

The aim of our own School Transition Project has not been to blame or stereotype low-income or single parents. Rather, we have sought to support the many positive and resilient qualities of families under stress. We agree with McKinney's (1975) belief that, despite increased educational resources in the school, true academic gains can better be attained by involving the parents of disadvantaged children in a meaningful way. Moreover, our staff presumed that family support systems often predominate over those provided by schools (Sandler, 1980). Thus, our goal has been to collaborate with caretakers in naturally existing support systems within the homes and neighborhoods of the transfer children.

How and When Parents Can Help

A key time for parents to offer support in the home is during a child's homework time. Through homework, children practice skills, increase the speed of skill application, and ensure the maintenance of skill levels (Epstein, 1983). In addition to boosting academic performance, homework can improve the way parents and children interact. Epstein contended that homework is sometimes the only serious form of communication about school and learning that occurs between children and parents. Through their attitudes toward homework, parents can help their elementary-age children set academic standards, select realistic goals, and determine values (Blai, 1985). Thus, homework provides an opportunity for parents and children to exchange information, facts, and attitudes about school achievement. Not surprisingly, Epstein discovered that children who like to talk about school and homework with their parents tended to be good students and were well behaved in class.

In contrast, parents who are unsupportive and critical concerning their children's school accomplishments are likely to discourage academic achievement. One study demonstrated that mothers' attitudes (positive versus negative) toward their male children's abilities influenced the students' attitudes toward reading as well as their subsequent achievement (Studholme, 1964). Negative parental responses tended to diminish children's interest and achievement in reading. Oftentimes, parents whose children are experiencing academic and behavioral difficulties in school are especially requested by teachers to provide home tutoring; however, those children who display serious problems in class can likewise be frustrating for parents, thereby creating great tension during "forced" homework periods with parents. Epstein (1983) cautioned that parents of children who have homework problems need to be trained how to help their children. Parents also need to be encouraged to believe in their effectiveness as home teachers. Otherwise, school problems could be exacerbated by ineffective teaching at home.

Preventive interventions that include school-based strategies and parent involvement can be effective for increasing children's academic achievement and social competence. Certainly, comprehensive intervention packages that enhance academic competencies through home tutoring are becoming more common (Anesko & O'Leary, 1982; Garcia, 1986; Harris, 1983). Walberg and others (1985) concluded that cooperative programs that provide specific materials and procedures for parents to use in tutoring their children can have a great impact on children's learning and achievement. In the authors' review of twenty-nine controlled studies involving parent-child homework interactions, 91 percent of the comparisons favored the academic achievement of program children over control groups.

Capability and Willingness of Parents

Home tutoring may be applicable for students who experience a wide range of academic difficulties. Shapero and Forbes (1981) reviewed studies addressing parent tutoring for learning disabled children and concluded that parent involvement can greatly benefit the academic performance of special education students. Parents from lower socioeconomic groups (Chandler, Argyris, Barnes, Goodman, & Snow, 1983; Shuck,

Ulsh, & Platt, 1983) and ethnic minorities (Oliva, 1986) have proven to be competent tutors for low-achieving children. In addition to improving achievement, parent involvement in school has been shown to foster a greater sense of control in children's lives and to reduce social problems (Conrad & Eash, 1983).

Undoubtedly, the content and quality of training are important to the success of these parent-tutors (Henderson & Glynn, 1986; McKinney, 1975). Gang and Poche (1982) developed a successful behavioral parent-tutor training program that focused on four categories of tutoring: presenting materials, giving instructions, using specific correction procedures, and providing reinforcements. Training parents in contingency management of their children's homework behaviors seems to be superior to other strategies in increasing both the quantity and quality of homework (Goldberg, Merbaum, Even, Getz, & Safir, 1981). Additionally, for monitoring progress or difficulties, researchers recommend consistent communication through home-notes signed by parents that attest to homework activity (Froelich, Blitzer, & Greenberg, 1967). In our own parent-tutor training we have relied on the wisdom of these earlier intervention efforts.

When we consider the promise and potential that home tutoring offers toward improving students' success in school, we are astonished at the low percentage of teachers who actually provide guidelines and suggestions for parent tutoring. Rather, teachers, who themselves have received at least college preparation for teaching, may tend to expect parents to know how to help their children with homework. A large survey of teachers revealed that only 7 percent of them actually provided some type of home-tutor training to parents at the beginning of the year (Epstein & Becker, 1982). In the survey, teachers reported that parent-teacher meetings, when they did occur, typically were used merely to outline homework expectations. Thus, an important goal of any parent-tutor training program should be to gain the cooperation, initiative, and leadership of classroom teachers.

Are parents really willing to participate in such training programs? Many studies suggest that most parents voluntarily

acquire skills and materials to help their children with homework (Robinson, McNaughton, & Quinn, 1979; Welsh, Doss,
& Totusek, 1981). Further, they are generally enthusiastic about
continuing the home-tutoring efforts after formal programs end
(Searls, Lewis, & Morrow, 1983). Such widespread acceptance
suggests that parent-tutor training can have an enduring impact on the course of students' school careers.

At the end of the first year of the School Transition Project, we asked parents of transfer children if they would have
been interested in participating in a parent training program
to increase their effectiveness in tutoring their children, and 81
percent said yes (Jason et al., 1989). Even among those children who scored lowest on the major postpoint adjustment measures, 79 percent of their parents said they would be interested
in training. Remarkably, 63 percent of these parents felt they
did not have the skills to tutor their children effectively. Such
broad appeal for parent training encouraged us to involve parents much more in the following years of our intervention.
Toward this endeavor, we realized that a minority of parents
would probably not enlist as home tutors — some for valid reasons, and regrettably, a few because they did not have a genuine
interest in their children's schooling.

Importance of Parent Involvement in Schools

Of course, beyond tutoring their child, parents should be
encouraged to become directly involved in their child's school.
The School Development Program has gained wide recognition
for improving inner-city schools through greater parent participation (Haynes, Comer, & Hamilton-Lee, 1988, 1989). The
program promotes three levels of parent involvement. At the
first level, most parents are involved in total school activities,
which consist of one or more social events during the year
(for example, School Carnival, Family Night). At the second
level, parents participate in the school and classroom through
the "Parent Stipend Program." Thus far, the authors report that
an average of eighteen parents per school participate for a max-
imum of fifteen hours per week. Parents help in classroom,

lunchroom, playground, office, library, and material preparation activities. At the third level, selected parents serve on the School Advisory Committee, playing an important role in the governance of the school.

Even the media appear willing to advocate widespread parent participation in schools. The *New York Times* reported that Comer's approach is successfully reshaping many blighted schools by reducing the sense of alienation some students and parents feel for school, thereby strengthening the relationships between school and home (Marriott, 1990). Such efforts seem to be imperative for bolstering children's and parents' esteem, competence, and commitment about school life. Our own program wholeheartedly endorsed such multiple levels of parent involvement, which was largely already taking place in the schools in which we worked.

In summary, the research in parent tutoring suggests that when parents are trained in specific tutoring skills and given appropriate materials and feedback, they can have a positive impact on their children's academic success in school. Based on these data, the School Transition Project implemented a collaborative intervention that combined in-school intensive tutoring with parent or home tutoring. We contracted with parents or other family members to assist transfer students in homework assignments using the same tutoring techniques employed by our paraprofessional staff. Overall, the goal of our parent-tutoring intervention was to capitalize on academic and social resources within home support networks to help transfer children who were at risk for academic failure. Certainly, greater involvement of parents in broader school activities and governance is another key way to build bridges between home and school.

How Our Parent Program Worked

The parent component was piloted in the second year and was fully functioning in the third and fourth years of the School Transition Project. The school-based tutoring program, developed in the first two years, continued unchanged except for the addition of parent training. Thus, one experimental group of transfer students rceived tutoring in school while the other group received tutoring at school *and* tutoring at home. Thus, throughout this book we refer to these two groups as the "school-tutored" and the "school-plus-home-tutored" groups. In this chapter we use "parent" and "home tutor" interchangeably, indicating that not just parents can tutor at home but also siblings, aunts, uncles, cousins, and close family friends and neighbors.

We designed this intervention as a four-step process:

- Select target children and make initial contact with parents (in late September)
- Have a "team" information meeting involving the parent(s), tutor, tutor supervisor, school principal, and teacher (in mid-October)
- Train the parent or home tutor in the same Direct Instruction approach used by the School Transition Project staff tutor (in October)
- Visit the families in their homes to check up on home-tutoring progress (November/December and February/March)

In addition, our staff communicated with the parents from October to May through biweekly written notes and periodic phone conversations. There are many innovative ways that school-home notes can be used to contract with the child, teacher, parents, and tutor. Regularly monitored and rewarded behavior, with good communication among all concerned, can motivate children to achieve goals. Some excellent ideas for consulting around implementing notes are offered in the book *School-Home Notes* by Kelley (1990).

Working with families demanded different and additional criteria for the tutors we hired, including high maturity, a strong desire to correspond with sometimes difficult parents, and a willingness to work long and often late hours for parent meetings and home visits. Finally, to increase the likelihood that tutors would become effective role models in the schools and be able to communicate well with parents, we tried to assign tutors to schools according to the tutor's race and bilingual status.

In the following sections, we describe in detail how we attempted to get the parents involved. Accompanying each description is a record of our *actual* experiences implementing the program. Like all service projects, this part of the program proceeded with a great number of snags and unexpected pleasures. The snags were most evident in our efforts to stick to the time line, whereas the pleasures involved the successes of the families with whom we worked. We learned much from our work with families, and we hope that this chapter will do justice to all that they taught us.

Select Students and Contact Parents

We chose children to be tutored according to their at-risk status, which was based on their academic achievement, their families' socioeconomic status, and recent stressful life events. After interviewing parents for the first time to determine this status, we contacted the parents again to offer them our in-school tutoring program and asked if the parent(s) would be willing to meet with us at the school to discuss their participation in the program.

This portion proceeded fairly efficiently. Contact with the parents was sometimes difficult to achieve, however, and schedules often conflicted when we tried to set up appointment times. With some parents, we decided to explain the program over the phone and train them during the first home visit. For other parents, initial meetings took place as late as January because of scheduling conflicts, missed appointments, or difficulty finding a translator. Persistence and flexibility were essential.

Overall, the parents responded very positively to our suggestion that they become involved in the program. Approximately 90 percent of the home tutors were trained before December in school meetings. Another 5 percent received training during home visits sometime during the first half of the year. The remaining families of tutored children were never trained because they were not interested in participating, they made another school transfer, they left the program some other way, or they knew no one that could act as a home tutor.

Have Team Meetings

The staff worked hard to determine the most effective way to interact with the parents so as to "hook" them into the program. Overall, we emphasized three principles in our initial meetings: (1) respect for the parent and family, (2) enthusiasm for the prospect of our working together, and (3) emphasis on the positive aspects of working with the developing child. These attitudes were conveyed through a number of tasks and meetings.

First, parent component tutors coordinated their schedules with those of the tutor supervisor, parent, teacher, and principal to involve as many as possible of the "team" players in the initial parent meeting. It was rare for the teacher or principal to be able to attend the meetings, and there were advantages and disadvantages to their absence. Primarily, their presence gave credibility to the program and increased the likelihood that parents would participate. In some cases, however, the relationship of the parent and the tutor suffered with the attendance of the school personnel. If a parent was intimidated by school personnel and viewed the tutor as part of "the system," she or he may have had a harder time accepting the tutor as an advocate.

Regardless, the meetings began with the School Transition Project staff introducing themselves and educating the parent about the tutoring program. The tutor explained to the parent that transfer students typically have gaps in their learning because academic curricula vary considerably from school to school. To demonstrate the child's need for the program, tutors showed parents the child's Wide Range Achievement Test scores and explained that the child had scored below grade level. The tutor emphasized that, by pooling their resources, the "team" had a good chance of bringing the child to the academic level of his or her classmates.

The tutor then described her or his initial efforts in tutoring the child by showing the parent graphs of the child's progress in the early tutoring sessions. Teachers (and principals, if present) then gave their view of the child's academic status. In addition, teachers presented to the parents the "Teacher Expectations Form" (see Resource G) to give them a written record of homework and other tasks expected of all children in the classroom. For example, one third-grade teacher's expectations included homework every night, spelling tests on Fridays, and quarterly book reports. Sometimes we would facilitate a discussion of how the teacher and parent could communicate about the progress of the target child during the school year.

We then assessed the parents' willingness to participate in home tutoring. In an extensive telephone interview with parents conducted at the beginning of the year, we had already administered the Parent-Tutor Assessment (PTA), which measures parent-tutoring support (Johnson & Jason, 1992; see Resource H). The tutor supervisor asked how the parents knew when their child had homework, and asked whether they routinely helped their child with homework. The tutor and supervisor were very careful at this point to encourage any help that the parents felt able to give, and they tried to identify and understand any barriers to parents' helping.

The supervisor and tutor gave the parents a packet of information that explained how beneficial home tutoring could be for children's academic success. The tutor then suggested that if the parent was willing to work with the child, the tutor could teach the parent a technique, Direct Instruction, that is particularly effective for one-on-one tutoring. He or she explained that because the tutor was already using the technique with the child, consistency in the language of instruction might facilitate the child's progress.

Of critical importance was the method by which the tutor, supervisor, and parent discussed the possibility of the parent using the Direct Instruction approach to tutor the child at home. The chief objective of the home tutoring was to empower family members to take an active interest in the academic development of children. Whether we trained them to tutor with perfect technique was secondary to supporting and encouraging them to rally behind the child in whatever ways they could. Encouraging healthy parent-child interaction was our primary goal.

Consistent with this notion, the tutor and supervisors were trained to understand the unique strengths of each family system.

They conveyed their belief that parents are the experts on their child, and the team was available as support staff only. If the parents agreed to try out the technique, the tutors tailored the technique to tap the parents' natural strengths as tutors.

Generally, we were relentless in our pursuit of *someone* to hook into the excitement of helping the developing child. Our strategies were many and varied for convincing parents or other able helpers within the family or community system to "sign up" for homework duty. For a surprising number of parents, previous home tutoring had been hindered only by their own insecurities about it. These parents were eager to learn greater competence in helping their children, and we found that the technique could be mastered easily by all family members. In other words, we did not lose many parents because the technique was too difficult for them to continue throughout the year.

The tutor and supervisor talked very frankly about the commitment that the parent would need to make as a home tutor and asked if there was someone else who might better fit the "job description." We learned from experiences during the pilot project that it was much easier to train the right person from the beginning than to find another home tutor mid-year. Sometimes, we trained back-up tutors during the initial home visits. From the first phone contact, we encouraged parents who did not read English and those who worked evenings to find alternate home tutors.

Generally, our School Transition Project staff completed initial meetings with the parents regardless of whether the parent could serve as the home tutor. The meetings were conducted in Spanish for many families, and translators were procured for a few other non-English-speaking families, such as Polish. It was our belief that parent involvement is critical even if it consists merely of knowing what the teacher and tutor expect of the child, supporting the child emotionally, supervising the home tutor, and providing adequate conditions for the child to do homework.

In most cases, the Spanish- or Polish-speaking parent or guardian could find a substitute home tutor among other extended-family members or neighbors. It was our experience that Spanish-speaking families were particularly resourceful in finding

English-speaking cousins or siblings to tutor the child at home. Gabriel, the transfer student who moved from his family's home in Mexico to live with his sister in the United States, was tutored by his niece. Although neither Gabriel's sister nor her husband spoke English, their ninth-grade daughter did, so every day after school, Gabriel and his older niece studied together, and she tutored him in reading.

In the fourth year of the program especially, the School Transition Project staff worked to reinforce the home tutors. We canvassed local businesses who provided free tickets and other prizes for participants of the program. For example, the Chicago Shedd Aquarium donated family passes and information books for all families involved in the parent component.

Train the Home Tutor in Direct Instruction

Once we secured a commitment from the parent and home tutor, training could begin. Although training may be difficult and protracted, if a few conditions are met, it can be an enjoyable experience. Specifically, the regular tutors must complement the parents' natural tutoring abilities, establish rapport with parents, and demonstrate the methods of tutoring with patience and humor. Training should give parents a sense of practical empowerment—a feeling that they not only have made a commitment to helping but are also skilled and able to help.

Ideally, after our training introduction, the parent was able to be the home tutor and agreed to learn the Direct Instruction approach. The staff tutor demonstrated the technique with the parent, who took the child's role by making mistakes while reading a fifth-grade story. The tutor emphasized two major points to the parent in teaching Direct Instruction: (1) repetition is central to learning, and (2) reinforcement encourages children's efforts by increasing their sense of mastery.

After the tutor modeled the technique, the parent switched to the tutor role and the tutor played the child. The tutor read the story with ten predetermined mistakes. If the parent did not (1) make the tutor (playing the child) repeat the word, (2) start over from the beginning of the sentence, and/or (3) reinforce the tutor for each corrected error, the supervisor reminded the parent of the procedure and encouraged the parent to try it again. In other words, we used the model-lead-test technique to teach the model-lead-test technique.

The "test" aspect of the technique occurred when the staff tutor read ten other predetermined mistakes in the story. If the parent achieved 90 percent accuracy with the technique, training was concluded. Otherwise, more practice and prompting ensued until the parent reached the mastery level.

Sometimes, empowering parents when they were in the "learner" position required delicacy. However, with a little humor and frequent encouragement, most parents appreciated and enjoyed the training. Some had a difficult time role-playing with the staff. One kept saying, "You know how to read — I'm not going to correct you!" Another parent caught the mistakes, but he thought it was disrespectful to correct another adult. In these cases, we explained the exercise more clearly, and we acted out reactions that were typical of their children to infuse some humor into the experience.

Finally, to emphasize further the teamwork aspect of the program, the supervisor reviewed a contract of expectations for each of the involved parties (see Resource I). In the contract, the parent agreed to tutor the child two days a week for one school year and to maintain contact with the tutor and teacher about the child's progress. If all agreed to its conditions, everyone signed the form.

Next, the tutor explained the home-tutoring materials to be sent home with the child. The tutoring program emphasized reading abilities. For reading materials, we used cards from Science Research Associates (SRA) (Parker & Scannel, 1982) because the cards are an attractive, easy-to-follow way for parents to help their children increase reading skills. The SRA cards have a short story followed by exercises for comprehension, phonics, and writing. Other tutoring materials included worksheets and flashcards for addition, subtraction, multiplication, and division. Also, parents tutored children particularly on their homework from the classroom, such as reviewing weekly spelling words.

Negotiation with parents was ongoing. For instance, the tutor negotiated with the parent how often to send home SRA and other materials with the child, and when to contact the parent. Finally, the tutor asked the parent if together they could set up another time in the next three weeks when the tutor could come to the parent's home to assess the home tutoring.

All year, tutors and parents communicated periodically. Tutors included notes to the parents in the folders with the SRA cards. In addition, the tutor phoned the parent an average of twice a month, or as needed, to ask how the home tutoring was progressing and to comment on how the tutor and the child were working together in school. As parents and tutors became better acquainted, conversations frequently covered not only schoolwork but family affairs and personal problems.

In some cases, the tutor was an advocate for the family. For example, when one school principal was worried about the reasons a boy was not in school, she asked the tutor to call his mother. The principal knew that the tutor's relationship with the boy's mother was secure enough that the mother would be honest. In the same school, several teachers asked the tutor to attend parent-teacher conferences to put the parents more at ease.

Visit Families in Their Homes

We visited homes of tutored children one to three times during the year to learn how home tutoring was progressing and to answer any questions the home tutor may have had regarding the program. Home visits were also an opportunity for the tutor to gain information about the unique qualities of each family that might help tutors work more effectively with each child.

Home visits can be a scary prospect for both families and school staff. Initially, tutors and supervisors expressed hesitation and concern that, when requesting home visits, we were invading the families' space. However, our experience over several years was that all parties perceived home visits as very enjoyable and worthwhile. Indeed, home visits proved to be a highly effective way for our staff to connect with families.

During the home visit, DePaul staff would ask for the family to enact a typical home-tutoring session using an SRA card. In a "Home Visit Diary" (see Resource J), a staff member recorded useful information about the home, the family, and the tutoring procedure. For example, we noted the physical location for home tutoring and often discussed with the parents ways to make the space quieter or better lit. Often the homework was completed at the kitchen table and several family members would participate in the sessions. Overall, we were pleased with the ways the parents ensured quality study time in apartments that were often quite cramped and sometimes chaotic.

Home visits were a time for candor, encouragement, camaraderie, and problem solving. Usually, the home visits consisted of casual exchange of information, suggestions and encouragement from our staff, and warm hospitality from the family. The tutor could usually give more complete information to the parents about the child's academic strengths and weaknesses than they had the first meeting. The home tutor and the staff tutor exchanged tips on teaching styles that seemed to work best for the child, and often the parents would ask for advice from the staff about discipline, homework sessions, and problems with the teacher.

Home visits seem particularly important for families of transfer students because of the tendency of these families to be isolated from the new school and community. Many parents told us they were lonely and in need of friends. Almost without exception, families were very grateful for the tutor's taking an interest in their child. We were likewise heartened by parents' genuine interest and commitment toward their children.

Conclusions

In the School Transition Project we experienced firsthand the value and importance of involving parents in the education of their transfer children. Our program goal was to enhance parents' ability to tutor their own children, thus extending the teaching resources available to children who were academically behind. We recognize the limitations, especially in terms of time, that classroom teachers face; most teachers are unable to provide all the one-on-one attention that at-risk students need. Even our own tutoring staff were able to tutor children individually for only two hours per week. By involving parents, we aimed to expand the amount of quality time during which children received instructive feedback in their basic subject areas. Our contact with the transfer children ended at the end of the school year, but through parent tutoring, the child could continue to make gains well beyond the termination of our program. We sought to empower families and schools, thereby creating self-sustaining resources for the children.

We discovered that most caretakers are eager to learn new skills to tutor their children, even when faced with seemingly insurmountable obstacles such as their own lack of prerequisite academic skills or fluency in the English language. Nonetheless, we overcame many of these obstacles by pursuing flexible options for home tutoring. The key to success was to foster the commitment of at least one responsible person within the child's home-support network.

Providing caretakers with effective, easy-to-learn tutoring skills increases the chances that both parent and child will experience homework time as positive and rewarding. These positive learning opportunities can enhance children's scholastic self-esteem as well as parents' confidence in their ability to help their child. Additionally, specific educational materials and learning objectives are critical for successful tutoring. We strongly urge school staff to follow up initial training with supportive phone calls and home visits. Parents could receive "after hours" information about their children's homework assignments through "homework hotlines." In one California elementary school, teachers prepare a prerecorded one-minute message each day telling parents what was worked on in school, what the homework is for the evening, and specific strategies to help their children (CBS News, 1991). School staff can capitalize on other technological resources such as producing videotapes demonstrating parent-tutoring techniques that can be viewed in households with VCRs, now prevalent in most American homes.

Of course, for most teachers such extensive contact may be possible only for the most at-risk children unless a school system provides adequate paraprofessional staff such as teacher aides. What are realistic ways to expand such support to caretakers? Certainly, the basic tools of parent tutoring could be presented in group training for parents at the beginning of the year, when parents could be paired up to practice newly learned techniques. Teachers may need to schedule several initial training sessions in order to adapt to different work schedules of parents. Extending these initial efforts, teachers could establish parent-tutor "teams," perhaps consisting of four parents each, which would form a nucleus of mutually accountable parent support. Throughout the school year, teachers could call or meet with one parent from each team, who in turn could share new information and skills with the other team parents through phone calls, home visits, or letters. Particularly in the case of transfer students, such a support network could hasten parents' integration into the new school and community. Of course, the traditional, individualized parent-teacher conferences should remain the regular means to communicate about a child's school progress.

Our bias has been that most parents can and should take partial responsibility for their children's education. Unquestionably, to integrate transfer students most completely into a new school, teachers need the full support and cooperation of caregivers at home. Later, in Chapter Ten, we present program evaluation results that confirm our beliefs that rallying parents to increase their attention to their children's schoolwork is a necessity.

9

The Influence
of School Climate

When we change houses, jobs, or schools, we enter new and different milieus. There are new customs, people, manners, norms, and decor. People may work harder, the furniture may be sterile or comfortable, the boss may be accommodating or demanding. A new temperature prevails, both physically and psychologically, along with unfamiliar smells, sights, and noises. Inevitably the new climate shapes us, and by our very presence we influence the setting's atmosphere as well. These notions of the climate and culture of peoples and places are central to organizational psychology.

A child transferring schools also enters a new environment filled with a startling array of unfamiliar people, rules, expectations, and rooms. Different stimuli bombard the child's senses. Unlike adults, who may be seasoned by experience, children undergoing unscheduled school transfer may be making the first significant move of their lives without much preparation as to how to adjust. Most of us have had the experience of entering a school for the first time and feeling something unique about it that we could not put our finger on, a certain pulse that may have been sluggish or erratic, invigorating or disheartening, warm or cold. In this chapter we discuss how such environmental differences might matter to transfer students. First, we examine the literature on organizational influences and then, through interviews, we look at our schools.

Organizational Perspective

Environmental and organizational effects have not been investigated in the literature on unscheduled transfer students, yet many researchers see the need for perspectives that reach beyond the student as an individual. Such perspectives may be ecological (Barker, 1968; Jason, Durlak, & Holton-Walker, 1984), environmental (Moos, 1979), cross-level (Shinn, 1990), multilevel (Bryk, 1987), or organizational (Maher, Illback, & Zins, 1984). An organizational development perspective emphasizes how norms, structures, and procedures interrelate to inform and influence individuals' behavior (Elias & Clabby, 1984; Schmuck, 1982). According to Maher and others (1984), "Developing and improving schools as organizations may very well be the most important challenge facing all school professionals during the remainder of this century" (p. 5).

The school as an organization embodies many elements. Maher and colleagues (1984) proposed a framework in which the school has organizational structure, processes, and behavior. In diagnosing an organization's need for change, Lippitt, Longseth, and Mossop (1985) suggested looking at many facets of the organization: its context, outputs, culture, task requirements, formal organization, people, and the physical setting and technology. Similarly, Moos (1973) offered six approaches for studying environmental characteristics: examining physical characteristics and architectural designs; analyzing behavior settings; studying organizational structure; analyzing characteristics of people in an environment; looking at reinforcement contingencies and other behavioral aspects of the environment; and assessing the perceived social environment. We were interested in many of these aspects of the schools, and a first step in looking at these was to see how our tutors understood the environment in which they worked.

An organizational perspective is helpful for planning interventions. Short and Short (1987) emphasized that one must consider teacher, student, and administrator behavior as important variables of the school milieu to discover a school's resources and constraints. Zins and others (1988) noted that organizational functioning may influence program implementation. Linney and Seidman (1989) cited studies concluding that "both elementary and secondary schools need to increase flexibility and design organizational structures more optimally matched to the personal problems and needs of students" (p. 338).

Organizational focus comes into play in consideration of ways to enhance social behavior. Advocates of social skills training remain divided on whether to target individuals and small groups or to take an organizational focus (Elias & Clabby, 1984). Since social behavior is rooted in the structure of a school, programmers seeking to affect children's social skills must also intervene in the organization of schools (Elias & Clabby, 1984).

A study by Gottfredson (1988) provides an example of how an organizational view aids a social intervention. She used an organizational developmental approach to reduce disorder in an urban school. In this study, the intervention was designed to increase the predictability of responses to students' disciplinary infractions, increase rewards for appropriate behaviors, and heighten prosocial peer and teacher support. A school improvement team, led by the principal, ran the intervention, which consisted of training teachers in classroom management innovations and classroom instructional innovation. Compared to a nonintervention school, the school improved dramatically on measures of organizational health and reduction of rebellious behavior.

Ecological Intervention with Schools

As discussed in Chapter Five, an ecological perspective is a helpful way to view school transfer. A prominent example of ecological research with transfer students is work by Felner and Adan (1988). We discussed this study in Chapter Three, but it bears reexamination. In this study, the researchers changed the social structure of schools to ensure better accommodation of transfer students. These students, however, were scheduled or normative transfers—from elementary to junior high school, or junior high to high school—in contrast to the unscheduled transfers discussed in this book. Still, their research applies well to work with unscheduled transfer students.

According to Felner and Adan (1988), characteristics of both the setting and the person can influence the extent to which negative outcomes follow transitions. The attributes of a setting can facilitate or impede students' adaptive efforts. For transfer students, two critical features of the school setting are the complexity of the school environment and how much the setting can respond to students' needs. The researchers implemented an intervention, the School Transitional Environment Program (STEP), which aimed to reduce the degree of flux students confront when entering the new school and to facilitate establishment of a stable peer support system.

Toward these goals, subgroups of sixty-five to one hundred students in an incoming class were identified to take all primary academic subjects together; also, in smaller groups of twenty to thirty students, they were assigned to a homeroom in which a teacher served as the primary administrative and counseling link among the students, their parents, and the rest of the school. Teachers received special training to enhance their counseling skills with students and their team-building skills with other faculty.

Outcome results indicated that, in comparison to matched controls, program participants evidenced higher self-esteem, better academic performance, and less absenteeism; they also saw their environment as more stable, understandable, well organized, involving, and supportive. A follow-up study indicated that program participants had less than half the dropout rate of controls, and had better grades and lower absenteeism in the first and second year following the transition.

This intervention provides precedent that transfer students can be helped by an ecological, systems-level intervention. This promising intervention, for scheduled transfer students, can be translated into use for unscheduled transfer students as well. Unscheduled transfer students could similarly benefit from less complexity in their environments, a close peer group of transfers, and a counselor and adviser. We need to think of similar ways to institutionalize programs for unscheduled transfer students. These might include training teachers about transfer students' special needs; centralizing administrative and counseling links for transfer students; allowing transfer students to spend regular time together so as to acclimate to the new school as a group rather than as individuals; and fitting transfer students with especially accommodating teachers and classrooms.

Thus, several studies point to the importance of considering organizational influences on transfer students. The next section offers a qualitative view of the schools in which we worked.

Perceptions of the Tutors

Qualitative assessment and naturalistic inquiry can enhance quantitative research in several ways. Qualitative data aid in interpreting findings from analysis of quantitative data (Price, 1987). Qualitative assessments can enlighten one's understanding of people and organizations by providing insight into nuances of concerns, motivation, and behavior. Furthermore, qualitative data can aid in hypothesis finding and intervention redesign (Price, 1987). Naturalistic inquiry and qualitative assessment have been advocated as an important new direction for community psychology research.

Halpin and Croft (1967) encouraged interpreting from both empirical data and abstract notions, using inductive and deductive reasoning. They delineated six organizational climates that made "good sense, both practically and psychologically" (p. 109). They suggested that further research on organizational climate should send observers into elementary schools to document case studies in order to validate quantitative data.

Interviews with Tutors

Tutors in the School Transition Project were valuable observers of schools. They were in the school on almost a daily basis yet were not subject to many of the pressures faculty feel. Also, many of our tutors tutored or tested in several schools, so they had some basis for comparison. Interviews with them were an important component of our evaluation.

Unlike interviews that are part of a rigidly designed research effort, these were more journalistic and exploratory in nature. Thus, from a strictly research point of view, validity and reliability were not established. Yet in the literature on education, there are many works that are journalistic, descriptive accounts of schools and educational issues. Such accounts have a complementary role to quantitative data. Thus, we think this information provides an interesting slice-of-life of the schools, and may provoke thinking about the nature of school transfer.

A member of our research team interviewed twenty-five staff of the School Transition Project (tutors, supervisors, project director, principal investigator) who altogether worked in twenty schools during one year of our project. The interviews, qualitative and open-ended in nature, attempted to assess each staff member's subjective characterization of a school, the "feel" of the schools. Interviews were also used to detect internal dynamics of the schools from the perspective of people who work there, to provide illustrations of some of the differences that may exist among schools, and to generate hypotheses and direction for future research.

Generally, we asked staff to talk about the schools in which they worked. They were encouraged to relate the "feeling" a school gave them and to describe what they thought was unique, different, and special about that school. Also they were asked to compare and contrast schools in which they worked. Finally, they were asked to discuss how they thought the school was experienced by teachers, parents, principals, transfer students, and students in general. Those who worked in only one school were asked to compare their schools with other project schools of which they had heard or about which they knew. Interviews with supervisors, who work in many schools, could be used to corroborate interviews with tutors who worked in only one school. Interviewees were encouraged to generalize when talking about their schools and to offer anecdotes to illustrate generalizations. The following are some of our findings.

Interview Findings

Overall, project staff perceived schools as unique along many dimensions. Such dimensions include the principal's behavior; teaching quality; schoolwide activities; involvement of children, faculty, principals, and parents; the physical nature of the school; and the surrounding neighborhood — race, ethnicity, degree of religious observance, wealth, and social class.

Criteria for school climate emerged from the interviews themselves. Criteria covered a wide range of dimensions, such as principal behavior, cohesiveness of teachers, student behavior and involvement, parents' investment of time and assistance in the school, parents' attitudes towards the school, the physical nature of the schools (decor, size, lighting, and number of open doors), teacher-student relationships, amount of schoolwide activity, office layout, teacher lounge activity, and school policies. Very important were comments of a general nature on the quality of climate.

We organized our interviews around three broad types of school climate that seemed to emerge from our tutors' remarks: the best schools, moderate schools, and schools needing improvement. The following are explanations of each type of school. After each explanation, selected quotes and paraphrases from interviews illustrate each type of school climate.

The Best Schools. Schools with the best social climate were characterized as very supportive environments for all students and especially for transfer students. These schools had extremely helpful and enthusiastic staff, involved parents, a great deal of interaction among different classrooms and grades, and many schoolwide activities. Halls and classrooms displayed a great amount of decoration and student work, such as honor rolls. Staff described these schools as having a tangible and very positive "school spirit." Often these schools had a principal characterized as dynamic and nurturing; teachers were friendly with each other. The school as a whole seemed very much a center of the neighborhood and community. Ethnic pride was encouraged in these schools.

What follows are selected data from interviews with project staff illustrating schools with the most favorable climate. Quotes are from project staff; those sentences not in quotes are paraphrases.

General comments:
"There is a support base . . . and consistency."
"There is a lot of warmth in the school. I think it comes from outside, from the parents. They're so involved—the grandparents, too. I think it softens the teachers."
"They seem to have a real spirit there."
"It is a word-of-mouth school—everyone's always talking about how great it is. It's like a family school—everyone goes there."
"It's a very united school."
"It's more like a friends' environment than a school environment."
"There's a kind of happy-go-lucky sense in the school."

Example of warmth:
"The priest and parents are always baking. There is always food on the kitchen table, always baked goods."

Examples of relaxed atmosphere:
The principal has a rocking chair at his desk.
"It even smells good! Some schools smell like pee. This one smells like cookies or cotton candy."

Example of teacher interaction:
The teachers' lounge door is always open; students can come to ask questions. Kids feel free to walk in.

Examples of warm, involved atmosphere:
The principal is really involved. She goes into all classrooms every day and knows all the kids by name.
There are after-school and evening programs. "It's one of those school buildings that never close. It's what a school should be."

Moderate Schools. Schools with a moderate social climate were described in mixed terms. Project staff saw both positive and negative characteristics. They also described the schools in mediocre terms, with no alluring or special quality, but also no serious detriments. These schools were not characterized as having any strong "school spirit" beyond an occasional sense of warmth from some faculty. Parents may or may not be involved in these schools. Project staff seemed unsure as to whether these schools were particularly good or bad for transfer students, or for students in general.

General comments:
"The principal is ever present, authoritarian, not warm. The parents would avoid her at any cost."

It has an "austere atmosphere . . . with steel lockers and tile floors."

"Parents get the sense that the school wants their money, period."

"There's a 'homeyness' there, a feeling of warmth and friendliness."

"The teachers have a drive . . . They're very altruistic and get their jollies by helping these kids and seeing their progress."

Examples of atmosphere:
"You can hear teachers shouting at students in the hallway."
The teachers' lounge door is locked. The kids must knock.
There are few decorations in the hallways.
The faculty seem to be doing just what's required of them, though some seem more dedicated.
Everyone is in class all the time.
"You don't walk in and think, 'Oh, it's *this* kind of school.'"

Schools Needing Improvement. These schools have many negative qualities of climate described at length by project staff. The schools were characterized as having an excessive and over-used policy of punishment, little cooperation among faculty, conflict between teaching and religious staff, distant principals, and uninvolved parents. There was little or no collective spirit, few if any schoolwide activities. Halls displayed little decoration or student work. These schools were isolated from the community and neighborhood. Some were on the verge of closing, or operated under the threat of being closed. For transfer students and students in general, these schools were described as having a decidedly negative influence on children.

General comments:
"No one seemed very open or friendly at the whole school. The secretary is grim. The principal is grim."

"Everything there is punishment."

"It's a war. It's like, 'We're going to educate you whether you like or not.'"

"It doesn't seem like it's a school. It's all these different classrooms, and that's it."

"The school is kind of like a little island."

Examples of physical condition:
The school is very cramped physically.

There are some very messy classes, out of control.

Radiators rattle and do not work.

Examples of confusion:
None of the clocks in the school work. "You walk down the hall and it's 8 A.M., 12 P.M., and 3 P.M.!"

"If you know the routine, you can do well—but it's the initial getting-used-to that's difficult."

Examples of teacher interaction:
Teachers are very independent among themselves. Walking past each other, they don't say "good morning."

"Teachers go for the academics and not for the personal relationship."

Examples of atmosphere:
Someone's always yelling at some kid for doing something.

Students eat lunch in their classrooms, so different grades of children do not interact much.

"Kids rebel against everything there."

Key Variables of School Organization

We gleaned more from the interviews than these classifications. Next we describe further research and data around important organizational variables. The focus here alternates between past studies and our own study; first we look at the literature on a certain facet of the school as an organization and then describe what we found relative to that particular facet. We focus on five key variables of a school's organization: size, principal's role, and involvement of students, parents, and faculty. These factors may function as telltale signs of the larger climate.

Influence of School Size

As a prime example of the fruits of ecological research in schools, Barker and Gump's study (1964) constitutes pioneering work in the influence of school size on students' behavior. Size significantly impinged on students' behavior in a number of ways. Students from small, underpopulated schools reported more attractions and pressures toward participation than did students from large schools. Unlike the small school, the large school contained a group of "outsiders," students who experienced little if any pressure to participate. Students from the small school felt more responsibility and obligation. Barker and Gump (1964) concluded that "a school should be small enough that students are not redundant" (p. 202). These findings seem to confirm the views of John Dewey, who regarded large school size as antithetical to the ideal school (cited in Sarason, 1971).

Since Barker and Gump's pioneering work (1964), research involving school size in urban areas has sharply increased rather than decreased (Linney & Seidman, 1989), thus further raising researchers' concerns about effects of size. A 1982 study by Glass, Cahen, Smith, and Filby (cited in Linney & Seidman, 1989) showed powerful effects of school size on achievement. Continued research needs to be conducted on the effects of school size.

Research is needed particularly on subgroups of populations who may be differentially affected by school size. Yet little research on school size has examined subgroups. Linney and Seidman (1989) promoted the idea of matching school environments with students' needs. They addressed the notion of fit between individual and environment, noting that students have different needs that are accommodated better in some environments than others. Applying the idea of fit — or matching — to size, further research could investigate subgroups' adjustment to size.

As an example, Willems (1964) found that school size significantly affected perceptions of marginal high school students. In particular, marginal students at large schools felt less social responsibility and fewer forces toward participation than did marginal students at small schools. Willems concluded that school size is an important variable in students' lives. Size, he maintained, affected motivation and participation.

One population of particular interest is that of transfer students, who may be especially more vulnerable to the harmful effects of size. One of our hypotheses is that school transfer may make certain high-risk subgroups of students vulnerable to the negative effects of large school size. Transfer students who participate in a preventive intervention may be shielded from these negative effects. While we could not fully evaluate this hypothesis, the following information provides some clues.

Class Size

In addition to the interviews, we also compiled a number of statistics on our schools, some of which yielded interesting results. School size correlated positively and significantly with class size. In other words, schools with a large number of students also had large classes. Conversely, smaller schools had smaller classes. Given the assumptions of this study, based on research by Barker and Gump (1964), that larger schools may be worse for children, this finding suggests that transfer students may suffer the doubly negative influences of larger school and larger class size. Both may offer fewer opportunities for participation, promote less affiliation, and offer more chances for children who are floundering socially to decline further in social as well as academic skills.

This finding suggests that the success of students in larger schools may be hindered by large class size, and that large schools may need to find ways to have smaller classes; or they may need to find other methods to increase per-student involvement (such as frequently breaking down into small groups in classes, or having more teacher aides, or having after-school programs similar to those in our project). Transfer students may be at greater risk in larger schools than smaller ones since they may receive less attention there and have more opportunities to "slip through the cracks." Therefore, aiding transfer students may be most important in larger schools.

These findings also imply that a student who transfers from a large school to a smaller one may find the transfer to be an advantage, not a risk. Thus it may be important in future research to take into account the size of a student's previous school.

Principal's Role

Another important element of school climate is the principal, who is a potentially powerful influence on students. Recently, researchers have paid more attention to the role of the principal as effective principal leadership seems to be an element of a successful school (Edington & DiBenedetto, 1988). In a desirable organizational climate, leadership acts emerge easily (Halpin & Croft, 1967).

Andrews and Soder (1987), in a study on principal leadership and student achievement, found that principals play a crucial role in the academic performance of students, especially for low achievers, blacks, and low-income students. Andrews and Soder analyzed teachers' perceptions of principals' instructional leadership, and how these perceptions corresponded to incremental growth of students' academic performance. Three characteristics of effective principal leadership were a visible presence in the school, a vision for the school, and ability to obtain resources for teachers. Schools with more effective principals showed measurable impact on student learning. The researchers found that for students as a whole, prior achievement best predicted future achievement; however, for black students, strong principal leadership best predicted future achievement. (The authors do not mention, however, the race of the principals, which may very well have influenced black student achievement in terms of a role-model effect.) If one assumes the authors controlled for the principals' race or found no effects for race, these findings seem to suggest that for average or high-performing students, principal leadership may have little or no effect. For marginal and at-risk students, though, principal leadership may be influential.

The principal's role and influence interests us for several reasons. Data on principal perceptions and behavior shed light on variation among principals' norms and styles. This variation may well influence the social structure of the school and life in the classroom (Sarason, 1971). In a trickle-down fashion the principal (along with other organizational variables) can affect children's learning. This may not always be the case, but it can be important in certain situations. As Halpin and Croft (1967) concluded, a principal's behavior is a necessary but not sufficient condition of school climate.

Nor does an appreciation of the principal's role place principals at the top of a hierarchy; instead, the principal is seen as an element in the school system as a whole, in a field of mutually influencing forces that includes teachers, students, parents, and the school board. What, then, do we want to consider as potentially important about the principal's role? This question we mostly allowed to emerge from the data themselves—that is, we left it to tutors to tell us what mattered about principals in their schools. Nevertheless, previous research provided us with some clues.

A component of principal role measured in previous studies is the way principals spend their time (Andrews & Soder, 1987; Halpin & Croft, 1967). It has been suggested that a principal who takes more active interest in teaching (by observing and supervising teachers, fostering their ability, and rallying resources for them) is more effective than one who is more an administrator. Halpin and Croft (1967) found aloofness in a principal to be ineffective; effective behavior consists of production emphasis, "thrust" (that is, motivation, modeling, and creativity) (p. 40), and consideration (humane treatment). From these studies on principal leadership, we conjectured that the principal who is more active with teachers and parents would promote a better learning environment than one who spends time on administrative and bureaucratic duties.

In our interviews, project staff were virtually unanimous in describing as ideal a principal who was frequently seen in school, involved in teaching and observing, accessible, and interacting often with students and teachers. Positive principals also welcomed after-school and other special programs while negative principals shunned them. Principals who were not seen in school were perceived as less effective. As for discipline and authoritarian style, project staff saw discipline in various ways. Some perceived it as good, affording structure and consistency that helped incoming transfer students, while others perceived discipline as completely negative. Most concurred that excessive use of discipline was harmful, as was the strong use of discipline without occasional complementary warmth.

Project staff had no idea what principals did outside of school, even principals whom they reported to be spending most of their time outside of schools.

We also had principals estimate the amount of time they spent doing various activities, including administration, instruction, and meetings with faculty, staff, parents, and students. When we correlated all activities of the principal, we found that administrative time clearly occurs at the cost of parent and student time. Principals who are likely to spend time with students are also likely to spend time with parents. Also, principals who spend time with parents are likely to spend time teaching. In correlations of principals' administrative time with other mean time ratings, significant results indicate that administrative time is distinct from and inversely related to combinations of other activities.

These results suggest a dichotomous picture of an *involved* versus a *bureaucratic* principal. Bureaucratic and administrative activities occur at the cost of principals' hands-on involvement in schools. This result also confirms data from interviews that a principal who is involved with one group (for example, students) is likely to be involved with many groups (parents, teachers, and community members). Interviews also suggested that a principal absorbed in administrative work was unlikely to be involved with people. These results support the notion that principals are faced with dichotomous demands on their time, resulting in a conflict between administrative tasks and hands-on involvement. The findings may indicate that principals need more support in their administrative work.

However, such results can be interpreted in different ways. A principal of a larger school who is less knowledgeable about administrative and staff affairs may risk being "out of touch" with his or her school and lacking influence. Conversely, he or she may be properly delegating responsibilities to others, and instead assuming a sort of lobbyist role outside the school. Thus a different dichotomy emerges: instead of an involved versus a bureaucratic principal, we may better describe a *school-centered* versus a *lobbyist* principal, especially in the private sector. Such a *lobbyist* principal may be more important and crucial in such affairs as raising money and smoothing relations with other agencies. Perhaps in this era when schools exist in a political and competitive climate that threatens their survival yearly, a principal active outside the school is necessary. This explanation seems particularly likely given the many recent closings among Chicago's Catholic schools in 1989 and 1990.

Overall, the principals' absence from school, a frequently reported phenomenon, points to the need for better study of what principals do outside of school. The lack of concentration on principals' outside activity constitutes a weakness of the current study. Future research should investigate the notion of a principal as an agent and lobbyist in the community and in the network of agencies.

Of course, people in the school environment as well as the principal may also influence transfer students' experience and the way a school functions. The interaction of these is discussed below.

Involvement of School Staff, Students, and Parents

According to open-systems theory (Katz & Kahn, 1978), an organization undergoes repeated cycles of input, transformation, output, and renewed input. Organizations import energy and resources, transform the energy into a product, and export the product into the environment. This flow of resources, crucial to effective organizations, is contingent on renewed input of resources.

For our purposes, we can consider commitment and involvement to be resources that enter a school and partially determine its effectiveness. The commitment and involvement of those within the school (principals, teachers, and students) and outside the school (parents and community agencies) may constitute important variables that influence student learning. A school with little investment on the part of its members or parents would, according to the open-systems model, function less effectively than a school with highly involved participants.

Past research has taken into account parent and teacher involvement and has found some relationship of this involvement to learning. For instance, Brookover, Beady, Flood, Schweitzer, and Wisenbaker (1979) found that in schools with predominantly high-SES white students, parent involvement was associated with lower student achievement. He concluded that these parents were not likely to be involved with the school unless students' achievement level was unsatisfactory. In contrast, a positive relationship between parental involvement and student achievement in schools with mostly African-American students suggested that African-American parents may impact or mediate the way school affects achievement. The latter conclusion is more appropriate than the first as a hypothesis for our study, which sampled schools of largely minority (African-American and Hispanic-American), low-SES populations.

Importance of Involvement and Commitment. Many tutors reported that positive school environments seemed to be due to the involvement of principals, maintenance workers, secretaries, teachers, or parents. Project staff described the dedication of these people in critical terms as making the difference between a school of average atmosphere and one with a great or poor climate. When giving examples of very positive or very negative school environments, they usually alluded to the participation of one or more of these groups. Sometimes, though, the commitment of one group would be undermined by the disinterest of another. Alternatively, commitment was seen as something that could easily "spill over" to affect other groups of people, or "trickle" up or down the hierarchy of community members or school personnel. For instance, a tutor reported how the parents' involvement "softened" the way teachers treated children. Another said, "One teacher can make a real difference."

Project staff also reported that the involvement of secretaries and maintenance workers had a very positive influence as well. Some secretaries in particular were seen as crucial gatekeepers, managers, and "everybody's second mom," whose influence seemed to even exceed the principal's.

Additionally, the quality of teaching was described as potentially crucial to a student's experience. A good teacher in an otherwise less effective school was seen as maintaining and boosting children's progress. Similarly, a poor teacher in an outstanding school could significantly impair a child's experience.

The Ecology of Elements in a School. As discussed earlier in this chapter, we conceptualize the transfer experience in ecological terms, with the student surrounded and influenced by other forces. Our interviews offered support for such a view. When we talked to tutors, we found that schools were commonly described as having interacting elements, such as involved parents influencing a school's faculty, or outstanding faculty being affected by a nondynamic principal. Thus, no one element on its own seemed to determine the quality of school climate. Rather, project staff described how one element of a school would offset or catalyze another.

For instance, large schools were not necessarily overwhelming or cold for students; project staff sometimes described the largeness as being compensated for by smaller classes or better school spirit.

Central to the ecology of elements in a school is the child, of course. Project staff described some children who seemed resilient and thrived despite a harsh transfer or a negative climate in the new school. For other children, tutors felt the transfer experience would have been more positive in a school with a better climate. Thus, staff seemed to perceive children as variously influenced by the quality of the school climate into which they transferred. Not all children were seen as influenced by a school's climate, yet often the at-risk students were perceived as being more deeply affected.

It was interesting to note in the interviews how some factors could be described in completely different terms. For instance, sometimes a physically large school was perceived as very positive, lending comfortable space to breathe, play, and wander, relieving the tension felt by students in smaller places. Other project staff described physically large schools as overwhelming, cold, amplifying noise, and lacking intimacy. One supervisor said of a physically big school, "It's inviting but intimidating at the same time." Another said, "Physically, it's kind of impersonal, an 'echoey' place, but it's big and bright and I think the kids like it." Overall, physical size was not expressed as the best overall indicator of a school's climate.

Similarly, the wealth of a school by no means determined the quality of its climate. Schools that were more financially sound or were located in neighborhoods with higher socioeconomic status were not necessarily described as having better school culture or climate. Likewise, poorer schools could exude warmth, commitment, and spirit, and were seen as having a positive climate despite a paucity of resources.

Indicators of Climate. The frequency and amount of hallway decor in schools emerged in virtually all interviews as a salient indicator of the schools' climate. Decor included posters celebrating ethnic or racial heritage, weekly honor rolls, art work by students, large calendars, photographs, religious pictures, and other works. Most tutors described this as a primary example of a school's quality. Good decor always described a very effective school with an overwhelmingly positive school climate, though poor decor was not always emblematic of a school with a poorer climate.

A second physical factor that emerged from interviews as telling of school climate was how many open doors there were in a school. Staff often used examples of open doors in explaining the atmosphere they sensed in a school. These included nearly all doors in a school: classroom doors, the principal's office door, the teachers' lounge door, and the main office door. In an "open-door school," teachers often visited each others' classes to seek assistance; there was more traffic of students among classrooms, delivering notes among teachers or watching over younger classrooms. There was also more traffic passing through the principal's and secretary's offices, with students or faculty seeking help or socializing; and the teachers' lounge door was always open, with students often coming for assistance. This finding is congruent with findings by Kelly (1979) on "fluid schools" (p. 192) as having more traffic in the principal's office, and his conclusion that fluid schools were generally positive and nurturing environments for students.

A third physical factor that arose in interviews was the layout of the main office and the teachers' lounge. Some staff perceived the layout to be emblematic of the school climate or the principal's management style. For instance, in one school the teachers' lounge is openly linked to the secretary's and principal's office suite; therefore teachers have little or no privacy, do not congregate there, and exhibit little cohesion or interpersonal warmth. In another school the principal's office stands on a level higher than the main office and the hallway itself; this height was seen as a sign of the principal's distant and authoritarian working style. As one supervisor said, "The set-up of the principal's office and the main office tells you a lot about the school. [It's important] how it's arranged, how many places there are to sit."

Summary

What, then, can we conclude? According to staff interviews, children seemed variously influenced by the quality of the school climate into which they transferred. Tutors, who worked closely with transfer students, thought that transfer children were influenced by school climate. As one tutor said, "The school I work in isn't warm enough. It would have been different for my transfer students in another school."

According to interviews with staff members, the wealth of a school does not seem to determine the quality of its climate. Thus, there is much that poorer schools can do to enhance their atmosphere of learning, and "throwing money" at a school may not influence its climate.

The interviews also suggest that positive qualities of a principal include high visibility within the school, high involvement in teaching and observing, easy accessibility, and frequent interaction with students and teachers. Positive principals also welcomed after-school and other special programs while negative principals shunned them. Principals who were not seen in school were perceived as less effective. Overall, a highly involved principal in a school that serves the entire community with activities was seen as ideal. These observations may enlighten what communities and transfer students need in a principal.

Project staff provided information on indicators of the quality of school climate. Hallway decor, open doors, and office layout were key indicators of climate. These indicators should be validated by future research. Knowing such signs can sensitize newcomers to what to expect from a school, and add to anthropological data on school environments. Moreover, schools can enhance their climates by posting much hallway and classroom decor (posters, graded papers, art work), designing office layout to welcome students and visitors (for example, the visitors' seating area, principal's office, and teachers' lounge), and having all doors stay open as much as possible to promote an atmosphere of openness. Our staff strongly reinforced the idea that environmental design matters.

One very practical way to acknowledge the change of climate a transfer student undergoes is to implement an orientation program. In Chapter Six, we outlined the orientation program we used in schools. It gives students the chance to express what their old school was like and how the new one seems different. They learn about rules, roles, layout, and environments. This is a prime time for students to comment on differences in climate. An orientation program is like a therapeutic debriefing from the old school and a welcoming beginner's course for the new school.

Furthermore, our study supports the use of qualitative methodology with an endeavor such as the School Transition

Project. Staff members' unique roles as part-time tutors, consultants, and advocates in schools present an ideal opportunity to utilize them as participant-observers. The rich data gleaned from qualitative interviews with staff show that they learn much about their schools. They gain a unique sense of climate that may be inaccessible to both "outsiders" of a school, who lack exposure and training in that place, and "insiders" of a school, who may be too immersed and invested in the environment to gain a critical perspective.

Therefore, we recommend that future programs try to understand the kinds of climate into which children enter. By understanding climate, programmers can then seek to modify climates and social systems to enhance transfer students' experience. A very helpful book by Maher, Illback, and Zins (1984), *Organizational Psychology in the Schools: A Handbook for Professionals,* elaborates on numerous ways professionals can improve the organizational nature of schools. Works on consultation, such as *Consulting with Human Service Systems* (Goodstein, 1978) and *Implementing Organizational Change* (Lippitt et al., 1985) provide many valuable ideas for helping organizations to change. In addition, studies by Moos and his colleagues (for example, Moos, 1974, 1979) discuss how environmental evaluations can be conducted with quantitative tools, and then used to change aspects of an organization. Finally, our inquiry reinforces the idea that climate remains an important—and, in some cases, crucial—factor to consider in helping students adjust.

10

Outcomes for
Transfer Students

Any social service should seek to prove that it has made
lasting, positive change, yet providing and explaining such proof
can be an enormously complex task. One must take into account how the program affects everyone; how subgroups such
as boys and girls responded differently; and how various participants, such as parents and children, affected one another.
Our aim in this chapter is to elucidate and summarize results
from our research analyses, for both lay and professional audiences. In-depth statistical description is sacrificed for the sake
of economy and brevity. Thus, research specialists may want
to refer to more elaborate descriptions in our other publications,
to which we refer throughout the chapter. Further analyses are
in progress as well, and will be published. Wherever possible
in this chapter, we attempt to draw conclusions from our results.
However, broader generalizations regarding future directions
for research will be deferred to Chapter Eleven.

During the first two years of the School Transition Project, our aim was to develop the various components of the tutoring program. We anticipated that initial program evaluation
findings would help us fine-tune our intervention efforts with
transfer students. In the following paragraphs, we discuss the
sample composition for the project and findings from the program (Jason et al., 1989).

Composition of Sample

In the four years of the program, each cohort's high-risk
group (school tutored, school and home tutored, and control)

consisted of about fifty to sixty children in each group. We also had a low-risk group of controls each year. Overall, there were nearly equal numbers of boys and girls in each group as well as equal numbers of third, fourth, and fifth graders. The largest racial group was black (35 to 53 percent), followed by Hispanic (20 to 39 percent), and white (8 to 19 percent); small percentages were designated "other" (mostly Asian, 2 to 9 percent). This was a largely minority population, reflecting the composition of the inner city. Altogether, we tested or worked with nearly 1,400 children.

Initial Findings

In our first year, ten schools were randomly assigned to an experimental condition and ten to a control condition. We then worked with our first two cohorts of children, in 1986–87 and 1987–88. As mentioned earlier, a high-risk group of transfers was identified based on low socioeconomic status, evidence of academic lags, and exposure to multiple life stressors. High-risk transfer children in the experimental condition were compared to high-risk transfers in control schools.

In addition, a high-risk group of nontransfer children were compared to the high-risk transfer children. Prior to the transfer, high-risk transfer children were similar to high-risk nontransfer children in academic performance. After the transfer, those who were entering the new schools received significantly lower grades than those high-risk children that had not transferred.

Whether the children's changes were due to decreased functioning after the transfer or higher standards at the new school, it is of interest that these high-risk transfer children had significantly higher risk factors and significantly lower achievement scores and grades than nontransfer high-risk children. Our findings indicate that the identified high-risk children were more at risk than other problem youngsters within the schools. The criteria used to identify the high-risk transfer children — lower SES, number of risk factors, and lags in achievement — were effective in identifying a subgroup of transfer children who were in need of help, even more so than nontransfer children who were perceived by their teachers as having social and behavioral difficulties (Jason, Filippelli, Danner, & Bennett, in press).

Findings from the first year's program illustrate the general results that emerged during our first two years with the project (reported in Jason et al., 1989; Jason et al., 1990). At the end of the first year, program and control children were compared on achievement, self-concept, and social adjustment. On the Wide Range Achievement Test-Revised (WRAT-R), transfer children who received the tutoring program made significantly greater gains in reading, spelling, and mathematics during the year compared to control transfers. None of the scores for the control children significantly increased over time.

Our findings on the performance of experimental children in our program were encouraging. As discussed in Chapter Six, the Direct Instruction approach to tutoring emphasized skill mastery, and our results seemed to reflect this tutoring strategy. For the overall sample of experimental participants, significant academic improvements were found based on comparisons of children's first and last three sessions of tutoring. The experimental children's rate of reading increased from 70.4 to 90.2 words per minute. Their accuracy of words read increased from 90.6 percent to 95.6 percent; comprehension rose from 78.0 percent to 83.1 percent. Children's spelling improved from 76 percent to 83 percent of words correct. Also, program students showed substantial gains in mathematics and phonics instructional hierarchies.

Because significant findings emerged for achievement scores, we decided to determine the percentage of children who, over the school year, changed from an at-risk to a *not* at-risk status. We identified transfer children who, on achievement tests, were one standard deviation below the norm. Among the experimental group, 42 percent of those identified at pretest as being one standard deviation below the norm moved out of this category at posttesting. However, for the controls, the figure was 28 percent. This result suggests that the intervention directionally aided more experimental than control children to move out of the poor achievement category.

Despite academic gains evidenced by program children, there were no apparent "spillover" effects in social and behavioral domains. These findings informed us that a tutoring intervention alone may not be powerful enough to change high-risk transfer children's behavior and social competence. Thus, in order to promote broader behavioral and social changes, more comprehensive interventions were needed.

A major objective of the first year's intervention was to assess whether the consumers of the program felt that the overall program was both needed and helpful. Data obtained from program surveys were most favorable. At program end, 89 percent of the program children said that they liked the program, 94 percent said that the program helped them with homework, and 98 percent said their tutor was helpful. Using a scale ranging from poor (1), fair (2), good (3), and excellent (4), parents of the tutored children rated the academic benefits of the program with an average score of 3.3. Teachers and principals were asked a question using a five-point scale, ranging from very negative (1) to very positive (5). For the question "How do you feel about the overall tutoring program?" average ratings for teachers and principals were 4.4 and 4.7, respectively. The tutors also completed an evaluation form at the end of the project year. When asked how they felt about the overall tutoring program, using a five-point scale [very negative (1) to very positive (5)], the average rating was 4.6. Thus, tutors, teachers, principals, parents, and transfer children alike tended to perceive the overall effects of the tutoring program as positive and helpful.

Parent-Tutor Assessment

Although we were encouraged by the positive impact of the tutoring program, a high percentage of transfers still were evidencing academic and social problems at program end. It became clear that more time was needed to help remediate the identified lags. Parent involvement seemed to be one realistic and viable means to accomplish this formidable task. Thus, we endeavored to assess caregivers' willingness and competence to tutor their children. Toward this objective, we administered the Parent-Tutor Assessment (PTA) (discussed in Chapter Eight) to parents and guardians of transfer children at the end of the first year (Johnson & Jason, 1992). What we discovered in our preliminary questionnaire about parent tutoring convinced us that indeed we needed to involve caregivers more fully in the program.

After the end of the program, parents were asked if they would have been interested in participating in a parent-training program to increase their effectiveness in helping their children, and 81 percent said they would have been interested. Surprisingly, 63 percent of interviewed parents believed they did not have the skills to tutor their children effectively.

As discussed in Chapter Eight, the PTA assesses parent-tutoring behaviors, parent-child communication, and parents' motivation and perceived competence to tutor their children. Based on the first-year sample, we found that the PTA total score significantly correlated with transfers' final classroom grades for reading, spelling, and mathematics. These correlations suggest that fewer parent-tutoring problems are associated with higher overall classroom achievement (Johnson & Jason, 1992). Based on the PTA total score, we identified children who received high versus low parent-tutoring support. The well-supported children achieved average grades, whereas low-support transfers achieved below average final grades in the major subject areas. For example, based on a grade scale ranging from 4 = A to 0 = F, the high-support students' mean reading grade was 2.54, compared to low-support students' mean of 1.75.

Parent Involvement

During the second year of our project, we piloted a program that trained parents to implement our Direct Instruction tutoring intervention in their home (Jason, Kurasaki, Neuson, & Garcia, in press). When the trained parents actively worked with their children at home, the students mean grades in reading, math, and spelling at the end of the school year were 2.44, 3.00, and 2.77, respectively (based on a grade scale of 4 = A, 3 = B, 2 = C, 1 = D, and 0 = F). In contrast, when the children were tutored only in the school by our trained paraprofessionals, and the parents were not actively involved in the program, the high-risk children's average grades in reading, math, and spelling at the end of the school year were 1.88, 1.92, and 2.00, respectively. These pilot data were supportive of our hypothesis that when parents and school-based personnel work together in our prevention program, the outcomes are more favorable.

Gender Differences in Students

In our first two years, we also became interested in gender as an additional factor of transfer students' academic and social adjustment (Orosan et al., in press). We examined gender differences among transfer students in their self-concepts, academic performance, teacher evaluations, and peer ratings. Gender differences were found in many measures. Girls started the year with higher mathematics grades but boys improved more than girls. As expected, female transfer students had lower self-concepts than males; teachers reported that boys exhibited more disruptive, aggressive behavior, and that they were more popular; peers also rated boys as more aggressive; however, they rated girls as more likable than boys. However, analyses determined that the program did not affect boys differently from girls.

These findings suggest that preventive interventions for transfer students should be tailored differently for girls and boys. Any intervention should have both social and academic components, as transfer students evidence problems in both areas, and their success in one sphere might enhance mastery in the other. Program components aimed at facilitating academic adjustment of transfer students need not be different for boys and girls, since their academic adjustment is similar. However, program components with the aim of easing social adjustment should focus on increasing girls' self-concept, and decreasing boys' aggression, withdrawal, and anxiety. These social adjustments may positively affect academic adjustment. Further research is warranted in designing and testing gender-sensitive interventions for transfer students.

Third-Year Findings

With the home-tutoring component designed and piloted, we implemented two experimental programs in our third year (1988–89): school tutoring alone, and school and home tutoring, both for high-risk students (we also continued to have a nonprogram control group of high-risk students). We present the findings from our third-year cohort only because at the time of writing this book, we were still analyzing the data from the fourth-year cohort. Significant overall program effects were found for achievement tests in reading scores, indicating that the two experimental high-risk groups (those tutored at school, and at both school and home) improved significantly more than did the high-risk controls, who were not tutored (as reported in Weine, Kurasaki, Jason, Johnson, & Danner, 1992).

Among academic grades, significant program effects were found between pre- and post-intervention grades for spelling. Here again, the two experimental groups improved at a greater rate than the high-risk controls. In this area, tutoring may have helped because spelling is a very concrete task with clearly defined mastery levels. Tutors could ensure near-perfect test performance, and the words taught were straight from the class work.

Our program was not aimed explicitly at teaching social skills, but the program children did improve on several social measures. Teachers reported seeing, among the home-and-school tutored children, decreases in social withdrawal and inattentiveness. The home-plus-school tutoring intervention seems to have been more effective in making children more attentive and less withdrawn in the classroom, based on teacher reports, than school tutoring only. Working with both parents and tutors seems to have fostered greater attentiveness and participation with friends and teachers. Our positive findings on teacher ratings indicate that an academic intervention may have spillover effects on social behavior.

We are at the beginning stage of analyzing the one-year follow-up data for this cohort of high-risk children. The initial findings are encouraging. For example, in the important area of reading grades, children in all three conditions declined by half to three-fourths of a grade (from a C to a D) after the transfer. Only those children provided the parent tutoring showed continued improvement both during the intervention year and through the follow-up period. In fact, at the one-year follow-up, children who received the comprehensive intervention had reading grades that matched their pretransfer grades.

Overall, we observed modest successes from our home and school tutoring of high-risk transfer students. However, it seems necessary to develop more individualized and intensive interventions directed at both academic and social adjustment. Our aim in the parent-tutoring intervention was to intensify the time and support given to youngsters. Clearly, even the combined home and school tutoring for several hours per week may not be enough for children with more entrenched academic and social difficulties. Some children may need greater amounts of one-on-one tutoring. Also, some transfers probably need specific counseling or social skills training. Later in this chapter, we examine the effects of the year 3 intervention on different subtypes of children, and whether program intensity had an effect on the most at-risk children.

Toward an Empirical Model of Transfer Student Adjustment

In attempting to understand the interrelationships between ecological and individual variables potentially influencing school transitions, we have been developing an empirical model of elementary transfer-student adjustment (Johnson, Halpert, & Jason, 1992) using Linear Structural Relations Modeling (LISREL) path analysis procedures (Jorskog & Sorbom, 1989). We have been interested in learning how individual student characteristics such as achievement, social competence, self-concept, gender, and grade level interrelate with external variables such as family SES, major stressful life events, and parent-tutoring support. Path analysis enabled us to test the plausibility of causal relationships between variables in quasi-experimental conditions (Jorskog & Sorbom, 1989).

Our current model highlights a number of plausible linkages and consistent results between student and environmental variables. Not surprisingly, the most robust linkages emerged for academic achievement and social adjustment. Transfer students' incoming (last quarter in previous school) and first-quarter reading achievement were strongly predictive of final reading grades. Thus, we suspect that transfer students who demonstrate poor incoming and first-quarter reading achievement are likely at great risk for yearlong academic problems. Similarly, transfer students' first-quarter social adjustment (manifested by their aggression, withdrawal, and likability among peers) seems to be a strong indicator of their social competence at the end of the school year. Concerning connections between academic and social performance, the clearest finding was that increased student aggression, both at the beginning and end of the year, is associated with decreases in reading achievement. We can speculate that student aggression, encompassing such problems as aggression toward peers and distractibility, may diminish reading achievement. Perhaps teachers are more inclined to give aggressive students lower grades, also. Additionally, our model shows that lower reading grades at the beginning of the year are linked to increased social withdrawal. Such potentially intractable academic and social problems among transfers underscore the importance of comprehensive prevention efforts to enhance simultaneously both academic and social performance for high-risk youngsters.

We have also seen evidence that transfers' self-perceptions of scholastic competence may be associated with initial social withdrawal, such that lower self-perceptions are associated with increased withdrawal in the classroom. The path analyses suggest that older transfer children are less accepted by their new peers as compared to younger transfer children. This finding leads us to consider implementing strategies to promote social acceptance for newcomers particularly in later grades.

Early Intervention Effects

Finally, there is some evidence that our intervention had early results. Based on a path analysis model of third-year data, we found an association between program support and high-risk transfer students' first-quarter social adjustment. High-risk transfers receiving the orientation and buddy interventions displayed lower social withdrawal and aggression than high-risk transfers in the control group.

There may be several ways to explain this trend. We expected the orientation program to familiarize transfers with school rules, expectations, and routines. The orientation likely reduced the initial sense of confusion and guardedness that transfer students bring to their new school. Moreover, assigning classroom buddies to newcomers was designed to foster accepting and supportive classroom peer networks. In addition, prior to the start of the school year, project staff consulted with teachers in the intervention schools about ways to ease new students' academic and social transition. Teachers' guidance and classroom management may have reduced some transfer students' aggression and withdrawal. Tutor support early in the year could have strengthened transfers' social adjustment as well. Also, targeting transfer students for a tutoring intervention may have prompted some high-risk children to behave better in class.

Identifying High-Risk Transfer Students

The School Transition Project, like all prevention and early intervention programs, has been faced with the challenging task of accurately identifying the most at-risk children in need of services. Our selection criteria were initially based on transfer students' low family socioeconomic status, multiple life stressors, and evidence of academic lags. We soon saw evidence that incoming (that is, last year) and first-quarter academic achievement and social competence might be even better indicators of overall transfer student adjustment. We are refining a method, discussed below, that we used to predict yearlong transfer student academic and social performance.

We have been conducting a series of exploratory analyses to identify more accurately groups of high-risk transfer students. First, we employed cluster analysis to identify subtypes of high-risk transfers. Based on first-quarter grade average for reading and math (GPA), students in the third cohort were divided into high (A's and B's), average (C's), and low (D's and F's) achievement groups.

To look at adjustment from a different angle, we examined transfer students' *social status*. Again using our third-year data, we divided transfers based on first-quarter GPA and their social status measured by the peer nomination procedure developed by Coie and his colleagues (Coie et al., 1982). Transfer students' first-quarter social status fell into one of five categories: popular, rejected, neglected, controversial, and average.

We grouped transfers into one of three "coping" categories according to their combination of first-quarter achievement and social status (Johnson, Jost, & Jason, 1992). *Good copers* were those transfers who achieved a 3.0 or better GPA and were popular or average in social status. Children who were popular and had average achievement were also considered good copers. *Average copers* achieved an average first-quarter GPA and were either average or controversial in social status. High achievers who were controversial or low achievers who were popular were also considered average copers. *Poor copers* were those transfers at any achievement level who were rejected or neglected by peers. Additionally, low achievers who were average or controversial were classified as poor copers. Thus, our classification scheme simultaneously took into account both achievement and social standing in the classroom.

In general, our findings suggest that first-quarter academic and social performance are strong indicators of year-long adjustment. We can tentatively conclude that many transfers who display poor initial adjustment are likely to continue to exhibit academic and social difficulties. We realize that social problems can occur at any achievement level, but students who experience both academic and social difficulties are especially at risk for chronic problems. Overall, we believe that first-quarter measures of classroom achievement and social performance are valid and reliable predictors of high-risk status for transfer students.

The most high-risk transfer children are those who are classified as poor copers at the beginning of the year. This conclusion is confirmed by the finding that in the control condition, among poor copers at the beginning of the year, only 21 percent had moved out of this category by the end of the year. In contrast, among poor copers at the beginning of the year for the school-only tutoring condition, 30 percent were able to move out of this high-risk category, becoming either average or good copers by the end of the year.

We next tried to determine whether program intensity might also make a difference in changing the risk status of these vulnerable transfer children. Our belief was that within the school-plus-home tutoring condition, there were parents who worked consistently and patiently to improve their children's abilities while others had less time or motivation to be as effective in this role. When we selected the high-involvement parents and examined those children who were poor copers at the beginning of the academic year, the more comprehensive intervention was able to move 50 percent of the poor copers out of this category by year's end. In addition, all of the small group of poor copers at the beginning of the year who received the very highest ratings on intensity of parent tutoring were able to move out of this high-risk group by the end of the year. These data provide additional support to our hypothesis that more comprehensive and intensive interventions might be more effective with the most at-risk children (Jason, Johnson, Danner, Taylor, & Kurasaki, in press).

We suspect that program intensity is indeed important for transfer children who display initial poor coping on entering a new school. Greater program intensity, marked by cooperative and well-coordinated home and school interventions, likely results in greater gains for at-risk transfer students as compared to efforts that are less intensive. We are continuing to explore the key factors that determine program intensity, which we discuss in the final chapter.

We are presently examining more fine-grained types of groupings of children over time. Some children with severe environmental and personal risk factors seem to succeed in coping with the demands of the new school whereas other children who have been exposed to more favorable circumstances have not met minimal academic and social expectations. By grouping children into categories having a similar set of developmental and environmental markers over the course of the year, we hope to understand better the complex ecosystem in which the children are embedded, and how multiple influences protect, or jeopardize, the coping process in children transferring into a new school.

Summary

Many of the findings cited in this chapter need to be interpreted cautiously until more long-term results are reported. In addition, care should be exercised before generalizing program effects to other population subgroups and educational settings. Still, even with these limitations, we have seen that our orientation-plus-tutoring intervention shows promise in improving transfer students' academic performance. As our project evolved, we struggled to widen such academic improvement and to make it generalize to social life as well. One way to strengthen the intervention was to enlist the help of home tutors. Results showed that such tutoring was linked with better academic and social adjustment. Further results indicated that boys and girls probably differ in what they need from a preventive intervention. Parents may need to be differently trained according to the gender of their transfer children. Also, we have looked at the different adjustment of certain clusters of transfer children: good, average, and poor copers. The intensity of an intervention may matter as well.

Based on these results, we offer a number of recommendations for evaluation of school transition programs. From our experience, we see the importance of ongoing evaluations to fine-tune interventions and to determine which components best match individual transfer-student needs. We recognize that typical school systems may not be able to commit evaluation resources comparable to those of our School Transition Project. Nevertheless, several worthwhile evaluation procedures can be conducted efficiently and cost-effectively. We direct our suggestions specifically to school administrators, school psychologists, teachers, and researchers who might become involved in different levels of program evaluation.

The vast majority of schools formally test students' academic achievement using standardized achievement measures; usually such testing is completed in the spring of the school year, which can be seen as a postpoint evaluation. As we have learned in our investigation, it is critical to measure transfer students' *incoming* or prepoint academic achievement. Many schools depend on previous schools to forward past academic records, but in our experience past records are not reliably sent to a new school. Of course, some schools routinely test newcomers prior to or near the start of the school year in order to place them in appropriate curricular levels. For example, teachers may evaluate student achievement using placement tests provided by publishers of academic curricula. We strongly urge all educators to evaluate transfers at the beginning of the year and obtain a detailed academic profile of students' skills in the various subject areas. The results will enable teachers and school staff to pinpoint specific skill gaps relative to nontransfer peers.

In our project, we first evaluated students using the standardized WRAT-R; once we identified children with significant achievement deficits, we followed up with a more detailed evaluation of their phonics skills, reading accuracy, reading rate, and mathematical skills. For those students manifesting more serious deficits, formal testing for learning disabilities should be initiated early in the school year. Unfortunately, all too often transfer students struggle through several grading periods receiving low marks before they receive the necessary evaluation and intervention. Overall, pre- and postpoint testing allows school personnel to determine academic adjustment for transfer students. Also in this regard, detailed report cards that reflect academic skill levels and gaps are more informative than merely grades in the various subject areas.

We see a particular need to assess transfer students' first-quarter social and behavioral adjustment. This is probably not a priority in most schools at the present time. However, many educators will readily agree that social and behavioral adjustments are an important concern for transfers. Our data show that a considerable percentage of transfers do experience peer rejection or neglect. How many of these troubled transfers are identified and really helped by school staff in our nation's schools? Timely administration of the social measurement instrument developed by Coie and associates (1982) (explained in Chapter Six) for transfers and nontransfers alike would enable teachers and counselors to identify students who are at risk for yearlong peer problems. School staff may question the potential drawback of stigmatizing students by using the peer nomination measure, but we affirm the greater benefits of identifying social problems early and offering social skills programs for high-risk groups or entire classrooms. In consultation with administrators or school mental health personnel, we believe that teachers can reliably identify social and behavioral problems using such measures as the Child Behavior Checklist (Achenbach & Edelbrock, 1986). If a teacher intuitively senses that a transfer child exhibits significant social or behavior problems, such measures completed before and after social interventions can document behavioral progress. Of course, teachers should be sensitive to changes in children's social status; changes in children's social skills may not necessarily translate into changes in status among peers.

Finally, we encourage school staff to consider administering measures of transfer-student self-perceptions or perceived coping, such as Harter's Perceived Competence Scale for Children (1982). Such paper-and-pencil questionnaires permit students to share their concerns about their academic and social performance, physical appearance, athletic abilities, and general sense of self-worth. Such information can give teachers and counselors invaluable insight into individual students' motivation, fears, and emerging social and behavioral difficulties. Having such information early in the year can help direct school staff's efforts to build self-esteem among newcomers. We do not recommend using a measure of students' self-perception as a sole criterion for program evaluation but as one of several measures. Our experience has been that children's self-perceptions can often be discrepant from their actual behavior and performance.

These are some of our specific recommendations for evaluating programs for transfer students. Broad conclusions about the transfer experience — including the future for transfer students — are discussed in the last chapter.

Part Three

Where Do We Go From Here?

11

Future Directions: Building Compassion into School Systems

Throughout this book we have looked at a variety of approaches for helping children who transfer into new schools. In Chapter Three, we indicated that there have not been many studies directed at helping transfer children, or high-risk transfer students specifically. This lack is regrettable, given these students' special needs. The findings reported in Chapter Ten from our studies conducted at DePaul University reveal that a variety of approaches involving orientation programs, tutoring, and parent involvement can be helpful for some transfer children. A considerable amount of research is needed to learn which transfer children have the greatest needs for preventive interventions, and what are the short- and long-term outcomes of providing children different types of programs. It is clear that we are really at the beginning of understanding how to develop comprehensive interventions for children at risk who transfer into new schools.

In developing preventive interventions for children at risk, we need to recognize that there are many different factors influencing children's adjustment before and during the program. An understanding of these ecological factors can enable us to understand better how children cope with the transition into new schools (Felner et al., 1983). As an example, our project revealed that the family's support of the child and the family's cohesion and structural climate can affect the child's academic ability and social adjustment prior to the transfer (Johnson & Jason, 1992). Children who are exposed to a supportive environment along with a social climate that facilitates academic and social skill development are at an advantage in the new school. Because of this exposure, their ability may be higher and they are typically better adjusted. For those children who have ability or adjustment difficulties, the transition into a new school is much more difficult. An important point to consider is that the difficulties these children manifest were probably influenced by their social environment (that is, both home and previous school) prior to entering the new school.

In addition, the school intervention itself may be strongly affected by organizational variables such as the support of the school and the social climate in the class. For example, the most effective interventions may have minimal effect in a highly disorganized classroom. Unless we perceive that a school transition intervention is couched within larger cultures (for example, school and neighborhood) that facilitate the child's school adjustment to varying degrees, our attempts to understand intervention effects are more limited. In Chapter Nine, we identified some of these larger ecological influences that we think have the following implications.

As exemplified by the research of Felner and Adan (1988), interventions for transfer students need to involve not just passing programs — of interest one year and discontinued the next — but a restructuring of school systems in a more permanent way. That is, orientation programs could be a regular, yearly or twice-a-year feature of a school's curriculum. Inservice training that sensitizes teachers to transfer issues should be standard. Extra help for transfer students, including tutoring, counseling, and advocacy, should be a firm part of the school's services. These services, like others (such as special education or speech therapy), should be well coordinated with regular teaching, not a jarring interruption. School faculty should meet regularly to discuss transfer students and ways that school and class environments can be changed to better acclimate new students. Such changes may include posting and better articulation of class and school rules, using art and schoolwork to make the walls more visually appealing and friendly, centralizing transfer-student services, and having a principal be seen more in classes and introduce herself or himself to transfer students (individually or assembled as a group). These are just a few ideas that emerge when one begins to consider the "universe of alternatives" educators may generate when they think about how their schools can welcome new students (Sarason, 1974, p. 128). Further organizational changes can be discussed by parents, teachers, administrators, and counselors meeting together.

We believe that some children benefit greatly by being provided the types of programs we have been piloting; however, we recognize the need for even more comprehensive and individualized interventions for many of the children with whom we have been working. In short, some high-risk transfer children need much more intensive interventions than we have been able to provide up until now — interventions targeting not only the child but also his or her family, and broader ecological processes in the classroom, school, and community.

Readers may raise the criticism that the participating Chicago parochial schools were especially conducive settings that did not exist elsewhere. We selected the parochial school system for the site of our interventions because the Chicago public schools were involved in a major decentralization effort during the period of our project, and teacher strikes and political upheavals were occurring at the beginning of almost every year. We needed schools that were going to open uneventfully at the beginning of each year, as this condition was necessary for us to standardize our procedures across schools. In our work over the past four years, we have found that transfer children come from families having a wide range of economic levels. One might argue that parents sending their children to parochial schools have considerable disposable income as the yearly tuition at these schools ranges from $1,000 to $1,500. However, many of the families in our project were living at the poverty level, and they could afford to send their children to these schools only by working at the schools part-time to pay the tuition. It is then possible that the parents in our project were more motivated to support their children's academic progress. While it is probably true that these parents as a group were more motivated, the range again was rather wide; some parents were extremely concerned and motivated, but many, particularly those of the most at-risk students, were considerably less motivated or had less time and energy to devote to their children's education. Some parents felt that because they were paying to send their children to school, the educational personnel should solve all academic difficulties without bothering the parents.

Many of the children in our project had social and academic problems that were at least as serious as those found in schoolchildren within the public schools. In addition, we found that remedial services in inner-city parochial schools were often relatively limited compared to those of public institutions. In inner-city Chicago and across the country, public and private schools share many of the same burdens and circumstances: school closings, a paucity of funds, high rates of transfer, and an abundance of social problems. It seems that both public and private sector schools could benefit from school transition interventions.

Looking Toward the Future

Our intention to focus on children of the early elementary-school years was based on our examination of high school dropouts' records. We learned that high school students who were dropping out had begun having grade point average differences from their peers in the early elementary-school years. In other words, if children in third, fourth, and fifth grades have difficulties, it is much more likely that these children will have even more problems in junior high and high school (Hess, 1987). A good percentage of these youngsters will also have serious problems later with peers and possibly in their occupations. Given these connections between early academic and social difficulties and later school problems, we conclude that we should be investing more resources in helping children during the early elementary-school years.

It is surprising that practically no research has focused on helping at-risk transfer children at these early ages. Most of this literature has focused on scheduled transitions: children transferring from elementary to junior high school, junior high school to high school, or high school to college (see Chapter Three). We acknowledge the importance of these studies, but we also see an opportunity for investigators to devote more time to intervening with children when they might be most in need of preventive help. Thus, we advocate school transition interventions targeting students in the early elementary-school years.

One day, we believe all schools will have programs developed to help children who transfer. We believe that schools are just beginning to develop a variety of interventions to help children who are at risk, partly because of the demands of parents and teachers to do something about this serious problem. However, if one examines the types of programs typically provided for transition children, most involve only orientation programs (Cornille et al., 1983). Sometimes attempts at limited tutoring are made, but often such tutoring efforts are not comprehensive, carefully monitored, or evaluated. We believe that the future needs of transfer children will be given considerably more attention by society and that a variety of programs will be available to these children. We also hope that some of the lessons we have learned in our research at DePaul University will inform and apply to future interventions.

We would like to speculate on the types of programming we believe need to be mounted for both low- and high-risk transfer children. In over ten years of programming at DePaul University, we have tried out a variety of intervention ideas, and yet we still believe that we are only at the beginning of understanding how to design interventions that meet the individual needs of each child. However, we do feel confident that we can suggest some of the types of things that should be done by school systems to meet the needs of those most at risk for academic problems after entering a new school. In the remainder of this chapter, we speculate about what those components might be and how transfer children might benefit, if, according to our future predictions, they were provided such interventions in schools throughout the country.

Before the first day of school, all children entering new school systems would undergo comprehensive assessments. Obviously, some children enter school just after the start of the year and at later points during the year; these children will be assessed when they arrive. However, a large percentage of children do register for a new school system during the summer and at least one week prior to the beginning of the year. Assessment of these children could be done and the results of these assessments would be important in planning for the children's academic and social needs. As a guide for such evaluation, Yoshida (1984) offers helpful ways for school personnel to manage assessment smoothly and effectively. When we talk about assessments, we are thinking comprehensively and including measures of academic abilities, self-esteem, and social skills. Assessment also should be made of the social support children are getting from their parents or other guardians. We would also be interested in learning the children's expectations and concerns about their new school. Also important to a comprehensive assessment would be discovering what elements of the class and school environment are important to children. It is clear that assessments need not be just a one-shot opportunity to view the child's functioning abilities, but that as the child comes into the school, his or her specific academic skills, social networks, and how he or she is perceived by others could be looked at several times over the course of the school year.

Of course, one might ask, where will the funding be for these kinds of comprehensive assessments? We believe that in the future there will be more standardized and convenient ways of measuring these different areas. Also, we think school systems will see that such attention makes psychological, educational, and economic sense. Early investment in students' competencies will pay off in later achievement. As more people are convinced of the value of early and frequent assessment, more resources will be provided to accomplish these types of goals.

Investigators have recognized that the variation in academic programs in schools around the country may have substantial impact on transfer-student adjustment (Cornille et al., 1983). Thus, newcomers and school personnel must deal with regional and even intra-city differences in the educational quality among schools. Such disparities often translate into large gaps in the skills of transfer students, due to incongruities between the curricula of their old and new schools. In this regard, when discussing the need for comprehensive, ongoing assessment, we also should bring attention to the currently great difficulty educators have in compiling academic records from previous schools. Improving information management systems has been identified as an important challenge that schools currently face (Bennett, 1984). In our project, we noticed that a considerable number of transfer children were missing previous school records at the beginning of the new school year. Most of the time, previous records were not sent until months later or not at all.

In order to provide timely and accurate records from previous schools, we advocate a national standardization of school records. We believe such records would include, as a minimum, documentation of children's achievement in specific reading, phonic, spelling, and mathematical skills; report card grades are simply not enough information to present a clear picture of academic skill mastery. The current call for standardized national exams comes close to meeting the need for such detailed records, which would give schools a valid appraisal of incoming transfer-student academic needs.

Schools throughout the country also need to become much more accountable, from a clerical and administrative standpoint, in sending accurate records in a timely fashion to new schools. Given technological advances in computer networking and facsimile services, we can envision schools forwarding student records via phone lines, an action that would take minutes, not months. For administrators, Bennett (1984) provides a helpful look at the ways and benefits of installing automated information management systems in schools. At the very least, procedures to mail records to new schools immediately on the transfer students' arrival should be prioritized by administrators. In short, quick transfer of detailed academic records would help teachers immensely as they plan remedial strategies for transfer students.

When children enter a new school, one of their most pressing concerns is whether they are accepted by other schoolchildren; literature supporting this was presented in the first chapters of this book. For such concerns to be addressed, we believe all newcomers should be provided an orientation program, possibly similar to the ones that we have described in this book. In addition, each child should be provided with a nontransfer "buddy" who tries to help the child acclimate into the new social support system. These orientation programs and buddy assignments should be done as early as possible in the new school year. This is because children's social status often crystallizes during the first critical days and weeks of the school year. If our program is not provided immediately, after one or two weeks of school the children might already be somewhat rejected, isolated, or neglected. These types of social statuses are much harder to change once the children's reputation has been made. The majority of children would be, and have been, very pleased with participating in these orientation and buddy programs, and they have often reported that their buddies have become friends. We believe these types of interventions are adequate for most children. Of course, some children come from other schools with past reputations, experiences, and behavior problems that require more serious attention to social skills. We will return to such children later.

Rallying Parents

Another component of comprehensive, preventive interventions for transfer children requires active efforts to involve their parents. Many parents are interested in learning both skills and orientations that will be helpful in facilitating their children's successful adjustment to the new school. Toward this goal, we believe that, as early as possible, training sessions should be introduced to all parents to provide them the reassurance, information, and skills needed to help their children in a variety of areas, from academic to social.

Some children probably will not have the benefit of their parents' involvement, and there are some legitimate reasons for this. Some parents cannot become involved because they are too busy with other children for whom they care, or with job responsibilities. Other parents might have psychological problems that prevent them from becoming actively involved in helping their children. Non-English-speaking parents are typically unable to tutor in academic subjects such as reading but can often tutor in mathematics. Barring these exceptions, the majority of parents should, and would, become involved if they were provided the opportunities to do so. We heavily stress the importance of involving parents in preventive interventions for children transferring into new schools.

In Chapter Eight, we also discussed ways to secure the home support of other family members — such as aunts or uncles, cousins or grandparents — or trusted family friends. When parents are unable to tutor their transfer child, we urge school staff to persistently seek another responsible person who can promise support. Families can be flexible and adaptive in assigning caregiver responsibilities. Admittedly, school staff will likely become disheartened and frustrated by some alienated home situations where children are seemingly abandoned. Nevertheless, the all-important goal is to gain the aid of a supportive person, or even several people, for the high-risk transfer child. In our experience, guardians, siblings, and relatives who were trained by our staff were often quite dependable and committed to tutoring transfer children. Of course, school staff should be discreet about soliciting support from appropriate helpers, and perhaps monitor the home tutoring with such helpers even more closely than they would with parents.

Parent training also should be sensitive to cultural differences and potential barriers to successful parent tutoring. For example, the United States has a rapidly growing Hispanic population, which heightens the need for bilingual services. In the fourth year of our project, nearly one-half of the transfer children we served were from Hispanic homes where Spanish was often the primary language. For these families, staff fluent in Spanish worked with parents. Although non-English-speaking parents could not tutor their child in such subjects as reading, they were typically supportive in securing the help of another person. Given our encouraging experiences with culturally diverse families, we believe school systems will need to continue experimenting with ways to gain optimal involvement of families from different cultural backgrounds whose children may be experiencing jarring cultural as well as school transitions.

In our attempts to understand and serve families better, we visited parents and transfer children in their homes. Undoubtedly, these visits forged a stronger tie between home and school. The literature indicates that school staff rarely conduct home visits, which is regrettable. Based on our positive home-visiting experiences, we urge teachers to reach out to families in their homes and neighborhoods. Home visits not only build relationships but also afford teachers and counselors insight into the dynamics and resources of families, knowledge of which is valuable in helping students in the classroom.

Besides the home, we see great opportunities for teachers and other school personnel to conduct parent orientation and training in school. Again, our survey of current teacher practices suggests that this is not frequently done. To reiterate, many parents are well motivated to participate in training. Of course, school boards and administrators need to be supportive of teacher efforts to conduct home visits and school-based parent training. Schools can help by compensating staff for their time, adjusting their salaries, offering staff training, and providing access to school facilities during hours that parents can attend training sessions.

Toward Comprehensive Interventions

Perhaps the biggest shortcoming of the interventions that we have piloted in DePaul University's series of programs has been the twice-a-week basis on which we conducted tutoring. It is now very clear to us that some children needed much more frequent help to gain the information and skills to be successful in school. Some fourth-grade children functioned at a first-grade level, and twice-a-week tutoring did not boost them to expected grade level achievement. There were some children whose parents worked with them, in addition to the tutors working with them, and still this was not enough. Our experiences suggest that some children may need minimal tutoring at the beginning of the year; they will catch up and perform well. For other children, some tutoring from a paraprofessional (like a tutor) and a parent would be enough to get them caught up. However, there is a significant minority of children who probably need much more intensive intervention which might, for example, involve one and a half hours of tutoring during or after school each day. Educators need to consider this type of programming if they seriously want to help these children catch up. This is particularly true with children whose parents or family members cannot be involved in the tutoring efforts.

We believe, therefore, that comprehensive academic interventions might involve paraprofessional tutoring, parent tutoring, and teacher tutoring, as well as after-school programs, and that different children will probably need varying levels of involvement and intensity. Mastery-oriented, well-monitored programming should help determine when a transfer child has advanced sufficiently. We hope that future progress is able to meet the individual needs of each child. In this respect, there is a lot more to learn in doing intervention studies with high-risk transfer children.

Social Success

Much of the focus up to now has been on trying to boost children academically; less attention has been given to their social needs. From our experience, it is clear that many children have serious behavior problems and, as a result of the combination of social and academic problems, they become either neglected or rejected by their peers and teachers. Schools need social intervention programs that provide the child an opportunity to develop appropriate social skills to meet their needs in more prosocial, as opposed to aggressive or negative, ways. This means learning to cooperate, share, make friends, resolve differences, and play and work well together. Sometimes children change schools because they have had serious behavior problems in the previous school. These children often have similar problems in the new school. We feel that these behavior problems can be identified very early by asking the parents how the child behaved in the previous school, or by simply observing the child's behavior during the first weeks of attendance at the new school. When children are identified as having significant social deficits or behavior problems, whether it is withdrawal or aggression, programming is needed to help them overcome these problems which have serious, long-term negative effects. In our project we piloted a social skills curriculum (Elias & Clabby, 1989) with a small group of students identified as exhibiting classroom behavior problems (Turner, 1990). Following the social skills program, participants displayed increased attentive listening during tutoring sessions and increased on-task behavior in the classroom. Thus, we have observed that social skills training can improve classroom behavior. Such interventions would likely have additive benefits for transfers when combined with academic tutoring.

Visions for Change: A New Agenda for Our Schools

Is this all possible? Yes. We are dreaming and thinking about future possibilities for effective interventions that might help children adjust better to new schools. We know that many schools throughout the country are introducing transition programs to help transfer students. What is needed now are more comprehensive interventions, interventions that meet the needs of each child. We believe that in the future, more comprehensive and individualized transition programs will be designed, mounted, and evaluated.

In this country, more and more people are interested in what is occurring in our schools; as a result, many ideas for improvement are being advocated. It was beyond the scope of this book for us to discuss the educational reform movement. We have focused on a particular group of needy children, those who transfer into new schools in unscheduled transitions. However, we would be remiss if we did not at least mention some of the larger issues.

In a recent book, *The Moral and Spiritual Crisis in Education,* Purpel (1989) asks whether our schools can be energized with new images that have a more vital spirit and meaning. Purpel strongly believes that an overemphasis on achievement and obedience is inappropriate preparation for an interdependent world, which needs an overriding sense of justice, community, compassion, love, and joy. The authors believe that our educational experiences must begin with problems and concerns that stir us to seek liberating techniques and answers. One might wonder how these types of idealistic concepts can be related to school transition programs; we see several possibilities.

A school transition program that incorporated some of Purpel's ideas (1989) might emphasize the need for teaching not only critical thinking and information processing skills but also compassion and how to care for others. School transitions could be seen as opportunities for entire school systems to think about how to welcome children and their parents into the new settings. All the activities of the school need not revolve around transitions, but school transitions could be seen as an opportunity for the principal, teachers, and students to unite in efforts to respond sensitively and compassionately to the ethnic, racial, religious, and individual differences of the transfer children. We think that children and teachers can learn to use concepts of compassion, caring, and love in smoothing transitions for children transferring into a new school system.

Is this really possible? Could school transitions really serve as a vehicle to help us gain a better understanding of our humanity, our caring for others, our sensitivity for those who are having difficulties? We think so. We believe that if principals, teachers, and students were to rally to the unique needs of children entering schools, this new orientation would reverberate throughout the entire school system. If children and school personnel had opportunities to participate actively in efforts to rethink the way they welcome new students and their parents into schools, we believe this experience would enrich them with attitudes and skills that might greatly benefit all participants not only during their school years but throughout their lives.

Resources

Sample Materials from the School Transition Project

For more information about the training manuals and materials implemented in the School Transition Project, please write to Leonard A. Jason, Department of Psychology, DePaul University, 2219 North Kenmore Avenue, Chicago, Illinois 60614.

RESOURCE A

Parent Interview

Child's Name _____ Birth Date _____

School _____ Contact Attempted: __

Interviewer _____ _____

Parent Interviewed _____ _____

Parent Questions Regarding the Move

1. Was the child's last school public or private?
   1. Public
   2. Private

2. Did your child move to another home, or just change schools?
   1. School change only
   2. Residence and school change

Questions Regarding Reason for Moving

Can you tell me a little bit about why you moved or changed schools?

3. Did the old school close?   Y   N

4. Were financial considerations involved in moving or changing schools?   Y   N
   If yes, what were the considerations?

1. New job
2. Loss of job
3. Promotion/increase
4. Demotion/decrease
5. Other_____ (specify)

5. Were relationships with your child's friends a reason for the school move?   Y   N
   If yes, why?
   1. Having trouble with the kids at the other school
   2. Wanting to be with current friends at the new school
   3. Other_____

6. Were your child's academics a reason for moving?   Y   N
   If yes, in what way?
   1. Having academic problems at the other school
   2. Was going to be put back a grade
   3. Needed/wanted more of a challenge
   4. Other_____

7. Was religion an issue when deciding to change schools?
   Y   N
   If yes, how so?
   1. You wanted religious training for your child
   2. You wanted a more solid school structure that the Catholic system could provide
   3. Other_____

8. Were there things about the schools themselves that made you want to move or change schools?   Y   N
   If yes, what were they?
   1. Problems with the old teacher
   2. Problems with the old principal
   3. Problems with the school policies/procedures
   4. Old school location wasn't convenient
   5. New school personnel attracted you
   6. New school location is better
   7. Old school was public; you wanted private
   8. Other_____

9. Did you move or change schools because of changes in your family or household?   Y   N
   If yes, what happened?
   1. Divorce
   2. Remarriage
   3. Other breakup of the household
   4. Other joining of a household
   5. Other_____

**School-move-only parents skip to question #14

Questions Regarding Residence and School Change

10. (If they changed residences) What was the distance of the move?
    1. Moved within the city
    2. Stayed inside Illinois
    3. Moved from another state
    4. Moved from another country

11. Did you move because of the apartment or house itself?
    Y   N
    If yes, what was the situation?
    1. Needed more space
    2. Needed less space
    3. Could afford better housing
    4. Couldn't maintain the cost
    5. Old place no longer available (forced to move)
    6. Wanted to be in a better neighborhood
    7. Other_____

12. How do you feel about the home move?

1	2	3	4	5
very negative		neutral		very positive

13. How do you feel about the new neighborhood?

1	2	3	4	5
much worse		same		definite improvement

**To be asked of all parents:

14. How do you feel about the school change?

        1   2   3   4   5
      worse   same   better

15. How many times has your child ever changed schools (including this time)? _____

Other comments on the move: _____

_____

_____

Family Background Information

16. Are you the natural mother?   Y   N
    If no,
    1. step
    2. adoptive
    3. foster
    4. none present
    5. other (describe)_____

17. Is the child's natural father living with you?   Y   N
    If no, is any father figure present?
    1. step
    2. adoptive
    3. foster
    4. none present
    5. other (describe)_____

	Mother Information	*Father Information*
Occupation	_____	_____
Education	_____	_____
Age	_____	_____
Race	_____	_____

18. What are the ages of the other children at home?

    _____ , _____ , _____ , _____ , _____ , _____

19. How many adult relatives live with you? _____

    What is their relationship to the child?   1. Aunt
    (circle)   2. Grandmother
                                                    3. Uncle
                                                    4. Grandfather
                                                    5. Other _____

20. How many other adult nonrelatives live in your home?
    (describe) _____

21. Do you presently own your home or rent? _____

Other comments: _____

_____

_____

Grades

22. What were your child's last year's final grades?

    Reading _____

    Writing _____

    Math   _____

    Spelling _____

23. How many days was he or she absent? _____

                                      late? _____

                          suspended? _____

24. Has she or he ever repeated a grade? _____

Other comments: _____

_____

Resources

Does your child have an ongoing medical problem? _____

Does your child have a physical handicap? _____

Does your child often get sick? _____

Tell me yes or no if the child was involved in these activities last year.

_____ Organized sports program

_____ School chorus, orchestra or band

_____ School recreational program

_____ Speech therapy

_____ Out-of-class extra tutoring

_____ Counseling

_____ Many visits to the doctor or the school nurse

_____ Many visits to the school principal

How does your child feel about the transition into the new school?

_____

_____

_____

_____

_____

_____

RESOURCE B

The Welcome Booklet:
Teacher Resource Packet for New Students

The Welcome Booklet

This booklet was designed to help the transfer student become acquainted with his or her new school. It includes

1. a welcome page
2. a list of important school personnel
3. pages for class schedule, etc.
4. pages listing special activities such as clubs, holiday activities, sports, and fund-raising drives
5. a helpful hints page
6. a page of bookmarkers
7. a puzzle addressing some concerns of new students

Some pages require a teacher or another school staff person to fill in various blanks to tailor the information to every particular school and classroom. By being individualized, the booklets will be more useful to the new students. Teachers need not use all of the pages.

Orientation and Buddy Activity Sheets

These sheets are specifically for teachers. They provide several suggestions for classroom activities to help assimilate students into their new classroom more smoothly. There are a variety of activities listed to meet the needs of different classroom teachers. Any of the procedures can certainly be modified to fit the classroom and management style of the teacher. These materials should help teachers provide a more sensitive and welcoming environment for their new transfer students.

Buddy Activities

Most transfer students lose some friends when they change schools and it is important that they make new friends in order to reestablish their social support networks. The following activities are suggested to help facilitate peer relationships between transfer students and other children in the classroom.

•Designate a "buddy" for each transfer child. Some general suggestions for buddy selection are choosing a child who is

- The same sex as the transfer child
- Outgoing
- Enthusiastic
- Responsive to others' needs
- Popular (not necessarily the *most* popular)
- Doing well academically

•Help facilitate interaction between the transfer student and the buddy. Some ideas include the following:

- If two children are required to deliver a message, run an errand or move equipment, let the pair work on these activities together.
- If teams are required for a classroom activity, let the pair be on the same team.
- If one of the pair is having difficulty with a particular assignment or subject, the other student in the pair could specifically "help out" his or her buddy during an appropriate time.

•Have the class discuss or write about

- How to be a good friend
- Why one should be a good friend

• Have one of the nontransfer students (preferably a buddy) interview a new child and make a presentation to the class about the new classmate. The interview can focus on information such as

- What his or her old school, teacher, and neighborhood were like
- Number of brothers and sisters
- Likes and dislikes
- Favorite movies, T.V. shows, music groups, cartoons, hobbies, songs, foods, places to go, subjects in school

Orientation Activities

When children are new to a school, they often feel anxious because they are unsure of the environment. In addition, they often experience mixed emotions in regard to their transfer. The following activities are suggested to aid children in becoming more familiar with their surroundings and also to help them feel more comfortable with the different emotions they may experience. By validating the experience of being a new student, teachers can help put children at ease and thereby aid them in becoming more attentive and productive early in the school year. Suggested activities:

- As a teacher, make it clear to new students that you are available if they have any questions about procedures, rules, or class work.
- Design a bulletin board that communicates to the children activities they can anticipate during the year.
- Spend one of the first recess periods indoors with the transfer students and review the "Welcome" booklet with them.
- Designate one or two students as "information officers" to whom transfer students may go for assistance with school assignments or general questions.
- Have one or two children take the transfer students on a tour of the school building. This time can also include formal introductions to various school personnel.
- Review the "Welcome" booklet with the entire class. Have

different children discuss/present a topic in the booklet. This could also be an ideal time to go over specific classroom rules, procedures, and activities.

- Have the transfer children express their feelings about being new through a collage, painting, or drawing. Display their work.
- Conduct a class discussion about being new. Have transfer students tell how they feel; nontransfer students can talk about how they would feel.
- Have older students write an essay or poem about their feelings and concerns regarding being new. Again, have nontransfer students write about how they would feel or how they have felt when they were new in another situation.
  - Conduct a class discussion about this topic after the assignment.
  - Display the work on a bulletin board.
- Have an informal welcome party one afternoon for the transfer students.
- Have the classroom put on a presentation for the new students about school rules, procedures, and activities. This presentation could include role-plays and skits, general information, and question-and-answer activities.
- Have a homeroom welcome party at lunchtime on one of the early days of school.
- Have the eighth graders (or the junior high) make a welcome poster for each new child in the school and have a specific welcome day.

RESOURCE C

Tutoring Curriculum

Spelling

Like reading, spelling materials come directly from the classroom. At the beginning of each week, you should get the weekly spelling list from the student or teacher.

1. *Placement.* Give the child a spelling test during your first session of the week. Use the spelling list the class is currently working on.
2. *Teaching.* As the child takes the test, praise him or her for correctly spelled words and immediately correct misspelled words using the model-lead-test procedure. Have the student rewrite the misspelled words on the right-hand side of the page so when the test is over the child will have a list of words to study before taking the test in class. Make flash cards of the missed words and encourage the child to practice.
3. *Mastery.* During the second session, have the child spell the misspelled words from the first test. If the child still misses some of these words, correct him or her using the same procedure as above.
4. *Data.* Record the number of words the student spelled correctly over the number of words given. Then, after the second session, add the additional number of words spelled correctly to the number of correctly spelled words from the first session. For example, if the student was given 20 words

at the first session and missed 3, but went on to get them all right at the second session, your data for the two sessions would look like this:

Day 1 = 17/20
Day 2 = 20/20.

Reading

The reading curriculum differs from that of math and phonics in two ways: the materials used come directly from the classroom, and stories are read in the order presented in the reader, so there is no specific hierarchy involved.

1. *Placement.* A Curriculum-Based Assessment (CBA) is used to place the student in the appropriate reader. Before you meet with the student, mark off 100 words in a story the student is reading in class. Have the child begin reading two to three paragraphs before the 100-word passage. When the child gets to the passage, time how long it takes him or her to read it. Also count the number of errors the student makes: mispronouncing, skipping, adding, or pausing on a word for more than seven seconds are all considered errors. If a student pauses on a word for more than seven seconds, say the word for the student, but make sure you record the word as an error. Otherwise, do not correct errors during the assessment. (You can, however, review the words when the assessment is completed.) After the student finishes reading the passage, ask him or her five comprehension questions (prepared in advance) based on the passage. Two of the questions should be factual (pertaining to the main idea), two should be inferential (requiring answers not explicitly stated in the text), and one should be sequential (stating what happened before, during, or after an event). If the student pauses for more than seven seconds before answering, the question is recorded as an error. When the student has finished reading the passage and answering the questions, you should have three sources of data:

   Accuracy = number correct words/100
   Rate = number of correct words × 60/time in seconds
   Comprehension = number of correct questions/5

For example, if a student reads 85 words correctly in 75 seconds and answers four questions correctly, he or she would receive the following scores:

Accuracy = 85/100 or 85%

Rate = 85 × 60/75 = 68 correct words per minute

Comprehension = 4/5 or 80%

These data will help you and your supervisor determine whether the classroom material is appropriate for the child or whether the child needs a different level of material.

2. *Teaching.* One-hundred-word assessments should be given at least once a week. When the assessment is over, teach the child the story by reading it with him or her, correcting mispronounced words as they occur and occasionally stopping to ask comprehension questions (try to focus on the types of questions the student has the most difficulty with). Stay in close communication with the classroom teacher so you know what stories are being read in class. If possible, try to work on stories that are coming up in the child's class; going over such stories in advance should help the child read them better in class.

Other activities can also enhance the reading of a story. Story mapping, for example, consists of drawing a picture containing the main idea of the story including the characters and sequence of events.

3. *Mastery.* The student has mastered a story if he or she has reached the following levels:

Accuracy: 95%

Rate: 35 correct words per minute

Comprehension: 80%

4. *Data.* Record the name of the story, and the accuracy, rate, and comprehension scores on the Tutor Weekly Data Sheet. If you are simply reading a story without giving an assessment, record the name of the story.

Math

The math curriculum consists of four hierarchies: addition, subtraction, multiplication, and division. A student can work on one math area or several areas at a time. Three factors should be considered when deciding how many areas to work on: the student's math deficiencies, the student's deficiencies in other areas, and the classroom teacher's wishes.

1. *Placement.* At the beginning of the year, students are given a math placement test containing problems from each step of the four hierarchies. If the student makes two errors in an area, such as addition, testing will stop in that area and the student will go on to the remaining areas of the test. When you start tutoring, instruction should begin on the step corresponding to the first missed item in each area.

2. *Teaching.* You can use any materials you like to teach math concepts (for example, work sheets with problems suitable for the different steps and flash cards). One good way to teach math skills is to talk through problems as you work them out step by step; this gives the student a good model to work from. Listening to the student talk through problems will also help you see which steps create difficulties for him or her. When you think the student understands a math concept, test the student by having him or her work on problems independently.

3. *Mastery.* The student should be given a mastery test at least once a week. A mastery test consists of five problems; if the student can answer all five problems correctly, he or she can advance to the next step in the hierarchy. The five problems can be given in written or oral form; they can come from flash cards or work sheets, or be made up by the tutor for the test.

4. *Data.* Record the area and the step being worked on in the Tutor Weekly Data Sheet by writing the operational sign followed by the step, for example, $\times 6$ (multiplication hierarchy, step 6). You should also graph the child's progress and show it to the child. Graphs can also be shown to the student's teacher, principal, and/or parents.

Phonics

The phonics curriculum consists of rules for reading regular, "sound out" words and of groups of the most commonly used

words. Both types of word groupings are arranged in a hierarchy—
also called the phonetic ladder—which is divided into 14 levels
from 1a through 4c. These levels are further subdivided into
a series of steps numbered from 1 to 70.

1. *Placement.* The phonetic ladder word list is used to determine
    at what level instruction should begin. The test begins one
    grade level below the child's present grade level and con-
    sists of ten single word items per step to be read orally by
    the student; if, however, the child reads less than nine out
    of ten words correctly in that step, the test will begin two
    levels below his or her present grade level. Once the start-
    ing point is determined, the child should proceed through
    the progressively more difficult steps. The test ends when the
    child fails to read nine out of ten words in a step. Instruc-
    tion should begin on the first step missed by the student.
2. *Teaching.* You will be given a list of rules to teach the stu-
    dents. For each rule there is a list of three to ten words and
    two sentences containing such words. Begin by teaching
    the child the rule using the model-lead-test procedure; then
    use the sample words and sentences to make sure the child
    understands the rule and can say the words correctly. Any
    words the child mispronounces should be reviewed using
    the model-lead-test procedure.
3. *Mastery.* The student has mastered a step if he or she can
    read nine out of ten words correctly. As the student reads
    the words, check off the ones he or she got right. Periodi-
    cally review the steps covered earlier, making sure you go
    over words the student previously missed.
4. *Data.* Record the phonics level worked on in the Tutor
    Weekly Data Sheet and graph the data.

Note: As the year progresses and you get to know your
students better, you will be able to assess better the curriculum areas in which the students need most help. You may
find that some of your students need help in curriculum areas
outside of our program, such as writing. One of the advantages of our program is that we can be flexible to adapt to
different students' needs.

RESOURCE D

Math Hierarchy

Counting and One-to-One Correspondence

1. The child can recite the numerals in order.
2. Given a set of movable objects, the child can count the objects, moving them out of the set as he or she counts.
3. Given a fixed, ordered set of objects, the child can count the objects.
4. Given a fixed, unordered set of objects, the child can count the objects.
5. Given a stated numeral and a set of objects, the child can count out a subset of stated size.
6. Given a stated numeral and several sets of fixed objects, the child can select a set of size indicated by numeral.
7. Given two sets of objects, the child can pair objects and state whether the sets are equivalent.
8. Given two unequal sets of objects, the child can pair objects and state which set has more.
9. Given two unequal sets of objects, the child can pair objects and state which set has less.

Numerals

10. Given two sets of numerals, the child can match the numerals.
11. Given a stated numeral and a set of printed numerals, the child can select the stated numeral.

12. Given a written numeral, the child can read the numeral.
13. Given several sets of objects and several numerals, the child can match numerals with appropriate sets.
14. Given two written numerals, the child can state which is more (less).
15. Given a set of numerals, the child can place them in order.
16. Given stated numerals, the child can write the numerals.

Comprehension of Sets

17. Given two sets of objects, the child can count the sets and state which has more objects or that the sets are equal.
18. Given a set of objects, the child can count the sets and state which has less objects.
19. Given a set of objects and numerals, the child can state which has more (less).
20. Given a numeral and several sets of objects, the child can select sets which are more (less) than the numeral; given a set of objects and several numerals, the child can select numerals which are more (less) than the set of objects.
21. Given two rows of objects (not paired), the child can state which row has more regardless of arrangement.
22. Given three sets of objects, the child can count sets and state which has most (least).

Seriation and Ordinal Numbers

23. Given three objects of different sizes, the child can select the largest (smallest).
24. Given objects of graduated sizes, the child can seriate according to size.
25. Given several sets of objects, the child can seriate the sets according to size.
26. Given an ordered set of objects, the child can name the ordinal position of the objects.

Addition Hierarchy

1. Recognizes inequalities of numbers less than 10.
2. Understands seriation of numbers less than 10.

3. Recognizes the word "sum."
4. Understands the " + " sign.
5. Computes sums less than 10 (memorize).
6. Understands place value of ones and tens.
7. Computes sums 10–18 in which both addends are less than 10 (memorize).
8. Computes 2D [two-digit number] + 1D [one-digit number] without regrouping.
9. Computes 2D + 2D without regrouping.
10. Understands place value concerning regrouping tens and ones.
11. Computes 2D + 1D with regrouping.
12. Computes 2D + 2D with regrouping.
13. Computes 2D + 2D with sums of ones greater than 20.
14. Understands place value of hundreds, tens, and ones.
15. Computes 3D [three-digit number] + 3D without regrouping.
16. Understands place value concerning regrouping hundreds and tens.
17. Computes 3D + 3D with regrouping.
18. Estimates sums.
19. Does addition word problems.

Subtraction Hierarchy

1. Finds missing addends (e.g., $4 + \underline{\quad} = 9$).
2. Understands the " – " sign.
3. Uses set separation as a model for subtraction.
4. Expresses a related addition statement in subtraction form.
5. Understands the word "difference."
6. Memorizes basic subtraction facts $0 – 9$.
7. Understands the place value of ones and tens.
8. Memorizes basic subtraction facts $0 – 18$.
9. Names the difference between a two-place whole number (2D) and a one-place whole number (1D) (not a basic fact and no regrouping).
10. Names the difference between 2D and 2D with no regrouping.
11. Names the difference between 2D and 3D with no regrouping.

12. Names the difference between 3D and 3D with no re-grouping.
13. Names the difference between two many-digit whole numbers with no regrouping.
14. Names the difference between 2D and 1D (not a basic fact) with regrouping.
15. Names the difference between 2D and 2D with regrouping from tens to ones.
16. Names the difference between 3D and 2D with regrouping from tens to ones.
17. Names the difference between 3D and 2D with double regrouping.
18. Names the difference between 3D and 3D with single regrouping.
19. Names the difference between 3D and 3D with double regrouping.
20. Names the difference between two many-place whole numbers with several regroupings.
21. Names the difference when a zero appears in a single place in minuend (top number).
22. Names the difference when zeros appear in the tens and ones places of the minuend.
23. Estimates differences.
24. Does subtraction word problems.
25. Does mixed addition and subtraction problems.

Multiplication Hierarchy

1. Recognizes sets as a model for multiplication (number of sets and number of objects in each set).
2. Understands the words "factor" and "product."
3. Understands the "×" sign.
4. Memorizes basic multiplication facts for a × b, where a is greater than 5 but less than or equal to 10.
5. Memorizes basic multiplication facts for a × b, where a is greater than 5 but less than 10, and b is less than 10.
6. Names the product if one factor is 10, 100, and so on.
7. Expands the basic multiplication facts (e.g., 4 × 3 to 4 × 30).

8. Computes 2D × 1D without regrouping.
9. Understands the place value of tens, ones, regrouping.
10. Computes 2D × 1D with regrouping, product less than 100.
11. Understands the place value of hundreds, tens, and ones.
12. Computes 2D × 1D with regrouping, product greater than 100.
13. Computes 2D × 2D with regrouping.
14. Computes 3D × 1D with regrouping.
15. Computes 3D × 2D with regrouping.
16. Computes 3D × 3D with regrouping.
17. Does mixed addition, subtraction, and multiplication problems.
18. Does mixed addition, subtraction, and multiplication word problems.

Division Hierarchy

1. Finds missing factor (e.g., $6 \times \underline{\hphantom{xx}} = 30$).
2. Uses symbols that indicate division ($2\overline{)6}$, $6 \div 2$, 6/2).
3. Expresses a related multiplication sentence as a division sentence (product ÷ factor = factor).
4. Computes division facts with one as divisor ($1\overline{)6}$).
5. Computes basic division facts (a divided by b, where a is less than or equal to 81 and b is less than or equal to 9).
6. Computes division of a non-zero number by itself ($12 \div 12$).
7. Computes 1D ÷ 1D with a remainder.
8. Estimates 2D ÷ 1D and computes 2D ÷ 1D with a remainder.
9. Computes quotients with expanding dividend (e.g., $3\overline{)9}$, $3\overline{)90}$, $3\overline{)900}$).
10. Estimates 3D ÷ 1D and computes 3D ÷ 1D (e.g., $6\overline{)747}$).
11. Computes quotients of many-place dividend with a one-place divisor (e.g., $4\overline{)78,743}$).
12. Estimates 3D ÷ 2D and computes 3D ÷ 2D where divisor is multiple of 10 (e.g., $20\overline{)684}$).
13. Computes quotient with divisors of 100, 1,000, and so on (e.g., $1,000\overline{)6,897}$).

14. Estimates 3D ÷ 2D and computes 3D ÷ 2D (e.g., $17\overline{)489}$).
15. Computes quotient of many-place dividend and many-place divisor (e.g., $3,897\overline{)487,876}$).
16. Does division word problems.
17. Does mixed addition, subtraction, multiplication, and division problems.
18. Does mixed addition, subtraction, multiplication, and division word problems.

RESOURCE E

Phonics

37	38	39	40	41
add	back	backtrack	shoe	than
cliff	black	bandstand	worm	that
egg	lack	bedlamp	about	them
fill	track	beltlift	what	then
inn	sack	helpless	their	this
bless	sick	milkman	more	thin
buzz	flick	sickbed	only	thank
ebb	clock	textbook	two	thong
mitt	lock	thinktank	its	thick
burr	mock	upheld	no	think

37a. Does a snake buzz or hiss?
37b. How much does an egg sell for?
38a. Dick lives on this block.
38b. Do not kick the clock.
39a. The milkman felt helpless in his sickbed.
39b. Let's form a thinktank by the bandstand.
40a. I saw only two worms in their shoes.
40b. Bess said, "We only have about two clocks left, no more."
41a. My brother and father are fun to bother.
41b. Put some lather on a cloth and then take a bath.

RESOURCE F

Peer Assessment Inventory

1. Which children are your best friends?
2. Which children are worried a lot?
3. Which children are too shy to make friends (easily)?
4. Which children start a fight over nothing?
5. Which children does everyone like to play with?
6. Which children always get into trouble?
7. Which children are sad a lot?
8. Which children are mean to others?
9. Which children make friends easily?

Scoring

The score for *aggression* is calculated from the scores for items #4, #6, and #8.

The score for *likability* is calculated from the scores for items #1, #5, and #9.

The score for *withdrawal* is calculated from the scores for items #2, #3, and #7.

For more information on this measure, write to Sheppard Kellam, M.D., Johns Hopkins University, School of Hygiene and Public Health, Department of Mental Hygiene, 624 North Broadway, Room 852, Baltimore, Maryland 21205.

RESOURCE G

Teacher Expectations

The ___ grade curriculum at _____ is a challenging one, making parent interaction and motivation essential. Your support is both appreciated and needed. The following is an overview of things to know that will make this year successful!

Homework

Students will have homework every night except on Friday. All work should be turned in on time. Please sign all homework papers. I will notify you if your child misses too many homework and class assignments. Please check your child's book bag nightly.

Communications

All notes and information from parents should be placed in your child's homework folder. If you wish to have a conference please make an appointment with me.

Reading

Please make sure your child studies and defines the reading vocabulary words.

Spelling

Each week the child will have a spelling test on Friday. Children will bring home their list of spelling words to study and define in their spiral notebook or composition book, due on every Friday. They will have sentence dictation on Thursday.

Math

Math facts are very important and should be learned and remembered. A math fact sheet on multiplication will be issued. It should be studied daily until all facts are learned.

Other

Book Reports: Students will read 4 books selected by me, one book for each quarter. They will be tested on each book, write a book report, and complete other follow-up activities.

Poems: Students will be expected to memorize two poems, one for each semester.

RESOURCE H

Parent-Tutor Assessment

Student: _____ School: _____

Primary Caretaker: Mother   Father   Guardian

Single Parent?   Yes   No

DIRECTIONS: Respond to each statement by circling either
Yes if you agree or No if you disagree.

1. Many times my child is not respectful toward me.   Yes   No

2. There are some academic problems that I just
   can't help my child with.   Yes   No

3. I have good reading and math skills which I can
   use to teach my child.   Yes   No

4. Many times I don't have the energy to work with
   my child.   Yes   No

5. I ask many questions about my child's school
   friends.   Yes   No

6. My child and I have not been communicating
   well lately.   Yes   No

7. I often help my child pronounce difficult reading words.   Yes   No

8. I've had some trouble communicating with his or
   her teacher.   Yes   No

9. My child listens to my advice.   Yes   No

10. I carefully look at schoolwork that my child
    brings home.   Yes   No

11. My child often argues with me.   Yes   No

12. I feel that I am not an effective tutor for my
    child.   Yes   No

13. Often, I don't know what my child is studying
    at school.   Yes   No

14. I usually check over and correct my child's
    homework.   Yes   No

15. My child reads aloud to me regularly.   Yes   No

16. I am good at motivating my child to succeed at
    school.   Yes   No

17. I get frustrated trying to teach my child.   Yes   No

18. My child is very willing to let me tutor him or
    her.   Yes   No

19. Recent events have prevented me from tutor-
    ing my child.   Yes   No

20. I haven't been very involved with his or her
    school.   Yes   No

21. I praise and reward my child very often.   Yes   No

22. I often put off helping my child with schoolwork.   Yes   No

23. If my child has a spelling test, I help him or her
    practice until he or she gets every word right.   Yes   No

24. I want my child to do better in school but haven't
    actually helped him or her improve.   Yes   No

25. I sit next to my child while he or she does home-
    work and help him or her with mistakes.   Yes   No

26. I usually don't ask questions about the stories
    that my child reads at home.   Yes   No

27. I correct many of my child's written sentences.　Yes　No

Estimate to the nearest half-hour how long you spend each week with your child directly tutoring him or her at home in such areas as math, reading, or spelling.

0 —— ½ —— 1 —— 1½ —— 2 —— 2½ —— 3

Other amount not shown _____

RESOURCE I

Teacher/Parent/Child/Tutor Contract

Teacher's Responsibility

Keep tutor well informed on child's progress/problems in class.

Parent's Responsibilities

Provide a quiet study area with little or no interruptions.
Regularly schedule tutoring sessions two to three times
a week for 20 minutes each session. (timed sessions)
Sit next to the child during the tutoring sessions and use
the Model-Lead-Test technique when corrections are
needed.
Give regular reinforcement to child for completing homework.

Child's Responsibilities

Participate in the regularly scheduled tutoring sessions
at home and school.
Bring home and return to tutor all the necessary materials
needed for homework assignments.
Finish all assignments and strive for 90% accuracy.

Tutor's Responsibilities

Provide the necessary materials for the home-tutoring sessions.

Will contact parents through notes and/or phone calls during an agreed-upon time to discuss the progress of student.

I have read and understood all of my responsibilities and agree to do my part in the home-tutoring sessions.

Parent_____ Child_____

Tutor_____ Teacher_____

RESOURCE J

Home Visit Diary

Child _____ School _____

Home Tutor _____ Date/Time of Visit _____

During observation of parent tutoring child note the following:

Is the space reserved for homework . . .

1. . . . quiet?   Yes   No
   (e.g., no distracting sound such as T.V., stereo)

2. . . . well lit?   Yes   No
   (e.g., light directly over desk, 75 watt bulb)

3. . . . used only for homework?   Yes   No
   (e.g., desk in bedroom vs. den)

4. . . . adequately neat and spacious?   Yes   No
   (i.e., desktop space)

Briefly describe the homework space: _____

_____

_____

5. Are all materials at the study area?   Yes   No
   (e.g., homework *folder*)

   If no, what is missing? (e.g., pencil) _____

Staff tutors ask parent-tutor the following two questions:

6. What are the days of the week and times that home tutoring occurs? (e.g., Tues/6 PM, Thurs/7:30 PM)

_____

7. Are there daily reward(s) given for homework completion?

   Yes   No

   If so, what? _____

While parent and child are reading SRA card, staff person tallies the number of mistakes child makes, parent's correct application of Model-Lead-Test (MLT) procedure, and the number of reinforcements given during the reading task. Put tally marks and total for each behavior in space below.

Child's mistakes _____ Total = _____

Parent's corrections _____ Total = _____

Reinforcements _____ Total = _____

(Number of corrections made by parent divided by actual number of child's mistakes = _____ × 100 = _____ = MLT accuracy).

Additional notes:

References

Achenbach, T. M., & Edelbrock, C. S. (1986). *Manual for the Teachers' Report Form and Teacher Version of the Child Behavior Profile*. Burlington: University of Vermont Department of Psychiatry.

Algozzine, B., & Maheady, L. (1986). When all else fails, teach! *Exceptional Children, 52,* 487–488.

Amatea, E. S. (1989). *Brief strategic intervention for school behavior problems*. San Francisco: Jossey-Bass.

Andrews, R. L., & Soder, R. (1987). Principal leadership and student achievement. *Educational Leadership, 24*(6), 9–11.

Anesko, K. M., & O'Leary, S. G. (1982). The effectiveness of brief parent training for the management of children's homework problems. *Child and Family Behavior Therapy, 4,* 113–126.

Asher, S. R., & Wheeler, V. A. (1985). Children's loneliness: A comparison of rejected and neglected peer status. *Journal of Consulting and Clinical Psychology, 53,* 500–505.

Babcock, N. L., & Pryzwansky, W. B. (1983). Models of consultation: Preferences of educational professionals at five stages of service. *Journal of School Psychology, 21,* 359–366.

Baker, I., Hughes, J., Street, E., & Sweetnam, P. (1983). Behaviour problems in children followed from 5 to 8½–9 years of age and their relation to educational attainment. *Child: Care, Health, and Development, 9,* 339–348.

Bandura, A. (1971). *Psychosocial modeling: Conflicting theories*. New York: Lieber-Atherton.

Barker, R. G. (1968). *Ecological psychology*. Stanford, CA: Stanford University.

Barker, R. G., & Gump, P. V. (1964). *Big school, small school.* Stanford, CA: Stanford University.

Barone, C., Aquirre-Deandreis, A. I., & Trickett, E. J. (1991). Means-ends problem-solving skills, life stress, and social support as mediators of adjustment in the normative transition to high school. *American Journal of Community Psychology, 19,* 207–225.

Barrera, M. (1986). Distinctions between social support concepts, measures, and models. *American Journal of Community Psychology, 14,* 413–446.

Barrett, C. L., & Noble, H. (1973). Mothers' anxieties versus the effects of long distance move on children. *Journal of Marriage and the Family, 35,* 181–188.

Beem, L. M., & Prah, D. W. (1984). "When I move away, will I still be me?" *Childhood Education, 60,* 310–314.

Bennett, R. E. (1984). Information management in educational service delivery. In C. A. Maher, R. J. Illback, & J. E. Zins (Eds.), *Organizational psychology in the schools: A handbook for professionals* (pp. 385–401). Springfield, IL: Thomas.

Bensen, G. P., Haycraft, J. R., Steyaert, J. P., & Weigel, D. J. (1979). Mobility in sixth graders as related to achievement, adjustment, and socioeconomic status. *Psychology in the Schools, 16,* 444–447.

Black, F. W. (1974). Self-concept as related to achievement and age in learning-disabled children. *Child Development, 45,* 1137–1140.

Black, F. S., & Bargar, R. R. (1975). Relating pupil mobility and reading achievement. *Reading Teacher, 28,* 317–321.

Blai, B. (1985). *Parents "always" matter in education* (Report No. PS 015 095). (ERIC Document Reproduction Service No. ED 256 490)

Blechman, E. A. (1984). Competent parents, competent children: Behavioral objectives of parent training. In R. F. Dangel & R. A. Polster (Eds.), *Parent training* (pp. 34–66). New York: Guilford.

Blyth, D. A., Simmons, R. G., & Carlton-Ford, S. (1983). The adjustment of early adolescents to school transitions. *Journal of Early Adolescence, 3,* 105–120.

Bogat, G. A., & Jason, L. A. (in press). Dogs bark at those they do not recognize: Towards an integration of behaviorism and community psychology. In J. Rappaport & E. Seidman (Eds.), *Handbook of community psychology.* New York: Plenum.

Bogat, G. A., Jones, J. W., & Jason, L. A. (1980). School transitions: Preventive intervention following an elementary school closing. *Journal of Community Psychology, 8,* 343–352.

Boivin, M., & Begin, G. (1989). Peer status and self-perception among early elementary school children: The case of the rejected child. *Child Development, 60,* 591–596.

Brockman, M. A., & Reeves, A. W. (1967). Relationship between transiency and test achievement. *Alberta Journal of Educational Research, 13,* 319–330.

Brookover, W., Beady, C., Flood, P., Schweitzer, J., & Wisenbaker, J. (1979). *School social systems and student achievement: Schools can make a difference.* New York: Praeger.

Brophy, J. E. (1983). Research on the self-fulfilling prophecy and teacher expectations. *Journal of Educational Psychology, 75,* 631–661.

Bryan, T. H. (1978). Social relationships and verbal interactions of learning disabled children. *Journal of Learning Disabilities, 11*(2), 58–66.

Bryk, A. S. (1987). Application of hierarchical linear models to assessing change. *Psychological Bulletin, 101*(1), 147–158.

Caplan, G. (1974). *Support systems and community mental health.* New York: Behavioral.

Cappas, C. L. (1989). *The effects of moving on children.* Unpublished manuscript. Bowling Green State University, Bowling Green, OH.

Cartledge, G., & Milburn, J. F. (1978). The case for teaching social skills in the classroom: A review. *Review of Educational Psychology, 1,* 133–156.

Cauce, A. M. (1987). School and peer competence in early adolescence: A test of domain-specific self-perceived competence. *Developmental Psychology, 23,* 287–291.

Cauce, A. M., Felner, R. D., & Primavera, J. (1982). Social support in high-risk adolescents: Structural components and adaptive impact. *American Journal of Community Psychology, 10,* 417–428.

Cauce, A. M., & Schrebnic, D. (1989). Peer social networks and social support: A focus for preventive efforts. In L. A. Bond & B. Compas (Eds.), *Primary prevention in the schools.* Newbury Park, CA: Sage.

CBS News. (1991, March 1). Parents helping children with homework. [Morning newscast edition] *This Morning.* New York: CBS.

Chandler, J., Argyris, D., Barnes, W. S., Goodman, I. F., & Snow, C. E. (1983). *Parents as teachers: Observations of low-income parents and children in a homework-like task* (Report No. SP 022 704). Cambridge, MA: Harvard University, Graduate School of Education. (ERIC Document Reproduction Service No. ED 231 812)

City of Chicago Education Summit. (1988). *An agenda for the reform of Chicago Public Schools.* Chicago, IL: Mayor's Office.

Clabby, J. F., & Elias, M. J. (1982). "Project Aware": A community partnership model for school-based consultation and education programming. In H. Fishman (Ed.), *Creativity and innovation* (pp. 289–303). Sacramento, CA: Pyramid Systems.

Cobb, J. A. (1972). Relationship of discrete classroom behaviors to fourth-grade academic achievement. *Journal of Educational Psychology, 63,* 74–80.

Coddington, R. D. (1972). The significance of life events as etiologic factors in disease of children-II. A study of a normal population. *Journal of Psychosomatic Research, 16,* 205–213.

Coie, J. D. (1985). Fitting social skills intervention to the target group. In B. H. Schneider, K. H. Rubin, & J. E. Ledingham (Eds.), *Children's peer relations: Issues in assessment and intervention* (pp. 141–156). New York: Springer-Verlag.

Coie, J. D., Dodge, K. A., & Coppotelli, H. (1982). Dimensions and types of social status: A cross-age perspective. *Developmental Psychology, 18,* 557–570.

Coie, J. D., & Krehbiel, G. (1984). Effects of academic tutoring on the social status of low-achieving socially rejected children. *Child Development, 55,* 1465–1478.

Colbert, P., Newman, B., Ney, P., & Young, J. (1982). Learning disabilities as a symptom of depression in children. *Journal of Learning Disabilities, 15,* 333–336.

Compas, B. E. (1987). Coping with stress during childhood and adolescence. *Psychological Bulletin, 101,* 393–403.

Conrad, K. J., & Eash, M. J. (1983). Measuring implementation and multiple outcomes in a child parent center compensatory education program. *American Educational Research Journal, 20,* 221–236.

Cornille, T. A., Bayer, A. E., & Smyth, C. K. (1983). Schools and newcomers: A national survey of innovative programs. *Personnel and Guidance Journal, 62,* 229–236.

Cowen, E. L., Lotyczewski, B. S., & Weissberg, R. P. (1984). Risk and resource indicators and their relationship to young children's school adjustment. *American Journal of Community Psychology, 12,* 353–367.

Cramer, W., & Dorsey, S. (1970). Are movers losers? *Elementary School Journal, 70,* 387–390.

Crockett, L. J., Petersen, A. C., Graber, J. A., Schulenberg, J. E., & Ebata, A. (1989). School transitions and adjustment during early adolescence. *Journal of Early Adolescence, 9,* 181–210.

Cullinan, D., Schloss, P. J., & Epstein, M. H. (1987). Relative prevalence and correlates of depressive characteristics among seriously emotionally disturbed and nonhandicapped students. *Behavioral Disorders, 12,* 90–98.

Curran, J. P., Farrell, A. B., & Grunberger, A. J. (1984). Social skills: A critique and rapprochement. In P. Trower (Ed.), *Radical approaches to social skills training* (pp. 47–88). New York: Methuen.

Curtis, M., & Zins, J. (1981). *The theory and practice of school consultation.* Springfield, IL: Thomas.

Curwin, R. L., & Fuhrman, B. S. (1975). *Discovering your teaching self.* Englewood Cliffs, NJ: Prentice-Hall.

Dodge, K. A. (1985). Facets of social interaction and the assessment of social competence in children. In B. H. Schneider, K. H. Rubin, & J. E. Ledingham (Eds.), *Children's peer relations: Issues in assessment and intervention* (pp. 5–22). New York: Springer-Verlag.

Dodge, K., Pettit, G., McClaskey, C., & Brown, M. (1986). Social competency in children. *Monographs of the Society for Research in Child Development, 51,* 1–85.

Dohrenwend, B. S. (1973). Social status and stressful life events. *Journal of Personality and Social Psychology, 28,* 225–235.

Dohrenwend, B. S. (1978). Social stress and community psychology. *American Journal of Community Psychology, 6,* 1–14.

Dolan, L. (1978). The affective consequences of home support, instructional quality, and achievement. *Urban Education, 13,* 323–344.

Donohue, K. C., & Gullotta, T. P. (1981, November-December). FIT: What corporations can do to ease relocation stress. *Mobility, 2,* 53–57.

Driscoll, W. D. (1984). Improving the coordination of special and regular education. In C. A. Maher, R. J. Illback, & J. E. Zins (Eds.), *Organizational psychology in the schools: A handbook for professionals* (pp. 121–142). Springfield, IL: Thomas.

Dubow, E. F., & Cappas, C. L. (1988). Peer social status and reports of children's adjustment by their teachers, by their peers, and by their self-ratings. *Journal of School Psychology, 26,* 69–75.

Dubow, E. F., & Ullman, D. G. (1989). Assessing social support in elementary school children: The survey of children's social support. *Journal of Clinical Child Psychology, 18,* 52–64.

Durlak, J. A. (1979). Comparative effectiveness of paraprofessional and professional helpers. *Psychological Bulletin, 86,* 80–92.

Durlak, J. A. (1982). Use of cognitive-behavioral interventions by paraprofessionals in the schools. *School Psychology Review, 11,* 64–66.

Durlak, J. A., & Jason, L. A. (1984). Preventive programs for school-aged children and adolescents. In M. C. Roberts & L. Peterson (Eds.), *Prevention of problems in childhood: Psychological research and applications* (pp. 103–132). New York: Wiley.

Edington, E. D., & DiBenedetto, R. R. (1988). *Principal leadership style and student achievement in small and rural schools of New Mexico.* Paper presented at the annual meeting of the American Educational Research Association, New Orleans, LA.

Elias, M. J., & Clabby, J. F. (1984). Integrating social and affective education into public school curriculum and instruction. In C. A. Maher, R. J. Illback, & J. E. Zins (Eds.), *Organizational psychology in the schools: A handbook for professionals* (pp. 143–172). Springfield, IL: Thomas.

Elias, M. J., & Clabby, J. F. (1989). *Social decision-making skills: A curriculum guide for the elementary grades.* Rockville, MD: Aspen.

Elias, M. J., Gara, M., & Ubriaco, M. (1985). Sources of stress and support in children's transition to middle school: An empirical analysis. *Journal of Clinical Child Psychology, 14,* 112–118.

Elias, M. J., Gara, M., Ubriaco, M., Rothbaum, P. A., Clabby, J. F., & Schuyler, T. (1986). Impact of a preventive social problem solving intervention on children's coping with middle-school stressors. *American Journal of Community Psychology, 14,* 259–275.

Englemann, S., Becker, W., Carnine, D., Meyers, L., Becher, J., & Johnson, G. (1975). *Corrective reading program: Teacher's management and skills manual.* Chicago: Science Research Associates.

Epstein, J. L. (1983). *Homework practices, achievements, and behaviors of elementary school students* (Grant No. NIE-G-83-0002). Baltimore, MD: Johns Hopkins University, Center for Social Organization of Schools. (ERIC Document Reproduction Service No. ED 250 351)

Epstein, J. L., & Becker, H. J. (1982). Teachers' reported practices of parent involvement: Problems and possibilities. *Elementary School Journal, 83,* 103–113.

Evans, I. M., Meyer, L. H., Kurkjian, J. A., & Kishi, G. S. (1988). An evaluation of behavioral interrelationships in child behavior therapy. In J. C. Witt, S. N. Elliot, & F. M. Gresham (Eds.), *Handbook of behavior therapy in education* (pp. 189–215). New York: Plenum.

Fawcett, S. B., Matthews, R. M., & Fletcher, R. K. (1980). Some promising dimensions for behavioral community technology. *Journal of Applied Behavior Analysis, 18,* 505–518.

Feldhusen, J. F., Thurston, J. R., & Benning, J. J. (1967). Classroom behavior, intelligence, and achievement. *Journal of Experimental Education, 36,* 82–87.

Felner, R. D. (1984). Vulnerability in childhood: A preventive framework for understanding children's efforts to cope with life stresses and transitions. In M. C. Roberts & L. Peterson (Eds.), *Prevention of problems in childhood: Psychological research and applications* (pp. 133–169). New York: Wiley.

Felner, R. D., & Adan, A. M. (1988). The School Transitional Environment Project: An ecological intervention and evaluation. In R. H. Price, E. L. Cowen, R. P. Lorion, & J. Ramos-McKay (Eds.), *Fourteen ounces of prevention: A casebook for practitioners* (pp. 111–122). Washington, DC: American Psychological Association.

Felner, R. D., Ginter, M. A., & Primavera, J. (1982). Primary prevention during school transitions: Social support and environmental structure. *American Journal of Community Psychology, 10,* 277–290.

Felner, R. D., Jason, L. A., Moritsugu, J., & Farber, S. S. (Eds.). (1983). *Preventive psychology: Theory, research and practice.* Elmsford, NY: Pergamon.

Felner, R. D., Primavera, J., & Cauce, A. M. (1981). The impact of school transitions: A focus for preventive efforts. *American Journal of Community Psychology, 9,* 449–459.

Fenzel, L. M. (1989). Role strain in early adolescence: A model for investigating school transition stress. *Journal of Early Adolescence, 9,* 13–33.

Fenzel, L. M., & Blyth, D. A. (1986). Individual adjustment to school transitions: An exploration of the role of supportive peer relations. *Journal of Early Adolescence, 6,* 315–329.

Field, T. (1984). Separation stress of young children transferring to new schools. *Developmental Psychology, 20,* 786–792.

Filippelli, L. A., & Jason, L. A. (1992). How life events affect the academic adjustment and self-concept of transfer children. *Journal of Instructional Psychology, 19,* 61–65.

Ford, M. E. (1982). Social cognition and social competence in adolescence. *Developmental Psychology, 18,* 323–340.

Forman, S. G. (1984). Behavioral and cognitive-behavioral approaches to staff development. In C. A. Maher, R. J. Illback, & J. E. Zins (Eds.), *Organizational psychology in the schools:*

A handbook for professionals (pp. 302–322). Springfield, IL: Thomas.

Freedman, R. (1964). Cityward migration, urban ecology and social theory. In E. W. Burgess & D. J. Bogue (Eds.), *Contributions to urban sociology* (pp. 178–200). Chicago: University of Chicago.

Freeman, E. M. (1984). Loss and grief in children: Implications for school social workers. *Social Work in Education, 6,* 241–258.

French, D. C. (1988). Heterogeneity of peer-rejected boys: Aggressive and nonaggressive subtypes. *Child Development, 59,* 976–985.

Froelich, M., Blitzer, F. K., & Greenberg, J. W. (1967). Success for disadvantaged children. *Reading Teacher, 21,* 29–30.

Galejs, I., & Stockdale, D. F. (1982). Social competence, school behaviors, and cooperative-competitive preferences: Assessments by parents, teachers, and school-age children. *Journal of Genetic Psychology, 141,* 243–252.

Gang, D., & Poche, C. E. (1982). An effective program to train parents as reading tutors for their children. *Education and Treatment of Children, 5,* 211–232.

Garcia, D. (1986, June). Parents assisting in learning (PAL). In C. Simich-Dudgeon (Ed.), Issues of parent involvement and literacy. *Proceedings of the symposium held at Trinity College* (pp. 93–95). (ERIC Document Reproduction Service No. ED 275 214)

Garmezy, N., Masten, A. S., & Tellegen, A. (1984). The study of stress and competence in children: A building block for developmental psychopathology. *Child Development, 55,* 97–111.

Gaylord, M., & Symons, E. (1986). Relocation stress: A definition and a need for services. *Employee Assistance Quarterly, 2,* 31–36.

Gersten, J. C., Langner, T. S., Eisenberg, J. G., & Simcha-Fagan, O. (1977). An evaluation of the etiologic role of stressful life-change events in psychological disorders. *Journal of Health and Social Behavior, 18,* 228–244.

Gettinger, M. (1984). Achievement as a function of time spent learning and time needed for learning. *American Educational Research Journal, 21,* 617–628.

Gilchrist, L. D., Schinke, S. P., Snow, W. H., Schilling, R. F., & Senechal, V. (1988). The transition to junior high school: Opportunities for primary prevention. *Journal of Primary Prevention, 8,* 99–108.

Gilliland, C. H. (1958). *The relation of pupil mobility to achievement in elementary school.* Unpublished doctoral dissertation, Colorado State University, Fort Collins.

Ginzberg, E., Berliner, H. S., & Ostow, M. (1988). *Young people at risk: Is prevention possible?* Boulder, CO: Westview.

Gips, C. J., & Burdin, J. L. (1983, November). *Parents and teachers as collaborating educators: A training model for emerging times.* Paper presented at the National Council of States for Inservice Education, Dallas, TX. (ERIC Document Reproduction Service No. ED 251 407)

Glass, G. V., Cahen, L. S., Smith, M. L., & Filby, N. N. (1982). *School class size: Research and policy.* Newbury Park, CA: Sage.

Goebel, B. L. (1981). Mobile children: An American tragedy? *Psychological Reports, 48,* 15–18.

Goldberg, J., Merbaum, M., Even, T., Getz, P., & Safir, M. P. (1981). Training mothers in contingency management of school-related behavior. *Journal of General Psychology, 104,* 3–12.

Good, T. L., & Brophy, J. E. (1972). Behavioral expression of teacher attitudes. *Journal of Educational Psychology, 63,* 617–624.

Goodstein, L. D. (1978). *Consulting with human service systems.* Reading, MA: Addison-Wesley.

Gottfredson, D. C. (1988). An evaluation of an organization development approach to reducing school disorder. *Evaluation Review, 11*(6), 739–763.

Gottman, J., Gonso, J., & Rasmussen, B. (1975). Social interaction, social competence, and friendship in children. *Child Development, 46,* 709–718.

Graham, E. (1990, November 14). Lost in the shuffle: In inner-city schools, endless transfers hurt some students' work. *Wall Street Journal,* pp. A1, A9.

Green, K. D., Forehand, R., Beck, S. J., & Vosk, B. (1980). An assessment of the relationship among measures of children's social competence and children's academic achievement. *Child Development, 51,* 1149–1156.

Green, K. D., Vosk, B., Forehand, R., & Beck, S. (1981). An examination of differences among sociometrically identified accepted, rejected, and neglected children. *Child Study Journal, 11,* 117–124.

Greene, J. E., & Daughtry, S. L. (1961). Factors associated with school mobility. *Journal of Educational Sociology, 35,* 36–40.

Greenwood, C. R., Granger, D., Terry, B., Wade, L., Stanley, S. O., Thibadeau, S., & Dalquandri, J. C. (1984). Teacher versus peer-mediated instruction: An ecobehavioral analysis of achievement outcomes. *Journal of Applied Behavioral Analysis, 17,* 521–538.

Gregory, R. P. (1984). Streaming, setting and mixed ability grouping in primary and secondary schools: Some research findings. *Educational Studies, 10,* 209–226.

Gresham, F. M. (1988). Social skills: Conceptual and applied aspects of assessment, training, and social validation. In J. C. Witt, S. N. Elliott, & F. M. Gresham (Eds.), *Handbook of behavior therapy in education* (pp. 523–546). New York: Plenum.

Halpin, A. W., & Croft, D. B. (1967). *The organizational climate of schools.* Washington, DC: U.S. Department of Health, Education, and Welfare.

Hansen, J. C., Himes, B. S., & Meier, S. (1990). *Consultation: Concepts and practices.* Englewood Cliffs, NJ: Prentice-Hall.

Harris, J. R. (1983). Parent-aided homework: A working model for school personnel. *School Counselor, 31,* 171–176.

Harter, S. G. (1982). The perceived competence scale for children. *Child Development, 53,* 87–97.

Harter, S. G. (1985). *Manual for the self-perception profile for children* (Grant HD 09613). Denver, CO: University of Denver.

Harter, S. G. (1988). Causes, correlates and the functional role of global self-worth: A life-span perspective. In J. Kolligian & R. Sternberg (Eds.), *Perceptions of competence and incompetence across the life-span* (pp. 67–97). New Haven, CT: Yale University.

Hartup, W. W. (1983). Peer relations. In P. H. Mussen (Ed.), *Handbook of child psychology* (Vol. 4, pp. 103–196). New York: Wiley.

Hatoff, S. H., Byran, C. A., & Hyson, M. C. (1981). *Teacher's practical guide for educating young children: A growing program.* Boston: Allyn & Bacon.

Hawkins, J. D., & Weis, J. G. (1985). The social development model: An integrated approach to delinquency prevention. *Journal of Primary Prevention, 6,* 73–97.

Haynes, N. M., Comer, J. P., & Hamilton-Lee, M. (1988). The school development program: A model for school improvement. *Journal of Negro Education, 57,* 11–21.

Haynes, N. M., Comer, J. P., & Hamilton-Lee, M. (1989). School climate enhancement through parental involvement. *Journal of School Psychology, 27,* 87–90.

Hazel, J. S., Schumaker, J. B., Sherman, J. A., & Sheldon-Wildgen, J. (1982). Social skills training with court-adjudicated delinquents. *Child and Youth Services, 5,* 117–137.

Hellem, D. W. (1990). Sixth grade transition groups: An approach to primary prevention. *Journal of Primary Prevention, 10,* 303–311.

Henderson, W., & Glynn, T. (1986). A feedback procedure for teacher trainees working with parent tutors of reading. *Educational Psychology, 6,* 159–177.

Hess, F. (1987). *Bending the twig: The elementary years and dropout rate in Chicago public schools.* Paper presented at the Chicago Panel on Public School Policy and Finance, Chicago, IL.

Hirsch, B. J. (1985). Social networks and the ecology of human development: Theory, research and practice. In I. G. Sarason & B. R. Sarason (Eds.), *Social support: Theory, research and application* (pp. 117–136). The Hague: Martinus Nijhof.

Hirsch, B. J., & Rapkin, B. D. (1987). The transition to junior high school: A longitudinal study of self-esteem, psychological symptomatology, school life, and social support. *Child Development, 58,* 1235–1243.

Hirschowitz, R. B. (1976). Groups to help people cope with the tasks of transitions. In R. G. Hirschowitz & B. Levy (Eds.), *The changing mental health scene* (pp. 171–188). New York: Spectrum.

Hobfoll, S. E. (1988). *The ecology of stress.* New York: Hemisphere.

Hofmeister, A. M., Atkinson, C., & Henterson, H. (1978). *What do I do now? Practical ways to develop good behavior in your child.* Allen, TX: Argus Communications.

Holland, J. V., Kaplan, D. M., & Davis, S. D. (1974). Interschool transfers: A mental health challenge. *Journal of School Health, 44,* 74–79.

Holland-Jacobsen, S., Holland, R. P., & Cook, A. S. (1984). Mobility: Easing the transition for students. *School Counselor, 32,* 49–53.

Holmes, T., & Rahe, R. H. (1967). The social readjustment rating scale. *Journal of Psychosomatic Research, 11,* 213–218.

Ingraham, C. L. (1985). Cognitive-affective dynamics of crisis intervention for school entry, school transition and school failure. *School Psychology Review, 14,* 266–279.

Jason, L. A. (in press). Eco-transactional behavioral research. *Journal of Primary Prevention.*

Jason, L. A., Betts, D., Johnson, J. H., Smith, S., Krueckeberg, S., & Cradock, M. (1989). An evaluation of an orientation plus tutoring school-based prevention program. *Professional School Psychology, 4,* 273–284.

Jason, L. A., Betts, D., Johnson, J. H., Weine, A. M., Neuson, L., Filippelli, L., & Lardon, C. (1992). Developing, implementing, and evaluating preventive intervention for high risk transfer children. In T. Kratochwill (Ed.), *Advances in school psychology* (pp. 45–77). Hillsdale, NJ: Erlbaum.

Jason, L. A., Betts, D., Johnson, J. H., Weine, A. M., Warren-Sohlberg, L., Shinaver, C. S., III, Neuson, L., Filippelli, L., & Lardon, C. (1990). Promoting competencies in high-risk transfer children. *Special Services in the Schools, 6,* 21–36.

Jason, L. A., & Bogat, G. A. (1983). Evaluating a preventive orientation program. *Journal of Social Service Research, 7,* 39–49.

Jason, L. A., & Burrows, B. (1983). Transition training for high school seniors. *Cognitive Therapy and Research, 7,* 79–91.

Jason, L. A., Christensen, H., & Carl, K. (1982). Programmed versus naturalistic approaches in enhancing study-related behavior. *Journal of Clinical Child Psychology, 11,* 249–254.

Jason, L. A., Durlak, J. A., & Holton-Walker, E. (1984). Pre-

vention of child problems in the schools. In M. C. Roberts
& L. Peterson (Eds.), *Prevention in childhood: Psychological research and applications* (pp. 331–341). New York: Wiley.

Jason, L. A., Ferone, L., & Soucy, G. (1979). Teaching peer-
tutoring behaviors in first and third grade classrooms. *Psychology in the Schools, 16,* 261–269.

Jason, L. A., Filippelli, L., Danner, K. E., & Bennett, P. (in
press). Identifying high risk children transferring into elementary schools. *Education.*

Jason, L. A., & Glenwick, D. S. (Eds.). (1984). Behavioral community psychology [Special Issue]. *Journal of Community Psychology.*

Jason, L. A., Hess, R., Felner, R. D., & Moritsugu, J. (Eds.).
(1987). *Prevention: Toward a multidisciplinary approach.* New
York: Haworth.

Jason, L. A., Johnson, J. H., Danner, K. E., Taylor, S., &
Kurasaki, K. S. (in press). A comprehensive, preventive,
parent-based intervention for high-risk transfer students.
Prevention in Human Services.

Jason, L. A., Kurasaki, K., Neuson, L., & Garcia, C. (in press).
Training parents in a preventive intervention for transfer children. *Journal of Primary Prevention.*

Jason, L. A., & Rhodes, J. E. (1989). Children helping children: Implications for prevention. *Journal of Primary Prevention, 9,* 203–212.

Jason, L. A., Thompson, D., & Rose, T. (1986). Methodological issues in prevention. In L. Michelson & B. Edelstein
(Eds.), *Handbook of prevention* (pp. 1–19). New York: Plenum.

Jastak, S., & Wilkinson, G. S. (1984). *Wide Range Achievement
Test-Revised.* Wilmington, DE: Jastak Associates.

Johnson, D. W., & Johnson, R. T. (1975). *Learning together and
alone: Cooperation, competition, and individualization.* Englewood
Cliffs, NJ: Prentice-Hall.

Johnson, J. H., Halpert, J., & Jason, L. A. (1992). *A path analysis
of transfer student adjustment.* Manuscript in preparation. DePaul
University, Chicago, IL.

Johnson, J. H., & Jason, L. A. (1992). *The development and evaluation of a parent tutoring assessment scale.* Submitted for publication.

Johnson, J. H., Jost, S., & Jason, L. A. (1992). *An empirical study of elementary transfer student adjustment: Developing a model of transfer student adjustment using path analysis and classifying transfer student subtypes based on cluster analysis.* Manuscript in preparation.

Jones, R. M., & Thornburg, H. D. (1985). The experience of school-transfer: Does previous relocation facilitate the transition from elementary- to middle-level educational environments? *Journal of Early Adolescence, 5,* 229–237.

Jorskog, K. G., & Sorbom, D. (1989). *LISREL 7 user's reference guide.* Mooresville, IN: Scientific Software, Inc.

Jussim, L. (1991). Social perception and social reality: A reflection-construction model. *Psychological Review, 98,* 54–73.

Kane, J. S., & Lawler, E. E., III (1978). Methods of peer assessment. *Psychological Bulletin, 85,* 555–586.

Kantor, M. B. (1965). Social consequences for residential mobility for the adjustment of children. In M. B. Kantor (Ed.), *Mobility and mental health* (pp. 86–122). Springfield, IL: Thomas.

Katz, D., & Kahn, R. (1978). *The social psychology of organizations* (2nd ed.). New York: Wiley.

Keats, D. B., Crabbs, M. A., & Crabbs, S. K. (1981). Facilitating the adjustment process of new students. *Elementary School Guidance and Counseling, 15,* 319–323.

Kelley, M. (1990). *School-home notes: Promoting children's classroom success.* New York: Guilford.

Kelly, J. G. (1968). Towards an ecological conception of preventive interventions. In J. W. Carter (Ed.), *Research contributions from psychology to community mental health* (pp. 75–99). New York: Behavioral.

Kelly, J. G. (1979). *Adolescent boys in high school: A psychological study of coping and adaptation.* Hillsdale, NJ: Erlbaum.

Kelly, J. G. (1985). The concept of primary prevention: Creating new paradigms. *Journal of Primary Prevention, 5,* 269–272.

Kelly, J. G. (1987, April). *Beyond prevention techniques: Generating social settings for public's health.* Paper presented at the Tenth Erich Lindemann Memorial Lecture, Harvard Medical School, Boston, MA.

Kelly, J. G., Munoz, R. F., & Snowden, L. R. (Eds.). (1979).

Characteristics of community research projects and the implementation process. In R. F. Munoz, L. R. Snowden, & J. G. Kelly (Eds.), *Social and psychological research in community settings* (pp. 343-363). San Francisco: Jossey-Bass.

Kelly, J. G., Snowden, L. R., & Munoz, R. F. (1977). Social and community interventions. *Annual Review of Psychology, 28,* 223-261.

Kendall, P. C. (1984). Social cognition and problem solving: A developmental and child-clinical interface. In B. Gholson & T. Rosenthal (Eds.), *Applications of cognitive-developmental theory* (pp. 115-149). New York: Academic.

Kessler, R. C., Price, R. H., & Wortman, C. B. (1985). Social factors in psychopathology: Stress, social support, and coping processes. *Annual Review of Psychology, 36,* 531-572.

Kicklighter, R. H., Bailey, B. S., & Richmond, B. O. (1980). A direct measure of adaptive behavior. *School Psychology Review, 9,* 168-173.

Kim, Y., Anderson, H. E., & Bashaw, W. L. (1968). Social maturity, achievement, and basic ability. *Educational and Psychological Measurement, 28,* 535-543.

Kranser, L. (1980). *Environmental design and human behavior: A psychology of the individual in society.* Elmsford, NY: Pergamon.

Kroger, J. E. (1980). Residential mobility and self concept in adolescence. *Adolescence, 15,* 968-977.

Lacey, C., & Blane, D. (1979). Geographic mobility and school attainment: The confounding variables. *Education Research, 21,* 200-206.

Lardon, C., & Jason, L. A. (in press). Validating a brief pupil evaluation inventory. *Journal of Abnormal Child Psychology.*

LeCroy, C. W. (1982). Social skills training with adolescents: A review. *Child and Youth Services, 5,* 91-116.

Levine, M. (1966). Residential change and school adjustment. *Community Mental Health Journal, 2,* 61-69.

Levine, M., & Perkins, D. V. (1987). *Principles of community psychology.* New York: Oxford University.

Levine, M., Wesolowski, J. C., & Corbett, F. J. (1966). Pupil turnover and academic performance in an inner city elementary school. *Psychology in the Schools, 3,* 153-160.

Linney, J. A., & Seidman, E. (1989). The future of schooling. *American Psychologist, 44,* 336–340.

Lippitt, G. L., Longseth, P., & Mossop, J. (1985). *Implementing organizational change.* San Francisco: Jossey-Bass.

Long, L. (1975). Does migration interfere with children's progress in school? *Sociology of Education, 48,* 369–381.

Maheady, L., Sacca, M. K., & Harper, G. F. (1987). Classwide student tutoring teams: The effects of peer-mediated instruction on the academic performance of secondary mainstreamed students. *Journal of Special Education, 21,* 107–121.

Maher, C. A., Illback, R. J., & Zins, J. E. (1984). Applying organizational psychology in schools: Perspectives and framework. In C. A. Maher, R. J. Illback, & J. E. Zins (Eds.), *Organizational psychology in the schools: A handbook for professionals* (pp. 5–20). Springfield, IL: Thomas.

Marchant, K. H., & Medway, F. J. (1987). Adjustment and achievement associated with mobility in military families. *Psychology in the Schools, 24,* 289–294.

Marriott, M. (1990, June 13). A new road to learning: Teaching the whole child. The home's link to school success. *New York Times,* pp. A1, B8.

Mayer, S. A., & Jencks, C. (1989). Growing up in poor neighborhoods: How much does it matter? *Science, 243,* 1441–1445.

McAllister, R. J., Kaiser, E. J., & Butler, E. W. (1971). Residential mobility of blacks and whites: A national longitudinal survey. *American Journal of Sociology, 77,* 445–456.

McKinney, J. D. (1975). *The development and implementation of a tutorial program for parents to improve the reading and mathematics achievement of their children* (Report No. CS 002 213). Baltimore, MD: Johns Hopkins University, Center for Social Organization of Schools. (ERIC Document Reproduction Service No. ED 113 703)

McKinney, J. D., Mason, J., Perkerson, K., & Clifford, M. (1975). Relationship between classroom behavior and academic achievement. *Journal of Educational Psychology, 67,* 198–203.

McKinney, J. D., & Speece, D. L. (1986). Academic consequences and longitudinal stability of behavioral subtypes of learning disabled children. *Journal of Educational Psychology, 78,* 365–372.

Meyers, J., Parsons, R. D., & Martin, R. (1979). *Mental health consultation in the schools.* San Francisco: Jossey-Bass.

Millet, L., Pon, J., Guibaud, J. M., & Auriol, G. (1980). "Demenager": *Annales Medico-Psychologiques, 138,* 212–221.

Milne, A. M., Ginsburg, A., Myers, D. E., & Rosenthal, A. S. (1986). Single parents, working mothers, and the educational achievement of school children. *Sociology of Education, 59,* 125–139.

Minskoff, E. H. (1982). Training LD students to cope with the everyday world. *Academic Therapy, 17,* 311–316.

Mischel, W. (1971). *Introduction to personality.* New York: Holt, Rinehart & Winston.

Moos, R. H. (1973). Conceptualizations of human environment. *American Psychologist, 28,* 652–665.

Moos, R. H. (1974). *Evaluating treatment environments: A social ecological approach.* New York: Wiley.

Moos, R. H. (1979). *Evaluating educational environments.* San Francisco: Jossey-Bass.

Moos, R. H. (1984). Context and coping: Toward a unifying conceptual framework. *American Journal of Community Psychology, 12,* 5–36.

Moos, R. H. (1987). Person-environment congruence in work, school, and health care settings. *Journal of Vocational Behavior, 31*(3), 231–247.

Morris, J., Pestaner, M., & Nelson, A. (1967). Mobility and achievement. *Journal of Experimental Education, 35,* 74–79.

Morrison, G. M., & Borthwick, S. (1983). Patterns of behavior, cognitive competence, and social status for educable mentally retarded children. *Journal of Special Education, 17,* 441–452.

Murrell, S. A., & Norris, F. H. (1983). Resources, life events, and changes in psychological states: A prospective framework. *American Journal of Community Psychology, 11,* 473–491.

Nelson-Le Gall, S., & Glor-Scheib, S. (1985). Help seeking in elementary classrooms: An observational study. *Contemporary Educational Psychology, 10,* 58–71.

Oden, S., & Asher, S. R. (1977). Coaching children in social skills for friendship making. *Child Development, 48,* 495–506.

O'Grady, D., & Metz, J. R. (1987). Resilience in children at high risk for psychological disorder. *Journal of Pediatric Psychology, 12,* 3–23.

Oliva, J. (1986, June). Why parent tutors: Cultural reasons. In C. Simich-Dugeon (Ed.), Issues of parent involvement and literacy. *Proceedings of the symposium held at Trinity College* (pp. 79–81). (ERIC Document Reproduction Service No. ED 275 212)

Olson, D. H. (1986). Circumplex model VII: Validation studies and FACES III. *Family Process, 25,* 337–351.

Orosan, P. G., Jason, L. A., Johnson, J. H., & Weine, A. M. (in press). Gender differences in academic and social behavior of elementary school transfer students. *Psychology in the Schools.*

Panagos, J. L., Holmes, R. L., Thurman, R. L., Yard, G. J., & Spaner, S. D. (1981). Operation Sail. One effective model for the assimilation of new students into a school district. *Urban Education, 15,* 451–468.

Parker, D. H., & Scannel, G. (1982). *SRA reading laboratory.* Chicago: Science Research Associates.

Patterson, G. R. (1982). *Coercive family process.* Eugene, OR: Castalia.

Pekarik, E. G., Prinz, J. P., Liebert, D. E., Weintraub, S., & Neale, J. M. (1976). The Pupil Evaluation Inventory: A sociometric technique for assessing children's social behavior. *Journal of Abnormal Child Psychology, 4,* 83–97.

Perkins, H. V. (1965). Classroom behavior and underachievement. *American Educational Research Journal, 2,* 1–12.

Perrodin, A. F., & Snipes, W. P. (1966). The relationship of mobility to achievement in reading, arithmetic, and language in selected Georgia elementary schools. *Journal of Educational Research, 59,* 315–319.

Piers, E., & Harris, D. (1964). Age and other correlates of self-concept in children. *Journal of Educational Psychology, 55,* 91–95.

Pillen, B. L., Jason, L. A., & Olson, T. (1988). The effects of gender on the transition of transfer children into a new school. *Psychology in the Schools, 25,* 187–194.

Price, J. M., & Ladd, G. W. (1986). Assessment of children's friendships: Implications for social competence and social adjustment. In R. J. Prinz (Ed.), *Advances in behavioral assessment of children and families* (Vol. 2, pp. 121–149). New York: JAI.

Price, R. H. (1987). Introduction. In A. Weine, *The anatomy of a preventive intervention: A qualitative assessment of the Employment Transition Program* (pp. 1–5). Ann Arbor, MI: Institute for Social Research.

Purpel, D. E. (1989). *The moral and spiritual crisis in education.* New York: Bergin & Garvey.

Reyes, O., & Jason, L. A. (1991). An evaluation of a high school dropout prevention program. *Journal of Community Psychology, 19,* 221–230.

Rhodes, J. E., & Jason, L. A. (1988). *Preventing substance abuse among children and adolescents.* Elmsford, NY: Pergamon.

Richmond, B. O., & Blagg, D. E. (1985). Adaptive behavior, social adjustment, and academic achievement of regular and special education children. *The Exceptional Child, 32,* 93–97.

Roberts, N. (1975). Parental influence in the elementary classroom: A computer simulation. *Educational Technology, 15,* 37–42.

Robinson, V., McNaughton, S., & Quinn, M. (1979). *Parents as remedial reading tutors: A report on the work of the Mangere home and school project* (Report No. CS 005 324). Wellington, New Zealand: New Zealand Council for Educational Research. (ERIC Document Reproduction Service No. ED 184 079)

Rogers-Warren, A., & Warren, S. F. (1977). *Ecological perspectives in behavior analysis.* Baltimore: University Park.

Rosenshine, B. V., & Berliner, D. C. (1978). Academic engaged time. *British Journal of Teacher Education, 4,* 3–16.

Roy, C. M., & Fuqua, D. R. (1983). Social support systems and academic performance of single-parent students. *School Counselor, 30,* 183–192.

Rutter, M. (1979). Protective factors in children's responses to stress and disadvantage. In M. W. Kent & J. E. Rolf (Eds.), *Primary prevention of psychopathology: Vol. 3, Social competence in children* (pp. 49–74). Hanover, NH: University Press of New England.

Rutter, M. (1981). Stress, coping and development: Some issues and some questions. *Journal of Child Psychology and Psychiatry, 22,* 323–356.

Sameroff, A. (1975). Early influences on development: Fact or fantasy? *Merrill-Palmer Quarterly of Behavior and Development, 21,* 267–294.

Sameroff, A. J. (1987). Transactional risk factors and prevention. *Preventing mental disorders: A research perspective* (pp. 74–79). U.S. Department of Health and Human Services (Pub. No. 87-1492). Washington, DC: U.S. Government Printing Office.

Sameroff, A. J., & Chandler, M. J. (1975). Reproductive risk and the continuum of caretaking casualty. In F. D. Horowitz, M. Hetherington, S. Scarr-Salapatek, & G. Siegel (Eds.), *Review of child development research* (Vol. 4, pp. 187–244). Chicago: University of Chicago.

Sandler, I. N. (1980). Social support resources, stress and maladjustment of poor children. *American Journal of Community Psychology, 8,* 41–52.

Sarason, S. B. (1971). *The culture of the school and the problem of change.* Boston: Allyn & Bacon.

Sarason, S. B. (1974). *The psychological sense of community: Prospects for a community psychology.* San Francisco: Jossey-Bass.

Sarason, S. B., Levine, M., Goldenberg, I. I., Cherlin, D. L., & Bennett, E. M. (1966). *Psychology in community settings.* New York: Wiley.

Schaller, J. (1974). Residential change and academic performance. *Goteborg Psychological Reports, 4*(6), 1–20.

Schaller, J. (1975). The relation between geographic mobility and school behavior. *Man-Environment Systems, 5,* 185–187.

Schaller, J. (1976). Geographic mobility as a variable in ex-post facto research. *British Journal of Educational Psychology, 46,* 341–343.

Schmuck, R. A. (1982). Organization development in the schools. In C. R. Reynolds & T. B. Gutkin (Eds.), *Handbook of school psychology.* New York: Wiley.

Searls, E. F., Lewis, M. B., & Morrow, Y. B. (1983). Parents as tutors—it works! *Reading Psychology, 3,* 117–129.

Seidman, E. (1991). Growing up the hard way: Pathways of urban adolescents. *American Journal of Community Psychology, 19,* 173–201.

Sell, R. R. (1983). Analyzing migration decisions: The first step—Whose decisions? *Demography, 20,* 299–311.

Sexton, P. (1961). *Education and income.* New York: Viking.

Shapero, S., & Forbes, C. R. (1981). A review of involvement programs for parents of learning disabled children. *Journal of Learning Disabilities, 14,* 499–504.

Sharma, P., Saraswathi, T. S., & Gir, S. (1981). Role of parents and teachers in promoting social competence in children. *Child Psychiatry Quarterly, 14,* 132–135.

Shaw, J. A., & Pangman, J. (1975). Geographic mobility and the military child. *Military Medicine, 140,* 413–416.

Shinn, M. (1978). Father absence and children's cognitive development. *Psychological Bulletin, 85,* 295–324.

Shinn, M. (1988). *Mixing and matching: Levels of conceptualization, measurement, and statistical analysis in community research.* Paper presented at the Community Psychology Research Conference, Chicago, IL.

Shinn, M. (1990). Mixing and matching: Levels of conceptualization, measurement, and statistical analysis in community research. In P. Tolan, C. Keys, F. Chertok, & L. Jason (Eds.), *Researching community psychology: Issues of theory and methods* (pp. 111–128). Washington, DC: American Psychological Association.

Short, P. M., & Short, R. J. (1987). Beyond technique: Personal and organizational influences on school discipline. *High School Journal, 71*(1), 31–36.

Shuck, A., Ulsh, F., & Platt, J. S. (1983). Parents encourage pupils (PEP): An innercity parent involvement reading project. *Reading Teacher, 36,* 524–528.

Simmons, R. G. (1987). Social transition and adolescent development. In C. E. Irwin (Ed.), *Adolescent social behavior and health* (pp. 33–61). New Directions for Child Development, no. 37. San Francisco: Jossey-Bass.

Simmons, R. G., Burgeson, R., Carlton-Ford, S., & Blyth, D. A. (1987). The impact of cumulative change in early adolescence. *Child Development, 58,* 1220–1234.

Sines, J. O. (1987). Influence of the home and family environment on childhood dysfunction. In B. Lahey & A. E. Kazdin (Eds.), *Advances in Clinical Child Psychology* (Vol. 10, pp. 1–54). New York: Plenum.

Sloan, V. J., Jason, L. A., & Bogat, G. A. (1984). A comparison of orientation methods for elementary school transfer students. *Child Study Journal, 14,* 47–60.

Snow, W. H., Gilchrist, L. D., Schilling, R. F., Schinke, S. P., & Kelso, C. (1986). Preparing for junior high school: A transition training program. *Social Work in Education, 9,* 33–43.

Soli, S. D., & Devine, V. T. (1978). Behavioral correlates of achievements: A look at high and low achievers. *Journal of Educational Psychology, 68,* 335–341.

Stokes, T. F., & Baer, D. M. (1977). An implicit technology of generalization. *Journal of Applied Behavior Analysis, 19,* 349–367.

Stubblefield, R. L. (1955). Children's emotional problems aggravated by family moves. *American Journal of Orthopsychiatry, 25,* 120–126.

Studholme, J. M. (1964). Group guidance with mothers of retarded readers. *Reading Teacher, 17,* 528–530.

Swift, M. S., & Spivack, G. (1968). The assessment of achievement-related classroom behavior. *Journal of Special Education, 2,* 137–149.

Swift, M. S., & Spivack, G. (1969). Clarifying the relationship between academic success and overt classroom behavior. *Exceptional Children, 36,* 99–104.

Thomas, K. M. (1988, March 24). Education chief still skeptical on city schools. *Chicago Tribune,* p. 1.

Thompson, D. W., & Jason, L. A. (1988). Street gangs and preventive interventions. *Criminal Justice and Behavior, 15,* 323–333.

Tolan, P., Keys, C., Chertok, F., & Jason, L. A. (1990). *Researching community psychology: Issues of theory and methods.* Washington, DC: American Psychological Association.

Tolan, P., Miller, L., & Thomas, P. (1988). Perception and experience of types of social stress and self-image among adolescents. *Journal of Youth and Adolescence, 17,* 147–163.

Turner, E. Y. (1990). *A school survival skills intervention with third and fourth grade children: Implementation and evaluation.* Unpublished master's thesis, DePaul University, Chicago, IL.

Turner, I., & McClatchey, L. (1978). Mobility, school attainment, and adjustment. *Association of Educational Psychologists Journal, 4,* 45–50.

Vernberg, E. M., & Wilcox, B. L. (1984, August). *Residential mobility and children's adjustment: An assessment of short-term effects.* Paper presented at the annual meeting of the American Psychological Association, Toronto, Canada.

Vosk, B., Forehand, R., Parker, J. B., & Rickard, K. (1982). A multimethod comparison of popular and unpopular children. *Developmental Psychology, 18,* 571–575.

Wagner, B. M., Compas, B. E., & Howell, D. C. (1988). Daily and major life events: A test of an integrative model of psychosocial stress. *American Journal of Community Psychology, 16,* 189–205.

Wahler, R. G. (1980). The insular mother: Her problems in parent-child treatment. *Journal of Applied Behavioral Analysis, 13,* 207–219.

Walberg, H. J., Paschal, R. A., & Weinstein, T. (1985). Homework's powerful effects on learning. *Educational Leadership, 42,* 76–79.

Warner, T. E. (1969). Student mobility at the elementary school level. *Dissertation Abstracts International, 31,* 940A.

Warren-Sohlberg, L., & Jason, L. A. (1992). School transfer and adjustment. *Psychology in the Schools, 29,* 78–84.

Weine, A. M., Kurasaki, K. S., & Jason, L. A. (1990). Correspondence between parental reports and children's actual grades. *Psychological Reports, 67,* 607–610.

Weine, A. M., Kurasaki, K. S., Jason, L. A., Johnson, J. H., & Danner, K. E. (1992). *An evaluation of preventive tutoring programs for transfer students.* Manuscript submitted for publication.

Weinstein, R. S., Soule, C. R., Collins, F., Cone, J., Mehlhorn, M., & Simontacche, K. (1991). Expectations and high school change: Teacher-researcher collaboration to prevent school failure. *American Journal of Community Psychology, 19,* 333–363.

Welsh, D. J., Doss, D. A., & Totusek, P. (1981). *Title I parents as reading instructors: Is there no place like home?* (Publication No. 80.58). Paper presented at the annual meeting of the American Educational Research Association, Los Angeles, CA. (ERIC Document Reproduction Service No. ED 204 073)

Wertlieb, D., Weigel, C., & Feldstein, M. (1987). Stress, social support, and behavior symptoms in middle childhood. *Journal of Clinical Child Psychology, 16,* 204–211.

Whalen, T. E., & Fried, M. A. (1973). Geographic mobility and its effects on student achievement. *Journal of Educational Research, 67,* 163–165.

Willems, E. P. (1964). Forces toward participation in behavior settings. In R. E. Barker & P. V. Gump, *Big school, small school* (pp. 115–135). Stanford, CA: Stanford University.

Williams, A. S., Jobes, P. C., & Gilchrist, C. J. (1986). Gender roles, marital status, and urban-rural migration. *Sex Roles, 15,* 627–643.

Winett, R. A. (1985). Ecobehavioral assessment in health lifestyles: Concepts and methods. In P. Karoly (Ed.), *Measurement strategies in health psychology* (pp. 147–181). New York: Wiley.

Yoshida, R. K. (1984). Planning for change in pupil evaluation practices. In C. A. Maher, R. J. Illback, & J. E. Zins (Eds.), *Organizational psychology in the schools: A handbook for professionals*. Springfield, IL: Thomas.

Zigler, E., & Trickett, P. K. (1978). IQ, social competence, and evaluation of early childhood intervention programs. *American Psychologist, 33,* 789–798.

Ziller, R. C., & Behringer, R. D. (1961). A longitudinal study of the assimilation of the new child in the group. *Human Relations, 14,* 121–133.

Zins, J. E., & Curtis, M. (1984). Building consultation into the educational service delivery system. In C. A. Maher, R. J. Illback, & J. E. Zins (Eds.), *Organizational psychology in the schools: A handbook for professionals* (pp. 213–242). Springfield, IL: Thomas.

Zins, J. E., Curtis, M. J., Graden, J. L., & Ponti, C. R. (1988). *Helping students succeed in the regular classroom: A guide for developing intervention assistance programs.* San Francisco: Jossey-Bass.

Index